Superfairness

Superfairness

Applications and Theory

William J. Baumol

with contributions by
Dietrich Fischer

The MIT Press
Cambridge, Massachusetts
London, England

This book was set in Palatino by Asco Trade Typesetting Ltd., Hong Kong, and printed and bound by The Murray Printing Company in the United States of America.

Library of Congress Cataloging-in-Publication Data

Baumol, William J.
  Superfairness.
  Bibliography: p.
  Includes index.
  1. Distributive justice.   2. Social justice.
I. Title.
HB72.B356   1986   305   85-15127
ISBN 0-262-02234-6

1507658

To Naomi and Sasha,
who are still too young to be
blamed

Contents

---

*Dietrich Fischer is coauthor of this chapter.
**Dietrich Fischer is author of this appendix.

Preface

I have a clear recollection of how I invented the theory of superfairness. One morning, perhaps in 1976 or 1977, I awoke earlier than usual and there flashed into my hazy consciousness the Edgeworth diagram representation of the fairness analysis, which occupies much of the second chapter of this book. My unconscious must have been working overtime that night, because the implications of the concept became apparent in minutes. I could hardly wait to report my wonderful discovery to the next available listener. I had an early meeting that day, and seated next to me was a friend and colleague, Ed Zajac, now of the University of Arizona, of whom the reader will hear more in this little volume. I scribbled a long note describing some of the ideas and passed it to him. Ed's responding note, phrased with characteristic kindness, took the wind out of my sails. As I remember it, his note read, "Is this related to Hal Varian's recent work? I'll send you copies of his papers."

Of course it *was* related to Varian's work and that of Foley, Schmeidler, Kolm, and others, beginning about a decade before my belated entry into the field. But I still maintain a proprietory interest in this field that I had the delight of discovering for myself. To atone for the false claim of parentage, however briefly it may have endured, I have tried to retrace the somewhat tangled history of fairness theory in the appendix to chapter 3. More important, this book has sought to provide what originality it does offer primarily in the application of the theory rather than in contributions to the theory itself.

In writing this book I have profited from the generous assistance of a number of prime contributors to the literature. As will be seen, their help went well beyond the mere requirements of professional courtesy. Both in Princeton and Tel Aviv David Schmeidler spent hours discussing with me both some of the analytic issues that arise here and the history of the emergence of the theory. Hal Varian provided me with bibiographical materials, and then helped me to improve the appendix on the *dogmenges-chichte* (as Duncan Foley also subsequently did). Later, revealing himself as an anonymous reviewer of the manuscript, he prevented me from making a number of errors in the propositions of chapters 2 and 3, which he was kind enough to reformulate more satisfactorily. Ed Zajac, too, abandoned his anonymity as a reader for the publisher (as did Bob Solow—about whom more anon), and sent me extensive and very helpful comments to which I shall allude in several later chapters. Another reader's identity has remained concealed, but that person's suggestions were also constructive and helpful, and I offer my thanks to whoever it may be.

When the *American Economic Review* published a paper derived from materials in this book, it elicited a small flood of comments, some building on the materials and others expressing hostility to the ideas, but always in a friendly and constructive way. I am no longer sure that I remember all the authors, and since the editor of *AER* decided that space constraints permitted publication of only two of these notes, we may never be able to reconstruct the list. Still, the comments did help, and led me to adopt some substantive changes and to try to clarify some of my exposition. I shall make no attempt to describe these contributions further except to report the title of the response submitted by Gordon Tullock—"The Tragedy of Fairness." I wrote to Gordon that I did not quite understand either his note or his title, but that I was certainly taken with the latter. He replied that my failure to understand it was symptomatic of the tragedy.

Just before sending off what I thought was the final manuscript I received a note from Bob Bolick of The MIT Press telling me that Bob Solow had suggested that the addition of a chapter on arbitration would enhance the value of the book considerably. This was a terrifying proposal given my monumental ignorance of the area. Happily, Bob Solow put me in the very capable hands of Orley Ashenfelter and Henry Farber, who sent me the collections of writings on which chapter 12 is based. In retrospect I am convinced it was all worthwhile, that a report on the remarkable work that has emerged in this arena is inherently valuable, and that its contribution to my education was a beneficial externality.

I am also delighted to have the opportunity to thank several other persons to whom I am indebted—to Bob Bolick for his most stimulating enthusiasm and consistently helpful support and to Bruno Stein, Andrew Schotter, and Janusz Ordover, who made useful comments on various parts of the manuscript. Finally, I must acknowledge the crucial support of the Economics Division of the National Science Foundation and of the C. V.

Starr Center for Research in Applied Economics at New York University, which greatly facilitated the work reported here.

I also thank the pertinent journals for permission to reprint materials from the following articles:

Baumol, William J., "Equity vs. Allocative Efficiency: Toward a Theory of Distributive Justice," *Atlantic Economic Journal*, 6, March 1978, 8–16 (see chapter 1).

Baumol, William J., "Theory of Equity in Pricing for Resource Conservation," *Journal of Environmental Economics*, 7, 1980, 308–320 (see chapter 5).

Baumol, William J., "Applied Fairness Theory and Rationing Policy," *American Economic Review*, 72, 1982, 639–651 (see chapter 4).

Baumol, William J., and Dietrich Fischer, "The Output Distribution Frontier: Alternatives to Income Taxes and Transfers for Strong Equality Goals," *American Economic Review*, 69, September 1969, 514–525 (see chapter 9).

Finally, and most important, I must express my deep gratitude to my associates, Sue Anne Batey Blackman at Princeton University, Mary Mateja and Karen Garner-Lipman at New York University, whose heroic struggles produced as orderly a manuscript as could be extracted from the chaotic materials I submitted to them.

Princeton
April 1985

Superfairness

1

On the Theory of Fairness versus Allocative Efficiency*

Probably the most persistent reason for noneconomists' resistance to our most cherished recommendations on micropolicy is our determined disregard of their implications for distributive equity. We do not run into that issue in macropolicy, for in opposing unemployment or inflation we are also on the side of what is generally considered to be "justice." But that is about where agreement ends.

The economist who testifies before a regulatory commission about some proposed rates for a public utility will usually discuss their implications for allocative efficiency. But he is likely to find somewhat to his surprise that the court or the regulatory agency is much more interested in the fairness of the rates to buyers of other outputs of the firm (is one customer class "cross-subsidizing" the other?), or their fairness to the firm's competitors (do the prices constitute "predatory" competition?).

Samuel Brittan reports the results of a survey in the United Kingdom soliciting opinions of MPs and economists on various economic issues. He finds a striking divergence of views on one of our favorite issues— peak, off-peak pricing in mass transportation—with almost all the economists (predictably) supporting it, but 60 percent of the conservatives and 80 percent of the labor MPs opposing it. Our conditioned response is to deplore the ignorance and narrow-mindedness of the many politicians who have not grasped the benefits that peak-period surcharges offer. But perhaps it is we economists who should take another look at the matter, from the point of view of fairness to captive low-income riders who have no other means to get them to work.

I believe that issues of fairness are often more to the point than the literature of welfare economics seems to suggest. Moreover, I suspect that

*I am very grateful for their helpful comments to Elizabeth Bailey, Robert Dorfman, and Dietrich Fischer.

economists' reluctance to deal with these issues is not a reasoned response to an analysis of the problem, but a reflection of their inability until recently to get any analytic handle upon issues of justice in economic decisions.[1]

1   On the Significance of Equity Issues

It would, of course, be unfair and inaccurate to argue that economists have denied the importance of distributive justice, or have been insensitive to related issues such as poverty. Though many of us may not consider the classical economists' antipoverty proposals terribly attractive, we can surely not deny that they were deeply concerned about the problem of the poor and the welfare of the working man.[2] More recently, many economists have supported progressivity in taxation and the economist advocates of the negative income tax have encompassed an astonishingly wide spectrum of political beliefs.

However, as soon as economists turn to matters relating to optimality in resource allocation, either in theory or in practice, equity considerations are effectively relegated to a very minor role. The general position seems to be that prices in the economy should somehow be set so as to achieve allocative efficiency, with the policy maker urged to take some *independent* action to correct any unpalatable effects upon income distribution. The effects of some proposed pricing policy upon distribution are rarely considered explicitly.[3]

Now this two-step approach is untenable logically. Only a simultaneous analysis of the two issues is generally defensible. Given the unreality of lump-sum taxes, i.e., taxes with zero incentive effects, except as a convenient fiction of welfare theory, it is clear that any attempt is redistribute income must also affect prices. For assume that prices are set initially so as

---

1. There are noteworthy exceptions, e.g., the work of Ordover and Phelps [1979] in determining the implications for tax policy of John Rawls's *A Theory of Justice*. There is also the important formal literature on equity in taxation. See, for example, Mirrlees [1971], Sheshinski [1972], and Atkinson [1973]. See also the illuminating work on optimal distribution when one person's income creates externalities for others. Here the basic article is Hochman and Rogers [1969].

2. On this, see, particularly, the excellent discussions by Lionel Robbins [1952, chapter III] and [1976, chapters 7 and 8].

3. A noteworthy exception is to be found in some of the recent writings on environmental policy that have stressed the apparently antipoor bias of programs for the improvement of the environment. On this see, for example, the writings of A. Myrick Freeman III [1972], Nancy Dorfman [1975], and Robert Dorfman [1977]. See also Baumol and Oates [1975, chapter 19], and Peskin, Gianessi, and Wolff [1979].

to satisfy the requirements of optimality. Any attempt to superimpose on these arrangements a set of taxes or other types of transfers designed to improve the distribution of income must then necessarily result in a set of prices *after taxes* that are virtually certain to violate the allocative optimality requirements.

But logical untenability is not the main charge that can be leveled at the preoccupation with efficiency in resource allocation, which leaves adjustments for inequities until later. Rather, I believe that this approach is still more vulnerable to the charge of insensitivity. There are some cases where it is obvious. A clear example is my own proposition (chapter 5), which shows that Pareto optimality is prevented by *any* compensation to the victims of externalities. If we provide any payments to those who suffer damage from air or water or noise pollution, we reduce the inducements of these victims to take steps to protect themselves from the resulting damage, just as burglary insurance may induce carelessness on the part of the property owner in protecting his possessions from theft (the problem of "moral hazard" in insurance).

But here what is (not so obviously) efficient, seems quite obviously unfair. Surely, most of us would agree that society owes something to the innocent victim of an exotic pollutant that causes permanent and serious damage to health and impairs mental faculties in the bargain.

Less obvious, however, is the case of a special program to subsidize the consumption of a product by some particular group. Consider, for example, a program that proposes to subsidize electricity production in some impoverished area with high local unemployment and assume with me that there is good reason to expect the program to make a substantial contribution to job opportunities, that the population in the area is fairly immobile, and that there is no promising substitute proposal that seems feasible politically in the near future. Our professional predispositions tempt us to argue that the price of electricity is not the right means to redistribute income. But is it really wrong in this case? Some inefficiency in resources use is, of course, apt to result (though the Lancaster-Lipsey theory of the second-best makes even this uncertain). Yet it is difficult to believe that the loss to society overall will be very significant, in our wealthy economy. It is likely to be diffused, and negligible in its effects on any one individual.[4] If we compare these losses with the pain and suffering of which unemployed

---

4. One might also argue, following the famous Harberger evaluation of the welfare effects of monopoly, that the total loss in consumers' and producers' surplus is not apt to be very great.

families may be relieved by the electricity subsidy, we certainly are entitled to surmise that the public welfare may well gain very substantially from the adoption of the program.

Similarly, a little consideration should lead us to sympathize a bit more than we are ordinarily inclined with the politician's reluctance to impose high peak-period fares on a local transportation system that would un-doubtedly fall most heavily upon the working people who have open to them little opportunity for an alternative. And we might well see some merit in the viewpoint of those who have criticized the Ramsey theory on Pareto-optimal pricing under a budget constraint. That theorem, it will be recalled, tells us the requirements of allocative efficiency when prices are constrained to bring in some predetermined amount of revenue, say, an amount sufficient to cover the production cost of the products in question. Where scale economies are present, marginal cost pricing will, as we know, not cover total cost, and the Ramsey theorem suggests that the prices of products whose demands are particularly inelastic should then be raised most substantially above marginal costs. But, to paraphrase the comments of one federal administrative law judge whose decision dealt with the issue,[5] this places the burden upon those customers who have no place else to go, whose demands are inelastic because they have no real alternative.

2   On Concepts of Justice

While there may be widespread agreement upon some of the economic arrangements that are considered unjust, we have of course no agreement upon what decisions deserve to be considered just. Indeed, despite Rawls's groundbreaking work, few of us would be prepared to claim that we have any tenable criteria of economic justice that are of general applicability.

The notion of a "just price" has clearly been a will-o'-the-wisp whose pursuers have sometimes been led into a morass of metaphysics bearing little resemblance to reasoned argument. It is important to recognize that "fairness" in a pricing arrangement depends heavily on consistency with the practices of the past to which people have become habituated.[6] Even though costs of telephone calls spanning long distances have become closer and closer to the (rising) cost of a local telephone call, many people seem to consider it unfair to charge the same price for a call that spans the

---

5. See the decision of Judge Kraushaar in FCC Docket 19129 Phase II, August 2, 1976.

6. "[The world] condones abuses but detests innovations," Liddell Hart, quoted by Paul Fussel [1975, p. 10].

American continent as for one that traverses a mere five miles. Yet no one seems to suggest that there is anything unfair about a uniform charge for postal delivery even though its costs may well be more sensitive to distance than those of telecommunications.

Similarly, where it is proposed to switch from a flat fee for transportation or electric power to a system of peak, off-peak prices, one frequently hears that it is unfair if it involves any rise in peak rates. Apparently, customers object less to an initial lowering of off-peak rates, holding all other rates constant, even if it is followed quickly thereafter by a uniform increase in all rates, both peak and off-peak.[7] It is all too easy to charge this viewpoint with irrationality, but it is nothing of the sort. I am not irrational when a member of my family tells me about an expensive purchase and I say that I would rather not know the price—I am merely avoiding a pointless moment of displeasure. A payroll deduction may well ease the pain of a tax payment consciously observed. There is nothing irrational about measures that reduce such pains even if the methods rest on no more than illusion.[8] Pricing decisions that give no weight to such psychic costs are simply inconsistent with the economists' usual position that it is some measure of the individual's utility and not income or material possessions that matters for an evaluation of that person's welfare. Yet economists are so used to working from a premise of rationality that anything that smacks of the irrational understandably leaves them uncomfortable. This is perhaps one of the reasons for our profession's reluctance to work upon concepts of equity.

But there are three other reasons that are probably much more important. First, we are suspicious of the search for configurations that claim to be the *uniquely* just solution. Second, we are afraid that an evaluation of equity forces the economist to inject his own value judgments into the analysis, rather than using as the standard of evaluation the preferences of persons affected—as we do in our analysis of resource allocation. Third, we seem to have no effective analytic machinery capable of yielding illuminating results about equity like those that the theory of allocation has provided us.

I hope to show that each of those concerns, while quite appropriate, can be, and to some extent already has been, dealt with effectively. First,

---

7. This is all part of the accumulating evidence that consumers' preferences and choices are heavily affected by the way in which the seller frames the options offered to potential purchasers. Here see the references in the footnotes that follow.

8. I discuss these matters further in chapter 10. See also the writings of Thaler (for example, [1980]) and Tversky (for example, Tversky and Kahneman [1982]).

however, let me offer a few general comments on each of those three concerns in turn.

Our unease about the uniqueness of just solutions probably is, in part, a reaction to vague impressions about the medieval discussions of the just price, which conjure up debates about the number of angels who can populate the head of a pin. The more recent performance of governments seeking to impose (uniquely?) just prices has hardly been such as to inspire a more sympathetic view of the matter among our colleagues. The power of the Rawlsian model to select that *one* solution among the available candidates that is deemed uniquely most equitable has not swelled the ranks of those prepared to adopt Rawls's fruitful approach. On the contrary, it has invited criticism by counterexamples, problem cases for which the critic is able to provide alternative solutions that seem to have no less claim than the Rawlsian solution to be considered equitable.

I suspect that a promising alternative is the viewpoint that there is no *one* just solution. Rather, there is a range of solutions that are not clearly unjust. Similarly, there are in most cases many other solutions that *are* surely unjust. While we are virtually certain to fail in any attempt to single out *the one* just price, it takes little imagination to think of pricing practices that "reasonable" persons will all consider grossly unfair. This suggests that it may be useful to look at the matter in the following way: In the multidimensional space of candidate solution points for any decision problem, rather than hoping to find one most equitable point, it may be more appropriate to look for a set of candidate solution points all of which are "fair," and another all of whose points are "unfair," without ruling out the possibility that the two regions will not exhaust the entire solution space. Viewed in this way, the region of fairness may be defined by a set of acceptability constraints that bound it, rather than by some objective function whose value is to be maximized.

The second issue that impedes the way to an analysis of economic fairness problems is the role of the analyst's value judgments. Now, it is generally recognized that in welfare economics there is no such thing as a value-free analysis. The usual basis for our analysis, the view that individual (consumer) preferences should count, is itself surely a value judgment of the investigator. Nevertheless, we are much more comfortable when, to the extent Professor Arrow's analysis permits, we can substitute the preferences of the individuals affected by a decision for the preferences of the person analyzing that decision. It would seem at first blush that in an analysis of equity issues this is precisely what we are unable to do. How can injustice be defined except through the analyst's personal valuation?

As the next two chapters will show, this is not quite true. There are analytic approaches to fairness issues that are every bit as individualistic as Pareto optimality analysis of resource allocation. In these analyses the affected individuals' preferences do count, and they are the only preferences that count. For the analyses are based on the preference sets of the affected individuals—one of the prime tools of individualistic analysis of resource allocation. Moreover, these approaches require no interpersonal comparisons of utility. Of course, this does not eliminate entirely the role of the value judgments of the analyst. After all, the view that the values of those affected should count is itself a value judgment, as was just noted. Moreover, the avoidance of interpersonal comparisons may in fact prove to be a weakness of the result rather than one of its strengths. If, as some of the leading analysts of the subject have concluded, some fairness issues cannot be analyzed without recourse to interpersonal comparisons, however subjective, then a method that leaves no room for such comparisons must be inapplicable to such issues.

We shall also see that these approaches lend themselves to formal manipulation and the derivation of theorems, just as standard value theory does.

3 Three Approaches to Fairness Analysis

It is clearly impossible to foresee all of the avenues that fairness analysis can or will eventually pursue. But to illustrate the analytic tractability of the subject I shall allude briefly to two rather familiar approaches, and then one that is rather less widely known. It will be seen that none of these requires case by case reliance upon the analyst's own judgments.

First, however, it is important to make clear the objective of our search. We are seeking tools that are capable of shedding light upon the equity of particular policy proposals, institutional arrangements, or solutions derived from analytic models. A legislature proposes to limit hours of labor; a market assigns the bulk of certain types of jobs to recent immigrants or new entrants to the labor force; an analytic model is used to indicate that Pigouvian taxes are an efficient means to control pollution. The basic question posed by policy makers is whether these arrangements are "fair" or whether they are "fairer" than some available alternative. Our objective, then, is to see whether there exist instruments capable of shedding light upon this subject.

One such instrument that should readily recommend itself to our colleagues has been described as the Pareto improvement criterion. This familiar criterion offers as a test of the equitability of any proposal for change the universality of participation in the benefits of that change. If *everyone* affected is expected to benefit, or at least not be harmed, we say that the change is a Pareto improvement. It should be noted that, despite their similarities, this is not the same as the criterion of Pareto optimality. It is obvious that a change that is a Pareto improvement need not get us all the way to a Pareto optimum; and it is almost obvious that a move to a Pareto optimum from an initial position that was not optimal will *not* generally be a Pareto improvement—some persons may well be harmed by such a change. I believe that, like Pareto optimality in allocation theory, the Pareto improvement criterion will prove an instrument for fairness analysis far more powerful than one might have expected from the apparently weak criterion upon which it rests.

An example of an application of the Pareto improvement criterion is readily provided. The regulation of public utility rates is a field in which equity issues are prominent, and among the most pervasive of such issues are the interrelated subjects of cross-subsidy and unfair competition that I have already mentioned. In brief, it is often argued that the multiproduct regulated utility (and they *are* all multiproduct firms) will be tempted to reduce prices of those of its products for which competition is most intense, subsidizing the sale of these items by unjustifiably large receipts squeezed from its remaining products. Thus, those who challenge the prices charged by a utility allege that the firm is "cross-subsidizing" low prices in its competitive markets at the expense of customers in markets where the firm has monopoly power. Such a practice, it is held rather persuasively, represents an inequity among customer groups as well as a competitive tactic that is not easily justified. The issue for fairness analysis is the formulation of a test that can be used to determine whether the prices of the utility do in fact incur such cross-subsidies. The Pareto improvement criterion gives us such a test: If the customers of the firm's *less* competitive products can be shown to *gain* financially from the offerings in the *more* competitive markets, that is, if the former group of customers is better off with the competitive products offered at the prices in question (in comparison with the situation if those competitive products were withdrawn or had never been offered), then the offering is clearly a Pareto improvement from the point of view of all of the utility's customers. There can be no cross-subsidy since no one customer group benefits at the expense of another—all groups are net gainers. In the last few years this analysis has in fact played a considerable role in regulatory hearings (for example, Baumol [1970]), has produced an interesting theoretical literature (see, for example, Faulhaber and Zajac

[1976]), and has led to the design of procedures for empirical evaluation. In short, the Pareto improvement approach can work.

A second avenue for fairness analysis involves the issues of income distribution. Most observers will presumably agree that if a Pigouvian tax were to be shown, in effect, to make the poor poorer and the rich richer, then this would imply that the tax is inequitable. Society might still consider it to be worth its inequity cost, on balance, but certainly that consequence would be a significant count against the proposal.

There is no point in trying to summarize here the many important contributions that have been made to the theory and measurement of income inequality. Professor Sen has provided us a wholly admirable summary of the literature as well as significant contributions of his own on this subject (see Sen [1972]). Rather, as an indication of the basis for my view that the subject is more tractable analytically than is commonly recognized, it will be shown analytically in chapter 9 that some attributes of the trade-off between equality and efficiency can be deduced from a priori considerations, and that these show that the trade-off may be far more serious than most of us had expected, so long as conventional methods are used to carry out the redistribution. Indeed, it will be shown from some rather minimal assumptions that if progressive taxes and income transfers are the only instruments used, then, at least in theory, measures sufficiently strong to guarantee full income equality must reduce total output to zero! The primary purpose of the analysis is to show that those who are seriously interested in reducing inequality significantly may well have to undertake a serious search for more innovative means to achieve that goal. But my main purpose in bringing the issue up here is as an encouraging piece of evidence of the analytic tractability of the subject.

I come finally to the third and most novel of the avenues of equity analysis that will play a central role in this book—the body of work that I like to call "superfairness theory." Superfairness analysis has recently been formalized by Foley [1967], Pazner and Schmeidler [1974], Varian [1974], and others. But their fruitful work derives from a somewhat older source, the games of fair division. Everyone knows the procedure that can be used to assure that two people will divide a cake fairly: one of them cuts the cake into two parts and the other then chooses. This process has been extended to more complex problems of fair division—those involving more than two persons, more than one product, etc. The point of this analysis is that this process achieves fairness only in terms of the preferences of the persons involved. On "objective" standards—weight, caloric content, or any other such criteria—the cake may end up being divided very unevenly. Yet the process—A cuts, B chooses—ensures that each party will receive a piece that he prefers to the other's or at least leaves him indifferent between them.

Happily, this approach can be generalized, rendered more abstract or more concrete, translated into the standard language of indifference maps and utility theory, and applied to concrete problems. The translation into the standard constructions of the economist is not difficult. One judges the fairness of a particular distribution via the indifference loci of each party in turn—asking whether a particular distribution puts individual A on a higher indifference locus than she would be if she received the combination that distribution assigns to (an)other individual(s). In this way we can judge which points are strictly superfair, which are not fair to one or more parties, and which points are just on the borderline of fairness to some particular person in the sense that this person is indifferent there between what she receives and what is received by other persons.

The analysis also lends itself to the derivation of significant welfare theorems. For example, a highly significant result contributed by Schmeidler and Yaari is that in an exchange problem there will always be at least one point on the contract curve that lies in the region of superfairness, i.e., at least one solution that has both the desirable allocative property of Pareto optimality and the desirable equity property of superfairness.

Much of the material in this book represents application of superfairness theory to several concrete economic issues. For example, I shall use it to examine the intertemporal redistribution achieved by the employment of pricing devices to conserve scarce resources (taxes on gasoline consumption), the fairness of different rationing devices considered for use in periods of scarcity, the fairness of peak-load pricing, and a number of other such subjects.

4   On the Philosophical Underpinnings of a Fairness Analysis

As I have noted, the objective of this book is to explore the possibility of application of fairness analysis, and not to contribute to its philosophical foundations, a subject on which much has been written by persons in a far better position to do so. Though I shall not always avoid the temptation to get into some of the underlying theory or to offer occasional remarks on justifiability, many critical foundation issues will deliberately be evaded.

For example, there will be no attempt to come to grips with the choice between reliance on procedural and end-state criteria of fairness. Is fairness a matter of equity in the opportunities offered to individuals and the type of access they are provided to the various economic processes (the *procedural* notions of fairness), or is it to be interpreted in terms of the state in which individuals emerge from those processes (the *end-state* fairness concepts)? These are issues that have been debated cogently by philosophers and have served as rallying cries for politicians, revolutionaries, and defenders of the current order.

Probably the evolution of a widely acceptable criterion of fairness must grapple with issues even less tractable than the choice between a procedural and an end state approach. As Zajac [1985] emphasizes, in popular discourse fairness is an amalgam of a multiplicity of ad hoc desiderata that no simple and analytically tractable formulation may be able to capture. Among others, Zajac lists, for example, the notion that an act is unfair if it deprives any individuals of their "... basic economic rights to adequate food, shelter, heat, clothing, health care, education, and in the United States, to basic utility services" (p.19). He also tells us that the retention of a benefit that accrues to an individual under the status quo "is considered a right whose removal is considered unjust" (p. 23). Moreover, failure to ensure individuals against damage from exogenous developments is considered unjust. Zajac goes on to list three more such conditions that he considers to be requirements of "fairness' as the term is used in common parlance. What then can be said for concepts of fairness that omit such considerations?

Yet such issues, fundamental though they be, are beyond the scope of this book. Rather, the book is intended to take the appropriate fairness criteria as given and to explore their applicability to various policy problems. For discussion of the philosophical problems that still beset these criteria, at least some of which will inevitably occur to readers, they are referred to the extensive literature, some of which is cited in chapters 2 and 3 and the bibliography. (On procedural and end-state notions, see particularly Rawls [1971], Nozick [1974], and Thomson [1983].)

5   Avoidance of Irrationality in the Pursuit of Fairness

Though I have just proposed to ignore quite blatantly the intractable difficulties besetting the formulations of any unexceptionable criterion of fairness, these problems will inevitably haunt the work that follows. One may ask, with considerable justice, how I can possibly hope to obtain applied results on fairness that command any credence when there is no agreement on what the concept of "fairness" should connote, and little defense is offered for the concepts utilized other than a demonstration of their analytic tractability supplemented by some casual remarks on their more attractive features.

Happily, the traditions of economic analysis help us to go one step farther. For similar problems have beset attempts to derive defensible and applicable results from theories and formal models that are admittedly highly oversimplified and, at least in some respects, highly unrealistic. Here I do not refer to the reasonable but not entirely persuasive response that without such oversimplifications rigorous analysis might well be impossible. Rather, I allude to the use of simplified models to identify pitfalls that policy makers might not have recognized without them, that is, to demonstrate possible consequences that unaided intuition, judgment, and experience may be unable to envision. Formal economic analysis rarely can tell a policy maker just what he should do, but it has been far more successful in telling him what he should seek to avoid if he is not to regret the consequences.

Fairness issues provide us many illustrations of opportunities for this sort of contribution, particularly examples centered about the concept of fairness in pricing, a few of which I shall describe next. The point is that while we may never hope to determine exactly what is fair and what is unfair, we can aspire to determine what constitutes inefficiency and even self-destructiveness in pursuit of whatever fairness standard one adopts. In other words, one can hope to use rigorous analysis to point out irrationalities in fairness policies, that is, measures that not only fail in their purpose but, in doing so, exact a social cost that may be substantial and may even exacerbate the unfairness (however defined) that the programs are intended to ameliorate. The avoidance of such inefficiencies and irrationalities in fairness measures is surely not an impossible goal of applied fairness theory.

Let me attempt to impart some life to this way of looking at the matter with the aid of a few examples. The most clear-cut case is provided by those LDCs (less developed countries) in which restrictive regulations prevent the establishment of large or even medium-size firms in many relatively industrialized sectors of the economy, carefully limit the outputs of those larger enterprises that are permitted, and systematically restrict the use of modern technological devices such as the computer, all with the objective of promoting fairness and equality. Expansion of firms is discouraged to prevent larger enterprises from getting too far ahead of the small business firms. New techniques are circumscribed to prevent unemployment from growing. Yet income distribution in some of these countries is among the most unequal in the world—much more so than that in some LDCs (and some recently ex-LDCs) in which no similar restrictions have been adopted. If it can be demonstrated, as seems plausible, that the regulations, despite their egalitarian purpose, have in fact exacerbated the difference between rich and poor, it is clear that they constitute an irrational fairness program—that they in fact impede attainment of the objective they seek to promote.

A second example is provided by rules against "unfair" profiteering by speculators and the setting of unfairly high prices in times of shortages. Such rules have an ancient lineage and were clearly encompassed in the medieval prohibitions of "engrossing," "forestalling," and "regrating." Economists have recognized the dangers posed by such prohibitions for well over a century. For example, in 1834, about a decade before the great potato famine in Ireland, Mounifort Longfield in his inaugural address as professor of political economy in Dublin discussed the role of price controls in a case of crop failure:

Suppose the crop of potatoes in Ireland was to fall short in some year one-sixth of the usual consumption. If [there were no] increase of price, the whole ... supply of the year would be exhausted in ten months, and for the remaining two months a scene of misery and famine beyond description would ensue .... But when prices [increase] the sufferers [often believe] that it is not caused by scarcity.... They suppose that there are provisions enough, but that the distress is caused by the insatiable rapacity of the possessors ... [and] they have generally succeeded in obtaining laws against [the price increases] ... which alone can prevent the provisions from being entirely consumed long before a new supply can be obtained.

In short, Longfield is telling us that laws against unfair pricing by speculators in times of severe shortages, which presumably are designed to protect the interests of the poor, in fact make it likely that those poor will later be exposed to enormous hardships—possibly to famine and starvation. These all too prescient observations obviously serve as yet another example of what economists judge to be extreme irrationality in the pursuit of fairness.

Price controls evoke a standard gallery of horror stories—minimum wages as an alleged source of unemployment among black teenagers; rent controls as an inducement for abandonment of buildings that exacerbates building shortages; controls on the prices of food smuggled into beseiged Antwerp in 1584, which before had held out quite nicely against the Spanish blockade—but the controls quickly caused supplies to dry up and forced surrender of the city. Then, there were the price controls imposed on army supplies in 1777 by the Pennsylvania legislature to which the suffering of Washington's troops at Valley Forge has been ascribed. All of these and other examples, easily supplied, illustrate how it is possible to adopt measures in the pursuit of fairness that economists can judge to be irrational, not just because they cause economic inefficiency through resource misallocation, but because they injure just those persons the protection of whose interests is presumably required for the sake of fairness.

In sum, it is self-defeating approaches of this sort that applied fairness theory can aspire to ferret out. Of course, the types of examples just listed are familiar enough and require no new fairness theory to bring them to the attention of economists. But their familiarity is just the reason for their selection for this point in my narrative. I expect that little objection will be evoked when I cite them as examples of irrationality in the pursuit of fairness. Obviously, however, if fairness theory is to prove its worth in dealing with policy, it must come up with some other application, perhaps describing other less obvious ways in which measures intended to promote fairness may in fact manifest irrationality. This is the goal that much of the book's discussion pursues.

6   Evaluative Comment

Enough has been said to suggest that fairness analysis *is* tractable, that it can make good use of familiar analytic tools, and that it can be used to obtain concrete and applied results relying little more on the value judgment of the investigator than the standard theorems of welfare economics do. This book will offer a number of tentative results of this sort.

I do believe the theory can do more than expose irrationality in policy design and that in some areas it has already begun to do so. But even if it can be used only to identify such irrationalities, it will have served a very valuable purpose.

I also believe that applied microeconomists will have to devote more attention to fairness analysis than they have in the past because without the ability to make some well-founded comments on the relevant fairness considerations it will remain difficult for them to persuade others of the virtues of their recommendations relating to economic efficiency, and because fairness is the area in which advice is often most urgently desired by policy makers and the general public. Without such work, those who seek the help of microeconomists are likely to continue to feel that they have asked for bread, but we have only given them stone.

2   Superfairness

This chapter offers a very simple diagrammatic description[1] of the elements of what I have called "superfairness theory," the analysis first proposed by Foley and then expanded by Schmeidler, Yaari, Pazner, Kolm, Varian and others. This analysis provides the foundations of a theory of fairness in the economy's distribution and production processes upon which we can build an analysis of some of the equity issues that arise in a number of areas of policy. In this book I shall use a variety of standards of fairness all of which evolve from one or both of two basic criteria: the Pareto improvement criterion and the criterion of superfairness.

Here I use the following definition (which will later be made somewhat more explicit):

Definition 1   A distribution is called (nonstrictly) *superfair* if each class of participants prefers its own share to the share received by another group, that is, if no participant *envies* the other.[2]

1   Superfair Distributions and the Fair Division Problem

As was already noted, the superfairness approach to analysis of equity issues is a straightforward generalization of the familiar solution to the problem of fair division of a cake between two persons—I cut, you choose.

---

1. These diagrams seem first to have been constructed by Kolm [1972].

2. Varian calls such a distribution "equitable," reserving the term "fairness" to refer to a distribution that is both equitable *and Pareto optimal.* I prefer to avoid his terms for they invite confusion between issues of allocative efficiency and equity, which it is one of our purposes to disentangle. On these issues, see Varian [1974, 1975].

Though it is less well-known, there also exist solutions to the problem of dividing the cake among n persons.[3]

For our purposes, two characteristics of the solution to the fair division problem are noteworthy. First, the approach can work even when each party has no information about the preferences of the others,[4] and, second, the solution is (nonstrictly) superfair in that everyone obtains what can be described suggestively (but not rigorously) as at least one $(1/n)$th of the total utility *to himself* of the entire collection distributed and, very likely, he obtains more than this.

The first of these attributes is the workability of the fair division solution even if no one volunteers damaging information about himself. The mechanism is straightforward. One simply cuts the cake in a way that guarantees the cutter against being left with an unacceptably small piece.

The superfairness of the solution is perhaps more surprising at first but equally trivial. *Strict* superfairness may arise if the cake is not homogeneous and the parties' tastes or perceptions are not identical. Suppose the cutter judges the two pieces of the cake to be equal but the chooser does not. In that case, the cutter will end up with what, to her, is half the cake, while the chooser will obtain what, to him, is more than half. A more substantial example arises where both parties recognize that the cake is non-uniform—say, one side of the cake has many nuts and the other has most of the raisins. If the chooser is known to have a strong preference for nuts while the cutter prefers raisins, the cutter's strategy will be to cut the cake so that the (slightly?) smaller piece contains most of the nuts. In that way each of the two parties may perhaps be interpreted to get more than half the utility of the cake *in his own perception*.[5] The distribution is strictly superfair.

---

3. The following solution seems to be due to Knaster and Banach. The procedure consists in assigning arbitrarily numbers 1 to n to the different individuals. Individual 1 then cuts a slice of the cake and passes it on to individual 2. Person 2 then has two options: (a) to pass it on untouched or (b) to pass it on after reducing it by cutting away some portion. When it is passed on, individual 3 has the same options as 2, etc. If n decides not to keep the slice, the last person to cut a piece from it is required to accept it. The process is then repeated until each participant has a slice. In this way no one will cut a slice so small that he is unwilling to accept it as a fair share. The solution is reported by Steinhaus [1948] and by Kuhn [1967]. Kuhn's brief survey of the literature and the state of analysis of the problem is particularly illuminating.

4. This is true at least where there is perfect divisibility. For problems that arise in cases of indivisibility, see Kuhn [1967, pp. 35–36].

5. Later we shall note a significant problem besetting this interpretation, one that will suggest an alternative criterion of equity that is more restrictive than superfairness. It is

I shall deliberately avoid any protracted discussion of the philosophical underpinnings of the superfairness approach and its pros and cons, since my primary concern is application. Yet a few words on the subject must be offered now, and I shall have to return to the subject later to suggest a somewhat modified criterion.

The relationship between the superfairness criterion and the solution to the classical cake division problems brings out the attractive features of the new theory as a reasonable way of approaching the analysis of equity issues. It is not difficult to persuade oneself that the superfairness criterion is neither inherently irrational nor repugnant in its implicit value judgments. Yet it is important to emphasize that some observers have reacted quite differently to this approach, which has elicited considerable hostility (see, for example, Holcombe [1983]). Perhaps the main objection to it is that it enshrines envy as the standard of economic desirability. Thus, consider a change from which everyone benefits to some degree so that it easily qualifies as a Pareto improvement. Yet if in *B*'s judgment *A* benefits a great deal while *B* benefits very little, the change may fail the (incremental) superfairness test.[6] Here, it is noteworthy that courts and legislatures have, at least sometimes, come down on the side of the superfairness criterion's value judgments, explicitly rejecting economists' arguments that because no group is harmed by a particular proposal and some groups clearly benefit, all of its equity problems are automatically settled. Later in the chapter we shall, however, consider an alternative criterion, equal division fairness, which does not use envy as its basis.[7]

---

relevant that the actual distribution of benefits in the divide-and-choose procedure will depend on how much the cutter knows about the chooser's preferences. The better he knows them the more closely he can trim the cake to offer the chooser the minimum surplus that assures her selection of the piece of cake the cutter wants her to take. More will be said about this later. For a systematic discussion of the issue and some alternative procedures that provide increased protection to the chooser, see Crawford [1977, 1979A, 1980].

6. Incremental fairness is defined and discussed in the next chapter.

7. Another cogent objection is provided by an anonymous referee of an earlier article based on some of the materials in this book. He writes, "So long as it is assumed, as it is here, that preferences are strictly selfish, who *cares* about fairness? The economist is here in the position of the utilitarian advising people who ... do not care about others, that total welfare will be maximized by the equal distribution of income." But, surely, there is more to the matter. Selfish people are selfishly worried that they may be treated unfairly, and they may, consequently, insist on rules of fairness. That is what the cake division game is all about. A rule of fairness is a sort of insurance arrangement that selfish people accept to make sure they will not be mistreated, and pay for it by providing assurance to others that they, too, will not be mistreated. Rawls's social contract interpretation of fairness is no more

It should also be noted that the superfairness criterion is inconsistent with principles of fairness such as that of John Rawls [1971], which, in effect, considers a change to be equitable if and only if it benefits the member of the community in the most disadvantageous position (or benefits others without harming any of those most "disadvantaged" individuals). For if such a change arouses the envy of the other members of the community, it will not be incrementally superfair.

I shall not discuss further in such general terms the issue of the philosophical acceptability of the superfairness criterion (for more on the subject, see, for example, Varian [1974, 1975]). Rather, I should like to end these remarks by pointing out that the value judgments underlying the theory have much in common with those at the foundations of the theory of allocative efficiency, i.e., of standard welfare theory. For both approaches rest on the preconception that the desirability of an allocation of resources and a distribution of its products should be judged exclusively in terms of the preferences of the individuals affected by it, rather than some criterion of intrinsic merit decided upon by an uninvolved judge who presumably considers himself peculiarly qualified to determine what is "just and equitable."

This, incidentally, brings out another feature of superfairness theory that should contribute to its attractiveness to economists. The analysis employs as its data precisely the same sorts of information needed in the theory of resource allocation: the preferences of individuals, the available quantities of resources, and the state of technological knowledge. As a result, superfairness theory can also use the same analytical constructs as resource allocation theory: utility functions, preference sets, production functions, etc. In other words, one embarks on work in superfairness analysis with a considerable head start by making use of the ideas, techniques, and many of the value judgments of standard microeconomics.

---

dependent on altruism of the members of society than is Foley's fairness theory, which we are discussing here. Both deal with, in effect, an insurance program for those who do not come out on top, or, rather, it is an insurance policy that is rational for all of us because we cannot know in advance whether we shall be among those who come out on top.

It should be added that altruism complicates the superfairness analysis but does not undermine it. Following Hochman and Rogers's many pieces on the subject (see, for example, [1969]), one need only assume that the quantities of goods accruing to an individual A may enter into the utility function of another individual B and proceed as before. The set of fair solutions will, of course, be affected by this premise, but the principles of the analysis will not be undermined.

2   Some Basic Concepts

In our discussions it will be convenient to employ the following definitions, which slightly modify the terminology of previous writers:

Definition 2   Envy:[8] A distribution of n commodities is said to involve envy by individual 2 of the share obtained by individual 1 if 2 would rather have the bundle of commodities received by 1 under this distribution than the bundle the distribution assigns to 2.

It should be emphasized that the concept of envy as defined here involves absolutely no interpersonal comparisons of utilities. If individuals A and B are, respectively, assigned commodity bundles a and b, and U^a and U^b are their respective utility functions, envy of B by A is not defined as $U^b(b) > U^a(a)$, whatever that may mean, but as $U^a(b) > U^a(a)$. Thus, A consults only his own preferences and decides whether he would rather have B's bundle or his own. He is never required to know or guess about B's preferences.

Definition 3   Fairness: A distribution is fair if it involves no envy by any individual of any other.

Definition 4   Strict superfairness: A distribution is strictly superfair if each participant receives a bundle that is strictly preferred by that individual to the bundle received by anyone else, that is, if his holdings could be reduced (in the case of divisibility) without giving rise to envy.

We shall see next that the existence of superfair distributions is a normal state of affairs whenever there exist fixed quantities of two or more commodities to be divided among several individuals with different tastes.

Thus, consider the distribution of n perfectly divisible commodities among m persons. Suppose each individual is initially assigned exactly $(1/m)$th of each good. That distribution is obviously fair on the preceding definition (but not strictly superfair) since no individual will prefer anyone

---

8. Where uncertainty or risk is involved, envy and, hence, superfairness must be interpreted in an *ex ante* sense. *Ex post* the concepts are not very helpful. Thus, in any fair gamble, the loser can be expected to envy (in the more usual sense of the term) the winner after the event, but it is not very illuminating to label such an outcome (necessarily) "unfair." Of course, people may also be envious, in the common sense of the term, over an *ex ante* distribution.

else's identical share. Now, let the individuals trade freely among themselves. If their tastes differ, they will generally carry out some exchanges, and if those exchanges are carried out through a competitive market at fixed prices, every participant must gain from such an exchange.[9] The resulting distribution must then be superfair in the sense that each individual ends up with a bundle of goods that does not lead him to envy any other person's bundle, and to all who have done any trading it must be even better than that. Thus, in this case superfair distributions must always exist, as we wished to show.

3   Graphics of Superfairness in the Two-Good Case

Much of the analysis will deal with the division of fixed bundles of commodities. Consequently, the Edgeworth box diagram can serve as a basic analytic tool. Most of the literature deals with the case of m persons and n

---

9. As Hal Varian has pointed out to me, unless it is done through a competitive market, an exchange from an equal division distribution need not be fair even if it is mutually beneficial. No one loses as the result of such a trade and some must benefit, but some may gain more than others, and that will give rise to envy. As Varian put it (in a letter to me),

Suppose that there are just two kinds of people, those who like raisins and those who like nuts, with raisin lovers deriving zero utility from nuts and vice versa. Originally the nuts and raisins are divided equally. Now one nut lover and one raisin lover get together and make a trade. So they are better off, but of course each of them will be envied by his own class of people.

Thus, partial trading can easily create envy. What if one goes all the way to a Pareto efficient allocation? Even there it doesn't work. It can easily happen that trade to a Pareto efficient allocation from equal division will create envy. For example, suppose that there is only one nut lover. Then it is Pareto efficient for him to trade his raisins to one of the raisin lovers and have all the other raisin lovers give him their nuts—but then the other raisin lovers will necessarily envy the lucky one who got to make the trade. Note that this trade is even in the core of the equal division game.

Of course there is some point in the core that preserves the envy-free nature of the original allocation—the equal income competitive equilibrium. However, just any old trade from equal division doesn't necessarily preserve equity—but a competitive trading mechanism does. This is basically because the competitive mechanism offers everybody the same opportunities for trade.

Other mechanisms, such as perfectly discriminating monopoly, can achieve efficiency but do not generally preserve equity. Later we shall see more explicitly why a competitive equilibrium achieved by exchange from an equal initial distribution of all items must always be fair.

Varian also has provided a proof [1976A] that in economies with large numbers of persons and continuous variations in tastes the *only* Pareto efficient allocations that are also fair (envy free) are allocations that would result in competitive markets with a perfectly equal distribution of income. Thus, there, competitive markets and equal incomes can be necessary as well as sufficient for fairness and Pareto efficiency.

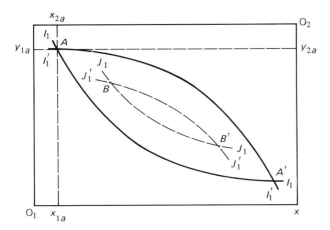

Figure 2.1

commodities, but for convenience in graphing it is obviously appropriate to deal with a world of two persons, 1 and 2, and two goods, X and Y.

Locus $I_1 I_1$ in figure 2.1 is simply an arbitrarily selected indifference curve of individual 1, as in the standard Edgeworth diagram. However, $I_1' I_1'$ is *not* one of individual 2's indifference curves. Rather, $I_1' I_1'$ is simply the mirror image of $I_1 I_1$—it is $I_1 I_1$ redrawn so that $I_1' I_1'$ relates to 2's origin, O_2, in exactly the same way that $I_1 I_1$ relates to O_1. This upside-down version of 1's indifference curve enables us to judge 1's evaluation of what 2 receives at a particular point in the box, as the concept of envy requires. I shall refer to $I_1' I_1'$ as the symmetric image of $I_1 I_1$ and henceforth the prime will be used to denote the symmetric image of the object represented by the corresponding unprimed symbol.

Now consider points A and A', the intersection points of our two renderings of the same indifference curve. The distribution represented by A must leave individual 1 indifferent between what A gives to him and what A gives to individual 2. For 1 receives the bundle $A_1 = (O_1 x_{1a},\ O_1 y_{1a})$, lying on his indifference curve $I_1 I_1$; while 2 receives $A_2 = (O_2 x_{2a},\ O_2 y_{2a})$, which lies on $I_1' I_1'$, the same indifference curve of individual 1 as A_1 does. Hence, 1 must be indifferent between A_1 and A_2 and so point A must involve no envy by person 1 of 2's commodity bundle. Consequently, point A is a distribution that is just *marginally* fair from the viewpoint of individual 1. The same is obviously true of A', the other intersection point between $I_1 I_1$ and its symmetric image indifference curve. Thus we say that points A and A' lie on person 1's *fairness boundary*. We can obtain two more such points from a second indifference curve, $J_1 J_1$, of individual 1 whose intersection points with its symmetric image $J_1' J_1'$ are boundary

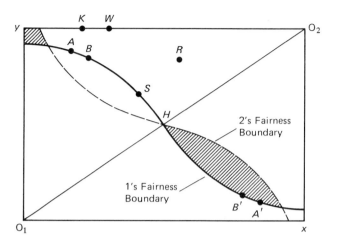

Figure 2.2

points B and B'. Continuing in this way we trace out all of individual 1's fairness boundary (figure 2.2), that is, the borderline between distributions that 1 considers unfair and those he considers more than fair.

In exactly the same way we can construct 2's fairness boundary, from her indifference curves and their symmetric images. This boundary is also shown in figure 2.2.

It is now easy to see how superfair solutions can arise. Assuming (as I shall throughout) that neither individual is sated in either good, then any point, such as R, above and/or to the right of 1's fairness boundary must be more than fair to him. For there must then exist points such as S on the fairness boundary that offer 1 less (or, at most, as much) of each good as R, and that offer 2 more (no less) of each good. Hence, since S is marginally fair to 1, R must be more than fair to him. Similarly, any point below 2's fairness boundary must be more than fair to her. Consequently, any point in a region that lies, simultaneously, above 1's fairness boundary and below that of person 2 (the shaded regions in figure 2.2) must represent a strictly superfair distribution.

4 Properties of the Fairness Boundaries

We can derive several properties of fairness boundaries.

Proposition 1   If each individual's preferences are continuous, they depend only on the quantities received by him, and if nonsatiation holds everywhere, the fairness boundary must (a) contain the midpoint, H, of either diagonal of the box; (b) its portion to the left of H must be the inverted mirror image of its portion to the right of H—that is, if (x^*, y^*) gives the dimensions of the box (i.e., x^* is the available quantity of x, etc.) and point $A \equiv (x, y)$ on the boundary lies to the left of H, then the symmetric image point $A' \equiv (x^* - x, y^* - y)$ must lie on the boundary to the right of H; (c) the boundary must have a negative slope everywhere.[10]

Proof Properties (a) and (b) follow trivially:

(a) *Midpoint*: At midpoint H, each individual receives exactly the same bundle as the other and so each must be indifferent between his own bundle and the other person's.

(b) *Symmetry*: By the construction of the boundary, if A lies on 1's boundary, person 1 must be indifferent between his bundle (x, y) and 2's bundle $(x^* - x, y^* - y)$. Hence, he must remain indifferent if the bundles are interchanged, so A' must also lie on 1's boundary.

(c) *Negative slope*: Let (x_1, y_1) and (x_2, y_2), respectively, be 1's and 2's possessions at point A on 1's fairness boundary; and let $(x_1 + \Delta x_1, y_1 + \Delta y_1)$, $(x_2 - \Delta x_1, y_2 - \Delta y_1)$ be their respective holdings at point $A + \Delta A$ on the boundary. If U^1 is 1's utility function, then, by definition of the fairness boundary, we must have

$$U^1(x_1, y_1) = U^1(x_2, y_2), \tag{2.1}$$

$$U^1(x_1 + \Delta x_1, y_1 + \Delta y_1) = U^1(x_2 - \Delta x_1, y_2 - \Delta y_1). \tag{2.2}$$

Taking $\Delta x_1 > 0$, if the slope were nonnegative, so that $\Delta y_1 \geqslant 0$, then by nonsatiety

$$U^1(x_1 + \Delta x_1, y_1 + \Delta y_1) > U^1(x_1, y_1),$$

$$U^1(x_2 - \Delta x_1, y_2 - \Delta y_1) < U^1(x_2, y_2),$$

which together with (2.1) contradict (2.2). Thus, if $\Delta x_1 > 0$ we must have $\Delta y_1 < 0$, and the boundary's slope must be negative.

Next, we turn to existence of the fairness boundary.

Proposition 2 Where the individual's utility function is continuous, and the individual is not sated in the commodities, the fairness boundary must extend to the edges of the Edgeworth box. The fairness boundary will then

---

10. This last characteristic was pointed out to me by Dietrich Fischer.

always exist. In particular, in the two-commodity case normally dealt with in the Edgeworth diagram it will extend from some point, K, on the upper or left-hand edges of the Edgeworth box, through the midpoint to the point K' symmetric with K on the lower or right-hand edges.[11]

Proof As we have seen, the midpoint, H, will always lie on the fairness boundary. If Varian's continuity condition is satisfied (see footnote 11), the boundary must always also exist in a neighborhood of H. Next, note (figure 2.2) that individual 1's origin, O_1, must be unfair to him because there individual 1 gets nothing and the goods all go to other parties. By the nonsatiety assumption 1 will envy the parties who do get goods. Analogously, O_2, the opposite origin, must be more than fair to 1 in his own opinion. As one moves along the boundary of the Edgeworth box from O_1 coming steadily closer to O_2, the degree of envy of individual 1 must decline steadily. By continuity, there must be some unique intermediate point, K, on this path at which 1 is indifferent between what is assigned to him and what is assigned to that other individual who in 1's opinion is most favored. By definition, K must lie on 1's fairness boundary.

Next, draw in a ray from O_1 to *any* point, such as W, that lies on the northeast boundary $O_1 y O_2$ of the box above or to the right of K; then by the same argument as before, a unique marginally fair point must lie somewhere on ray OW. The remainder of proposition 2 follows immediately by the continuity assumption, and the symmetry property of the fairness boundary.

We come next to a remarkable property of the fairness boundary apparently discovered by Kolm [1972, p. 50ff] for the two-person case and applied further by Crawford [1977]. This property is given by

Proposition 3   If everyone's indifference curves are differentiable and convex to the origin (i.e., their utility functions are quasi-concave), then at the equal division point, H, any individual's fairness boundary, F_i, must be tangent to his indifference curve, I_{Hi}, through H, and H must be preferred

---

11. Varian comments: "It is not obvious that the boundary can't have jumps/discontinuities. According to the implicit function theorem, the boundary will exist and be differentiable when

$$\frac{\partial u}{\partial x_2}(x_1, x_2) \neq \frac{\partial u}{\partial x_1}(w_1 - x_1, w_2 - x_2)$$

at all (x_1, x_2) on the fairness boundary."

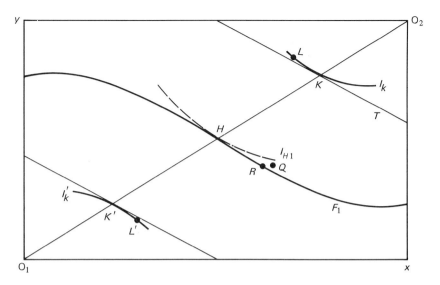

Figure 2.3

to any other point R on F_i, i.e., any point R on F_i must lie on an indifference curve less preferred[12] by i than I_{Hi}.

This is illustrated in figure 2.3, where I_{H1} is tangent to 1's fairness boundary, F_1, at H and is the highest indifference curve attained anywhere on the fairness boundary.

Before dealing rigorously with the n-person case we shall first sketch a geometric argument for the 2-person, 2-good case that permits use of the Edgeworth diagram. This requires two preliminary observations: (i) From

---

12. An intuitive (if not perfectly accurate) explanation is not too difficult to provide. The convexity (declining MRS) of 1's indifference curve through H means that if the equilibrium point moves farther and farther from H, in order to keep person 1 indifferent to H, person 2 must in effect give up disproportionately increasing quantities of goods, thereby making 1 prefer his holdings to 2's. Specifically, suppose the equilibrium point moves away from H along 1's indifference curve I_{H1} in steps, from point a to b to c ..., which involve equal decrements $\Delta x = \Delta x_a = \Delta x_b = \cdots$ in 1's holdings of x. Then, declining MRS requires that to remain indifferent, 1 must receive in exchange an increasing sequence of increments in his holdings of y, $\Delta y_a < \Delta y_b < \cdots$. It follows that in these moves individual 2 is giving up successively larger decrements of y, and receiving in exchange only constant increments of x. Hence, (in either individual's opinion) the value of 2's holdings must have successively lower and lower utility than her holdings at H. Thus, with 1 indifferent between his own holdings at, say, point b and point H, at b he must consider 2's holdings inferior to his own. That is, any such point b, on individual 1's indifference curve, must lie above his fairness boundary.

the construction, every point on individual i's fairness boundary must be the intersection of one of his indifference curves $I_k(x, y) = 0$ and its symmetric image $I'_k(x, y) = I_k(x^* - x, y^* - y) = 0$, where (x^*, y^*) are the available quantities of the two goods. This is so because otherwise individual i would not be indifferent between his own holdings at point (x, y) and those of the other individual. (ii) Our second observation is that if I_k is an indifference curve of individual k and I'_k is its symmetric image, and L and L' are symmetric image points on I_k and I'_k, respectively, then the slope of I_k at L must be the same as the slope of I'_k at L'. A moment's consideration suggests that this follows[13] from the symmetry of I_k and I'_k.

Proof We are now in a position to provide our geometric proof of proposition 3, which relies on the observation that any of individual 1's indifference curves I_1 that lies farther from 1's origin than the midpoint indifference curve I_{H1} will contain no intersection points with its symmetric image, I', and hence will contain no points on 1's fairness boundary.

Specifically, in figure 2.3 we know that I_{H1} lies on individual 1's fairness boundary. Let I_k be any indifference curve farther from individual 1's origin than I_{H1}, with point K the intersection of I_k and the upward sloping diagonal and T the support (tangent) of concave indifference curve I_k at K. Let I'_k, K', and T' be the corresponding symmetric images. Then by observation (ii) T' and T must be parallel and they cannot intersect since K and K' are on opposite sides of the midpoint. Therefore, by their convexity, I_k and I'_k can have no intersection point and so they cannot contain any point on the individual's fairness boundary.

By exactly the same reasoning I_{H1} and I'_{H1} can have only one intersection point, H, at which they are tangent to one another. Hence, all points other than H on fairness boundary F_1 must lie on indifference curves below I_{H1} and, by differentiability, F_1 and I_{H1} must be tangent at H.

To generalize this result to m persons we must first deal with the following difficulty. When individual 1 receives (x, y) (or the corresponding vector of n commodities), we do not know from this how the remainder of the available quantities of goods $(x^* - x, y^* - y)$ is distributed among the other $m - 1$ individuals. But without this information we cannot judge directly from information on the magnitude of (x, y) alone whether 1 envies

---

13. Formally, I_k satisfies $I_k(x, y) = 0$ whose slope $dy/dx = -I_{kx}/I_{ky}$ (where we write I_{kx} for $\partial I_k/\partial x$, etc.). But if (x, y) are the coordinates of L, then $(x', y') = (x^* - x, y^* - y)$ are the coordinates of L', and at L', I'_k satisfies $I_k(x', y') = I_k(x^* - x, y^* - y) = 0$. Therefore, at L', $dy'/dx' = -I_{kx'}/I_{ky'} = -I_{kx}/I_{ky}$, since $I_{kx} = I_{kx'} \cdot \partial x'/\partial x = -I_{kx'}$, etc.

anyone else. There are two extreme cases: (a) where all of the residue goes to one individual (the case most likely to arouse 1's envy)—but then we are essentially back at the two-person case in which the preceding argument holds;[14] and (b) at the other extreme, the residue is divided equally among the remaining $m - 1$ persons so that each receives $[(x^* - x)/m - 1,$ $(y^* - y)/m - 1]$ (and, of course, then individual 1 is least likely to envy any one other person). Dealing now with case (b) we proceed formally by defining 1's fairness boundary for this situation:

Definition 5   *The equal division of residue fairness boundary* (EDR fairness boundary) for i is the set of vectors (points), y, such that individual i is just indifferent between y and the amounts received by every one of the $m - 1$ other individuals if the residue $(y^* - y)$ is divided equally among them so that each receives $(y^* - y)/(m - 1)$. In other words, y is on i's EDR fairness boundary iff $U^i(y) = U^i[(y^* - y)/(m - 1)]$, where $U^i(\cdot)$ is i's utility function.

Then we have

Proposition 4   If all the individuals in question have utility functions that are quasi-concave and twice differentiable, then for any individual i: (i) along any ray through his origin, O_i, his EDR fairness boundary, F_i, must lie at least as close to his origin as I_{Hi}, his indifference curve through the equal division point, H; (ii) F_i must be tangent to I_{Hi} at H.

Proof   Let y^* be the vector of available quantities of the n products, so that the equal division point is y^*/m. Then given any $y \leqslant y^*$

$$U^i(y^*/m) \equiv U^i[y/m + (y^* - y)/m]$$

$$\equiv U^i\left[\frac{y}{m} + \frac{m-1}{m}\frac{y^* - y}{m - 1}\right] \tag{2.3}$$

$$\geqslant \frac{1}{m}U^i(y) + \frac{m-1}{m}U^i\left(\frac{y^* - y}{m - 1}\right),$$

where the inequality follows from the quasi-concavity of i's utility function.

Since (2.3) holds for any $y \leqslant y^*$, we may next consider the special case in which y lies in i's EDR fairness boundary, so that by definition

14. That is, it holds if H is interpreted as the point of equal division only between the two individuals who receive any goods, which obviously raises questions about the interpretation of this situation as an m-person case.

$$U^i(y) = U^i\left(\frac{y^* - y}{m - 1}\right) \equiv \frac{1}{m} U^i\left(\frac{y^* - y}{m - 1}\right) + \frac{m - 1}{m} U^i\left(\frac{y^* - y}{m - 1}\right)$$

$$= \frac{1}{m} U^i(y) + \frac{m - 1}{m} U^i\left(\frac{y^* - y}{m - 1}\right).$$

(2.4)

Consequently, by (2.3) for y any point on i's EDR fairness boundary

$U^i(y) \leqslant U^i(y^*/m)$.

Therefore y must lie between I_{Hi}, i's indifference curve through the equal division point y^*/m and i's origin, O_i, thus proving part (i) of the proposition. Next, part (ii) follows at once from the differentiability property and the result (proposition 2) that i's fairness boundary must include $H = y^*/m$.

The preceding argument immediately also provides a rigorous proof for the case of 2 persons and n commodities, which was treated by Kolm and Crawford. In that case we need not, of course, employ the construct of the EDR fairness boundary, since with only two persons present everything not going to person 1 must be received by 2 and so 1's fairness boundary will be unique.[15]

Propositions 3 and 4, which will prove of fundamental importance at a number of points in the discussion that follows, cry out for economic interpretation. What exactly goes on at points like R or Q in figure 2.3, that is, a point that is at least marginally fair to individual 1 but leaves him with a lower utility level than the equal division point? The answer is that while 1 likes what he gets at Q less than he likes $H/2$, he may accept it because he likes what individual 2 obtains at Q even less. Thus, it is true that 1 does not envy 2 *her possessions* at Q. He has, in effect, been blackmailed into accepting the inferior distribution at Q by making her holdings still less palatable *to him*.

But this does not necessarily mean that to the other person Q is less desirable than $H/2$. On the contrary, we shall soon see that the opposite will be true in a significant class of cases. This must inevitably raise some

---

15. In the m-person case, the EDR boundary for individual 1 may be taken to constitute a rough lower bound for the fairness boundaries of individual i corresponding to different distributions of the residual quantities of the goods. To see this consider a ray O_1R through 1's origin in the "Edgeworth hyperbox." Let E be the point on O_1R that lies on 1's EDR fairness boundary. If one now replaces the equal distribution of the residues from 1's holdings at E with an unequal distribution, call it V, that favors some individual j, then 1 is likely to envy j at point E. The distribution V fairness boundary for person 1 is therefore likely to intersect O_1R at a point farther from O_1 than point E.

question about the superfairness concept itself. If H is necessarily fair, as in some fundamental sense an equal division must be, and if at Q individual 1 is less happy than he is at H while 2 is happier at Q than she is at H, how can we say with any reason that point Q is fair? What sense does it make to say 1 does not envy 2 when the distribution is given by Q?

We shall return to this issue very soon and see that it seems to argue for a more restrictive definition of superfairness. It will suggest, in other words, that without further restrictions, the entire class of criteria stemming from the "I cut, you choose" procedure may sometimes yield rather blatantly unfair results.

5   Properties of the Regions of Superfairness

Having discussed some properties of fairness boundaries, we turn next to attributes of regions of superfair distribution points. We see from figure 2.2 that the set of (nonstrictly) superfair distributions must contain H, but it is generally not symmetric about H. Given one such region to the right of H, the symmetric region to the left of H will never be superfair since in the former, 1's fairness boundary *must* lie below 2's so that in the latter, 2's fairness boundary must lie above 1's.

We see also that the superfair regions may be disconnected and may contain portions of the axes. Thus we obtain

Proposition 5   The superfair region will generally not be located symmetrically within the Edgeworth box and it may not be convex or a single connected set of points.

Next, let us discuss the existence of *strictly* superfair solutions. It was remarked earlier that their existence is ascribable to differences in tastes. Indeed, it is easy to show

Proposition 6   If both individuals have identical preferences, then their fairness boundaries must coincide and so there can be no region of strictly superfair solutions, for such a region must lie between the two curves.

The proof is obvious. If point A lies on 1's fairness boundary yielding basket A_1 to 1 and A_2 to 2, then, by definition, 1 must be indifferent between A_1 and A_2. But, with identity of tastes, the same must be true of 2 so that A must also lie on 2's fairness boundary.

Thus, differences in tastes are necessary for the existence of strictly superfair solutions. The geometry also suggests a related sufficient condition.

Proposition 7   Assume that the utility functions are quasi-concave and differentiable. If in the neighborhood of the equal division point the two fairness boundaries have continuous first derivatives that are different from each other, then some strictly superfair solutions must exist. That is, there must exist at least some strictly superfair distributions if at the point of equal division the individuals involved have different marginal rates of substitution between at least two of the commodities in question.

Proof   If at H the slopes of the two boundaries are not identical, they must intersect there. Then 2's boundary must lie above 1's boundary either immediately to the right of H or to the left of H (but not both). There, any point between the two boundaries must be strictly superfair.

The connection between the slopes of the fairness boundaries and the marginal rates of substitution between x and y (the ratio of their marginal utilities) follows directly from propositions 3 and 4, which tell us that at H individual i's fairness boundary must be tangent to his indifference curve through H. This argument obviously holds for the n-commodity case, since if for any pair of commodities the ratio of their marginal utilities differs between two individuals, we can hold constant the quantities of all other commodities they possess and change the quantity of the two commodities in question, yielding the same sort of relationships as before in the corresponding two-dimensional cross section of their n-dimensional Edgeworth diagram.

6   Superfairness, Pareto Improvement, and Pareto Optimality

There are a number of connections between the concept of superfairness and the Pareto improvement and Pareto optimality criteria. First, we have shown in the case of quasi-concavity of utilities (propositions 3 and 4) that each individual prefers the equal division distribution to that of any other points on his (EDR) fairness boundary (see definition 5). It follows that any point he prefers to H must lie farther from his origin than the fairness boundary. Consequently, any point Pareto superior to H must lie above everyone's (EDR) fairness boundary and so must be strictly (EDR) superfair. More formally,

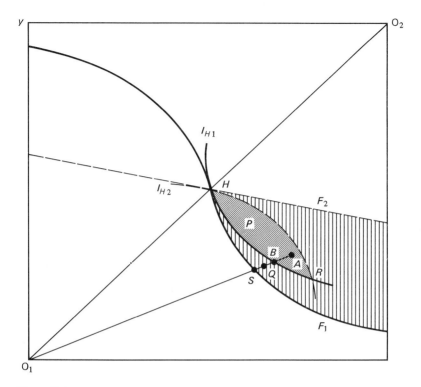

Figure 2.4

Proposition 8 (Kolm)   If all the pertinent utility functions are quasi-concave
and twice differentiable and the equal division point, H, is not Pareto
optimal, then there will exist a set, P, of points each of which is a Pareto
improvement over H. P must then be a proper subset of S, the set of EDR
superfair distributions (proposition 4), which in the two-person case is the
set of superfair distributions. Moreover, the equal division point, H, will be
the only point of P's boundaries that lies on any fairness boundary.

Proof   It is easy to show this diagrammatically. In figure 2.4 the lightly
shaded region between F_1 and F_2 is the set of superfair distributions. By
propositions 3 and 4 we know that none of the points on F_1 and F_2 is
Pareto superior to H. But we also know that I_{H1}, individual 1's indifference
curve through H, is tangent to his fairness boundary, F_1, at H and that a
similar relationship holds for person 2. Therefore, the region of distributions Pareto superior to H, the heavily shaded area, P, must lie entirely
within the region of superfair distributions.

We come next to a fundamental theorem that seems first to have been discovered by Schmeidler and Yaari. It deals with the relationship between Pareto optimal solutions and solutions that are superfair. Specifically, it tells us that among the available solutions to a problem involving the distribution of a *fixed* stock of commodities among a fixed number of individuals there will always be at least one solution that is at the same time superfair (though not necessarily strictly superfair) and Pareto optimal. To see why this is so, consider an initially equal distribution of all goods (point H). If the contract curve happens to contain H, the result follows since H is fair by definition. Assume next that the contract curve does not go through H and consider the intersection point L of the two individuals' offer curves that begin from H, as in the usual international-trade diagram. Then the standard proof shows that L must lie on the contract curve. But L must also be superfair because at the prices given by the slope of the common price line each individual has the same range of choices available. Letting L_1 and L_2 be the bundles chosen by 1 and 2 at L (where, by construction, the two bundles add up to the available quantities of the two goods), 1 thus reveals a preference for L_1 over L_2 and the reverse is true for 2. Consequently, L is necessarily superfair as well as Pareto optimal. Thus, we have a result now well known in the fairness literature:

Proposition 9   Assume the utility functions are quasi-concave and continuous. Then in the exchange of fixed quantities of n commodities among m individuals, there always exists at least one Pareto optimal solution that is superfair.

So far there would seem to be remarkable compatibility between the Paretian and superfairness concepts; and the latter, which lies at the foundation of the analysis of this book, would appear to behave in a reasonable manner that involves nothing that smacks of the pathological. Unfortunately, as we shall see, that happy state of affairs does not extend very far. The literature abounds with manifestations of curious behavior of the superfairness concept and its relation to the Pareto criterion. Several results of this sort will be described in this chapter and the next.

The first such proposition is due to Philpotts [1983] (and follows directly from the results of Feldman and Kirman, discussed in the next chapter):

Proposition 10   A distribution, D_s, that is strictly superfair may nevertheless be strictly Pareto inferior to another distribution, D_u, that everyone considers to be unfair; i.e., unfair distribution D_u may be one in which each

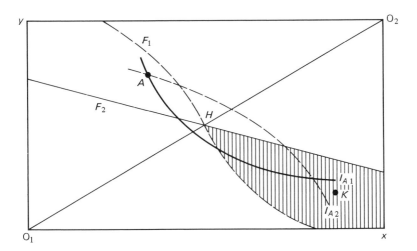

Figure 2.5

individual prefers what he receives to what he gets under strictly superfair distribution D_s.

Proof The proof, of course, requires only a single example in which the posited relationship holds. Such an example is shown in figure 2.5, which also indicates that this sort of situation does not require what appears to be extreme or implausible behavior of the indifference curves. Thus, in figure 2.5 the region of superfair distributions is represented by the shaded area between the fairness boundaries, F_1 and F_2. Consequently, K is strictly superfair. But it lies below I_{A1}, 1's indifference curve through unfair point A, and the same relation holds for person 2.

It is, perhaps, hardly surprising that the efficiency criterion constituted by the Pareto principle does not necessarily agree with the independent fairness criterion. However, Philpotts's example shows that the lack of correspondence may be rather extreme.

To get at the source of the problem which is even more fundamental than Philpotts's analysis indicates, we first prove

Proposition 11 If preferences are quasi-concave, continuous, and transitive, for any individual i there must exist superfair points, Q, that lie between his origin, O_i, and the (nonempty) set P of points Pareto superior to the equal division distribution, H (figure 2.4). For any such Q, while person i will prefer what he receives at H to what he gets at Q, at least one other individual must prefer what she gets at Q to what she obtains at H.

Proof   Let A be any point in set P (figure 2.4). Form the line segment O_1A. By continuity, there must be a point B on O_1A at which 1 is indifferent between[16] B and H. Then B is on the boundary of P nearest O_1. By proposition 8 there must be points such as Q on O_1A between B and the point S at which O_1A crosses F_1, individual 1's fairness boundary.

It is clear that since Q lies below B, 1 must prefer H to any such point Q. Moreover, since at Q person 1 receives less of each good than he does at A, that decrement in A's holdings must be divided up among other individuals. Assuming this is done in such a way that for each individual this constitutes a nonnegative addition to his holdings at A, then at least one person, w, must prefer Q to A. But since A is in the set of points Pareto superior to H, it follows by transitivity that w must prefer Q to H.

This proposition, in sum, tells us that there normally exist distributions that are superfair even though they make some people better off than they would be at the benchmark equal division distribution, while others simultaneously suffer a loss in welfare relative to that reference point. This raises serious questions about the concept of superfairness and suggests that we may want to replace it with a more demanding equity requirement. I shall indicate now that the requirement of Pareto superiority or Pareto equivalence to the equal division point H may reasonably be considered as such an alternative. Here I use

Definition 6   A distribution is called *superequal* if it yields to each individual a utility level equal to or superior to that offered by equal division of all commodities. (Note the relation to Pazner and Schmeidler's [1978] concept of egalitarian equivalence.)

By proposition 8 we know that any point A not Pareto inferior to H must be strictly superfair while there can exist points Q that are strictly superfair but not Pareto superior or equivalent to H. Thus, with quasiconcave and continuous preferences the superequality requirement is indeed more demanding than superfairness. But this does not tell us what is at stake in the choice.[17]

---

16. I mean, of course, that he is indifferent between what he receives at B and what he gets at H. The briefer wording will henceforth be used except where it may create confusion.

17. The equal division point, H, arises as a natural benchmark only in this pure exchange problem in which x^* and y^* can be taken to have descended like manna from heaven, without any of the participating individuals having contributed anything to their output. We shall see later in the chapter that where productive activity enters the picture the benchmark point must shift according to the modification in the fairness standard one uses

To see what is at issue we must again consider what goes on at a point such as Q that is eliminated from the set of fair distributions by the superequality test, but is accepted by the superfairness criterion. At Q we have seen that i is worse off than at H. On the other hand, individual w is better off at Q than at H. Yet at H, by *definition*, they are equally well off.[18] If so, it can be argued that in commonsense terms i does have grounds for envying w at Q, that Q is in some sense better off than i at that point.

A parable will bring out the issue. Consider an economy composed of two persons: Mr. Poor and Ms. Rich. There are also two goods: truffles and gin. Mr. Poor vastly prefers gin while Ms. Rich prefers truffles. With 200 pounds of truffles and 200 bottles of gin available, H gives each person 100 of each item. Now suppose Mr. Poor is indifferent between $1/2H$ and the bundle composed of zero truffles and 120 bottles of gin, and that Ms. Rich far prefers the residue (200 pounds of truffles and 80 bottles of gin) to $1/2H$. Thus, if instead (point Q) he is offered only 115 bottles of gin and no truffles, he will have suffered a distinct loss of utility in comparison with H. Yet he may still prefer this inferior bundle to what it leaves over for Ms. Rich, with her bundle so heavily skewed toward truffles.

In other words, the superfair solution supposedly reconciles Mr. Poor to his fate by putting in Ms. Rich's hands a bundle that is rather distasteful to Mr. Poor. In a cut-and-choose process, given these options, he would indeed select the 115 bottles. But it still remains true, in the classic Brooklyn phrase, that "he wuz robbed"—he received a loss in utility relative to the equal division point while Ms. Rich was enabled to cater most effectively to her preferences.

Put in another way, it does not seem irrational for the poor person to have envied Mr. Onassis his wealth even if he despises the opera performances and fine foods Onassis consumed and if yacht trips would only make him seasick. It is true that superfairness does mean absence of envy by the poor man of the rich man's *consumption bundle*—which is perhaps only a secondary concern—but it does not preclude the (higher priority?) envy of the rich man's *wealth* or *welfare level* (however defined). The paradoxes of superfairness appear to arise because the criterion seems, on

---

to take contributions to output into account. Here, one may also cite the widespread acceptance of the fairness of the I divide-you choose process as justification for the use of H as a benchmark. For in that process if the cake is cut into two identical portions, it is clear that the result must pass the implied fairness test.

18. This, of course, neglects differences in their utility functions, which may in some undefined sense lead them to derive different amounts of pleasure from the identical commodity bundles they receive at H.

superficial consideration, to require absence of all forms of envy when in reality it rules out only consumption bundle envy and not welfare level envy.

Partly to deal with this problem, Varian [1976A] has proposed the concept of *opportunity fairness*, a criterion that requires the incomes of the parties in question to be such that none of them can *afford* to buy any bundle that any of the other persons would envy. As already noted, in the same paper Varian also proves that where the population is large and tastes vary continuously *only* equal incomes are compatible with Pareto efficiency and fairness, so that in that case wealth envy is ruled out if there is to be no consumption bundle envy. Varian explains the reasons intuitively thus [1984]: "... consider a large economy where each agent has just *slightly* different preferences from his neighbor ... then if one agent had a higher income than his neighbor he would choose a bundle that his neighbor envied—since both of them have similar tastes" (p. 5).

It is easy to see that the superequality criterion, which by proposition 8 also rules out consumption bundle envy, also makes some provision against wealth envy. This is so because, by definition, if a distribution is superequal, it must put *every* person in a position of utility greater than or equal to what he would obtain at H, with all goods distributed perfectly equally. That is, surely, a substantial impediment to a very lopsided distribution of welfare, and suggests why the superequality criterion seems immune to many of the paradoxes to which superfairness is subject.

We shall return in the next chapter to a discussion of the two criteria, superfairness and superequality. But for the moment we may merely prove by contradiction that, unlike the superfairness criterion, the superequality criterion does not give rise to the Philpotts paradox of proposition 10.

Proposition 12   Any distribution that is Pareto superior to a superequal distribution must also be superequal.

Proof (by contradiction)   Consider any distribution, D_u, that is *not* superequal, and assume that it is nevertheless Pareto superior to another distribution, D_f, that is superequal. Then since D_u is Pareto superior to D_f, which is in turn Pareto superior or equivalent to H, D_u must also be Pareto superior to H. Therefore D_u must itself be superequal, contrary to the hypothesis that D_u is not.

To end our discussion of the relation between envy and the Pareto criterion, I report a nice result contributed by Varian [1974]. By definition, in any superfair distribution no person envies the commodity bundle possessed by any other. But can we say anything about patterns of envy in a distribution that is Pareto optimal but not superfair? Varian has shown

Proposition 13   In any Pareto optimal distribution among a finite set of individuals (i) there must be at least one individual whose commodity bundle no one envies and (ii) there must be at least one individual who envies no other person's commodity bundle.

Proof   The proof is trivial. We shall prove (i) by contradiction, the proof of (ii) being perfectly analogous. Suppose, contrary to (i), that everyone's commodity bundle, C_i, were envied by someone else. Then let C_1 be envied by person 2, C_2 be envied by 3, etc. With the number of persons being finite, a cycle must eventually occur. That is, there must be an individual i whose bundle is envied, say, by person 1. In that case, if 1 gave his bundle to 2, then 2 gave his bundle to 3, . . . , and i gave his bundle to 1, everyone could be made better off by this simple exchange. But that contradicts the assumption that the initial assumption was Pareto optimal.

Varian comments that this proposition may constitute an operational test to determine for purposes of Rawlsian analysis which persons should be considered "most disadvantaged" and whose improvement in welfare becomes the overriding priority of Rawlsian justice. For, Varian suggests, are not the persons whom no one envies those who are most disadvantaged? That is, is not the operational Rawlsian goal to make them as "well off" as possible—in the sense of guaranteeing that they envy no one, with the resulting allocation one where no one envies anyone else? Yet we know that if a distribution is superfair, everyone must fall into that category even if, like Ms. Rich in my parable, she is at the fortunate end of the income distribution. Varian's theorem is, of course, valid and illuminating, but his interpretation is, perhaps, somewhat premature.

7   First Mover Advantages in the Classic Fair Division Problem

It has long been observed that while the "I cut, you choose" solution to the classic fair division problem is necessarily superfair, it may nevertheless offer a systematic advantage to one of the participants. In particular, it has been noted that the cutter of the illustrative cake has an advantage over the chooser if the former is reasonably well informed about both parties' preferences. What is perhaps not always recognized, however, is that ignorance may move the balance of advantage the other way.

This can also be brought out with the aid of our Edgeworth diagram.

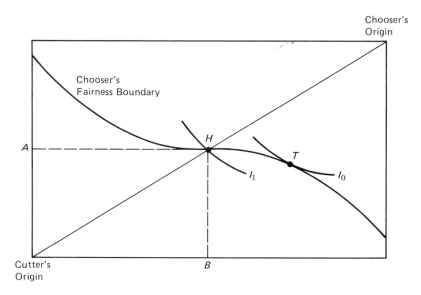

Figure 2.6

Figure 2.6 shows only the chooser's fairness boundary, where the fair division involves apportionment of two items (for example, cake and nuts). Obviously, if the cutter knows the other person's boundary precisely, he will select point T, the (tangency?) point where he reaches his highest indifference curve, I_0, on the chooser's fairness boundary. On the other hand, if the cutter does not know the chooser's fairness boundary, he can make conjectures about it, perhaps adding an extra amount to the portion he wants the chooser to select, to help ensure the "right"choice by the latter. The most conservative (maximin) strategy of the cutter is to assume that the chooser's fairness boundary has the piecewise linear form AHB. By proposition 1, since that boundary must go through H and have a negative slope throughout, the chooser's true boundary cannot possibly be closer to the cutter's origin than AHB; i.e., it cannot possibly be less advantageous to him.

The problem raised by the cutter with perfect knowledge is another example of the difficulty that arises from the existence of distributions that are superfair but not Pareto superior to the equal division point H. The perfectly informed cutter in our example has driven the chooser to a point T on her fairness boundary that, as we know by propositions 3 and 4, she considers inferior to equal division point H.

We may end our brief review of the advantage of the knowledgeable cutter with a proposition in the spirit of the preceding discussion of the limitations of the superfairness criterion and the possibility of using the superequality approach as a substitute. This proposition was contributed by Crawford [1980] and also later derived by Philpotts [1983]. Crawford, who has studied extensively the problem of bias in the divide and choose process (see [1977, 1979A, 1980]), has proposed the following modification of the standard procedure. A random choice is first made of the person to be assigned the position of divider. That person then is required to offer the chooser a choice of either of the bundles (the two parts of the divided cake) that the divider selects, or the equal division allocation (his share of the equal division point, H). Crawford calls this the EDDC (Equal Division Divide and Choose) method. Crawford then demonstrates the following result:

Proposition 14   If the utility functions are quasi-concave and each party is a utility maximizer, then the two-person EDDC division process will always yield a distribution that is Pareto optimal and fair.

Proof   Pareto optimality is proved in the following way: The chooser, 2, must at least end up with as high a utility level as she receives at H, i.e., she must end up on or above her indifference curve I_{H2} through H. Then, 1 maximizes his utility by picking a distribution, D, at least equal in 2's judgment to that which puts 1 on his highest indifference curve attainable from I_{H2}. Such a distribution is, by definition, Pareto optimal. Fairness follows because this process will end up either with distribution H or a distribution D that must be Pareto superior to H since both parties accept it voluntarily. But H is necessarily superfair, and by proposition 8, if D is Pareto superior to H, it must be strictly superfair.

It will be noted that the EDDC solution still offers an advantage to the perfectly informed divider of the cake. But this advantage is reduced from that which the divide and choose process offers because, by propositions 3 and 4, H is preferred by the chooser to all other points on her fairness boundary and, by continuity, to a nondenumerable infinity of other super-fair distributions as well. In other words, H gives the chooser a better lower bound to the benefits that may accrue to her in the process.

8   Production and the Superfairness Criterion

So far we have dealt only with cases in which the vector of relevant outputs is somehow given from outside the analysis, with the fairness criterion applied to the resulting exchanges. But both the theory and applications require us to go beyond this and include decisions on production as well as those relating to exchange. Unfortunately, as is well-known in the literature, this causes considerable trouble. I shall now seek to provide a brief and superficial review of the theory of fairness in production.

The basic problem besetting the evaluation of fairness in the presence of production has long been recognized. Different people differ in their native productive abilities and the intensity with which they are willing to use them. Just how and to what extent does equity require us to take them into account in the resulting distribution of society's products? In the *Critique of the Gotha Program*, one of his last pieces of economic writing, Marx describes the issue very clearly: A very new socialist state is "... morally ... still stamped with the birth marks of the old society from whose womb it emerges. Accordingly each individual receives back from society—after the deductions [for capital formation, etc.] have been made—exactly what he gives to it ... his individual quantum of labor." It is only after "a higher phase of communist society" has been reached, that the community can ignore the individual's contribution to output and follow the famous precept, "From each according to his ability, to each according to his needs" (*Critique*, part I, section 3).

It is clear which one of these principles is preferred by Marx, though not everyone is apt to agree with it, even as a vision of an ideal world. For many persons undoubtedly feel that the individual who is willing and able to work harder and to contribute more deserves *some* material recompense.[19]

19. Marx implies that in his ideal communist society the grounds for such a distinction disappear; for in that society work will lose its disutility. "Labor has become not only a means of life but life's prime want" (ibid.). He sees a basic source of alienation and dislike of labor in "... the enslaving subordination of the individual to the division of labor." Indeed, abolition of the division was the one characteristic of a communist society to which Marx and Engels committed themselves throughout their writings, from their early, joint work, the *German Ideology* [1845–1846] to Engels's *Anti-Dühring* [3rd ed., 1894]. Thus they wrote in the former, "... in communist society, where nobody has one exclusive sphere of activity but each can become accomplished in any branch he wishes, society regulates the general production and thus makes it possible for me to do one thing today and another tomorrow, to hunt in the morning, fish in the afternoon, rear cattle in the evening, criticize after dinner, just as I have a mind, without ever becoming, hunter, fisherman, shepherd or critic" [1845–1846, p. 47]. This extreme antipathy to the division of labor remained throughout their lives. In *Anti-Dühring* Engels repeats this view in very similar terms: "... in time to come there will no longer be any professional porters or architects, and ... the man who for

A basic dilemma for the definition of "fairness in production" is posed by the choice between these two ethical viewpoints, the view that each person should receive in accord with what he or she contributes to output and the contradictory view that people should ideally be compensated without regard for the inequality in the talents with which nature has endowed them and for the degree of their willingness to exercise them. Indeed, there is even a third and not unreasonable ethical viewpoint that goes beyond the second and holds that people with poorer working abilities, say, the physically handicapped, should in an ideal world receive greater compensation than those who suffer no such disadvantages.

The theory of superfairness, as we shall see, has flirted with each of these three ethical concepts. Preserving the individualistic framework it adopted for the theory of exchange, the analysis continues to rely upon the evaluations of the persons affected. Fairness continues to be defined as a state in which no pertinent individual has any basis for envy of any other. But, even so, the problem arises in the form of the choice of the list of the items to be considered in deciding whether person 1 envies person 2. The criterion, as before, is whether A would like to trade—whether he prefers what accrues to B to what he gets himself. But what are the proper objects to be considered for exchange? A's and B's earning abilities? The bundle of their consumption goods plus the labor each expends? Their incomes? A decision among these, as we shall see, is tantamount to a choice among the three ethical viewpoints that were just described.

9   Proposed Formal Criteria of Fairness in Production[20]

In addition to the fundamental problem we have just discussed, that of the appropriate reward for effort and ability in a standard of equity, there is a second difficulty that has been emphasized in the recent literature. This is the problem that the criterion that may be taken to be closest to Marx's ultimate ideal may be incompatible with a Pareto optimum. That is, unlike the case of fairness in pure distribution (proposition 9), depending on the nature of the production set and the utility functions, it may be impossible to find a solution that is superfair in terms of the goods and services people

---

half an hour gives instructions as an architect will also push a barrow for a period, until his activity as an architect is once again required. It is a fine sort of socialism which perpetuates the professional porter!" [1894, p.221].

20. The discussion in this section is based on Pazner and Schmeidler [1974] and Varian [1974, 1975].

enjoy (disregarding their relative contributions to output) and that, at the same time, allocates society's resources efficiently.

Before we discuss the implications of this result let us first consider three formal criteria of equity in production and distribution that have been proposed in the literature. These may be referred to, respectively, as consumption fairness, contribution fairness,[21] and income fairness. In each case we assume that each individual, i, has a given amount of time, t, available that is divided between labor, q_i, leisure, $t - q_i$, and that the individual receives a vector of consumption goods, x^i, and contributes an (incremental) output vector, z^i.

Definition 7 Consumption fairness simply considers the complete bundle of outputs, *including leisure*, enjoyed by the individual, and requires that no individual, i, envies any individual, j; i.e., i prefers his own complete consumption bundle to j's or is indifferent between them, and where i does not envy j's consumption iff $U^i(x^i, t - q_i) \geqslant U^i(x^j, t - q_j)$. Here, U^i is i's utility function.

Then a production-consumption vector is consumption superfair if no individual envies any other individual's complete consumption bundle. This criterion assigns some weight to effort expended, but absolutely no reward for differences in ability. Two people who work an equal number of hours, and therefore enjoy an equal number of hours of leisure, are considered to be treated equally on this score. Fairness is then judged in terms of their consumption of goods and services alone. Roughly speaking, this test proposes to give to each according to his (leisure-consumption) preferences, regardless of ability.

A diagrammatic treatment of this criterion is not quite as useful as that which was employed in the analysis of fairness in exchange. However, a graph may nevertheless help to bring out the issues involved. In figure 2.7 we show the output-leisure space for two individuals, simply adding together $t - q_1 + t - q_2$ as the leisure enjoyed by the two of them together. To keep the diagram to two dimensions we assume that their hourly labor is identical in quality so that output depends simply upon the sum of the two labor inputs, $q_1 + q_2 \equiv q$. The curve YY represents the total output of x as a function of q, which is measured leftward from point $2t$, the total (labor-leisure) time available to the two-person community.

---

21. Varian [1975] calls this "wealth equitability," but I think (and he now agrees) that his terminology does not suggest the content of the idea.

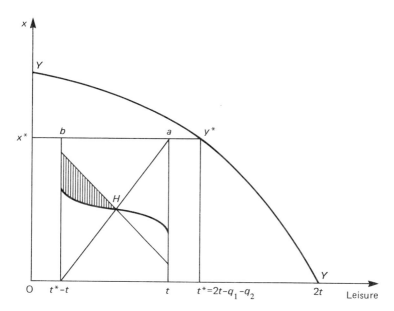

Figure 2.7

Now, for each point on YY there will be a different menu of complete consumption bundles available to the two individuals, since the total available output and the total available leisure will differ. Thus, at each output point, such as y^*, there will be a different Edgeworth box.

The relevant Edgeworth box at y^* is not the entire rectangle $t^*y^*x^*O$, where $t^* = 2t - q_1 - q_2$ is the total leisure time available to the two individuals at output x^*. Regions of that box are not feasible because they assign to one individual or the other more than the maximum amount of time t (24 hours per day) that he has available. This is so because t^*, the total amount of leisure that output x^* leaves to the two individuals together, is greater than t. Thus we must eliminate as infeasible any point in the box to the right of t, which assigns to person 1 more leisure than the time he has available, and similarly we must eliminate any point to the left of $t^* - t$, because it assigns to person 2 more leisure than the time available to 2. The relevant Edgeworth box, then, is tab $(t^* - t)$, containing the shaded region of superfair distributions shown in the figure.

There will be one such (set of) superfair region(s) corresponding to each output point, y^*. The sum (union) of these regions constitutes all distributions that are superfair under the criterion of consumption fairness, with its denial of any reward for ability.

Contribution fairness, the second criterion of fairness in production and distribution, was proposed by Varian. This criterion uses an ingenious device to take account of individuals' differences in their abilities. In effect, in comparing the goods and leisure assigned to two individuals, the criterion considers not the leisure each actually obtains. Instead, each compares his own leisure time with the amount that would have accrued to him if he had matched the other person's *output* contribution. Thus, if individual 2's net contribution to output is z_2, and the amount of labor time it would take individual 1 to duplicate z_2 (or its equivalent in market value?) is $Q^1(z_2)$, then individual 1 compares his own leisure time, $t - q_1$, with $t - Q^1(z_2)$. Note that if 2 is more able than 1, then we expect $Q^1(z_2) > q_2$ and $Q^2(z_1) < q_1$.

Definition 8   Contribution fairness requires absence of envy, where i is said not to envy j iff $U^i(x^i, t - q_i) \geqslant U^i[x^j, t - Q^i(z_j)]$, that is, iff i prefers his own consumption and labor contribution to j's consumption and the labor it would take i to make j's output contribution.

In effect, contribution fairness considers it equitable for the abler person, j, to retain the rewards of his ability. It implies that no individual, 1, is entitled to envy 2's consumption if 1 is unwilling to put in the additional labor needed, because of 1's inferior abilities, for 1 to match 2's output.[22]

Here again, a graphic translation is not terribly helpful, but it is suggestive. Suppose individuals 1 and 2 each work a 6-hour day, leaving 36 hours of leisure between them. If an hour of 2's labor is exactly twice as productive as 1's, then from 1's point of view 2's 6 hours of labor are equivalent to 12 of his own. This means that in his view the total amount of labor expended is 18 hours, leaving 30 hours of leisure to be divided between them. Therefore, for 1 the equal division point is $(x^1, t - q_1) = (x^*/2, 15)$, where x^* is the vector of available consumption goods.

Similarly, in 2's adjusted time calculus the two individuals together expend only 9 hours of labor, meaning that equal division of the available leisure gives each 19.5 hours, so that 2's equal division point is $(x^2, t - q_2) = (x^*/2, 19.5)$.

We see (figure 2.8) that because of their negative slopes neither person's fairness boundary will go through the midpoint $H = (x^*/2, 18)$ of the diagram. Instead, individual 1's boundary will go through his transposed midpoint $H_1 = (x^*/2, 15)$. Similarly, 2's fairness boundary will go through

---

22. An anonymous reader comments, "Contribution fairness is only well-defined with complete separability in production; hence it is practically useless for most applications."

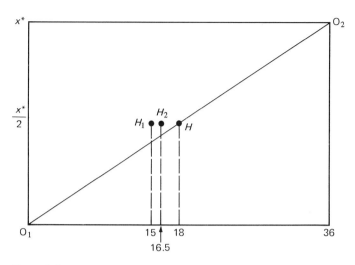

Figure 2.8

her transposed midpoint $H_1 = (x^*/2,\ 16.5)$, which gives 16.5 hours to individual 1, because it leaves to 2 the $19.5 = 36 - 16.5$ leisure hours that she considers her equal share of the available 36 hours of leisure time.

We see that both transposed midpoints lie to the left of H, meaning that with equal division of consumption goods, contribution fairness requires more than half the available leisure to go to the more capable individual, 2. Thus, the contribution fairness criterion in effect gives to each according to his ability, *not* according to his needs. However, the numerical illustration suggests that the compensation for ability under this criterion is rather modest. Even under the strong assumption that person 2 is twice as productive as 1, the amount of leisure assigned to 2 at the point of "equality" is at most 40 percent greater than that assigned to 1 (15 hours to 1 and 21 hours to 2, with the rest of their consumption bundles identical).

Finally, we come to the third criterion offered by the literature. *Income fairness* uses as its standard the purchasing power that would accrue to each individual if everyone were given the same purchasing power over the consumption of all goods, and *everyone's* leisure. The trick here is the fact that the market places different values upon an hour of leisure of different persons. An hour of the more able person will be more valuable in terms of opportunity cost, as measured by wage rate in a perfectly competitive market. Thus, on this criterion, if 1's wage rate is $10 per hour and 2's wage rate is $15 per hour, equal leisure consumption occurs when both persons receive leisure worth the same amount of money.

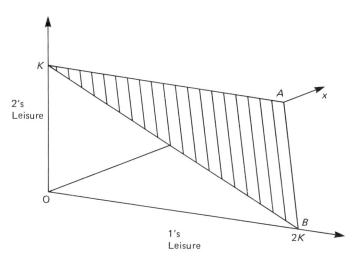

Figure 2.9

Definition 9   Income fairness: Let p_k be the competitive price of good k, x_{ik} = individual i's consumption of good k, w_i = i's competitive wage rate, and $t - q_i$ = i's leisure. Then the implicit income of individual i is defined as

$$y_i = \sum_k p_k x_{ik} + w_i(t - q_i),$$

and income fairness is defined to hold for individuals 1 and 2 iff $y_1 = y_2$.

This concept, due to Pazner and Schmeidler, has been likened by Varian to an arrangement in which each person is incorporated, with shares issued to equal in total value the market value of that person's available time. Fairness is achieved when these shares are distributed equally to all persons so that in an *n*-person community individual 1 holds $(1/n)$th of the shares in each other individual's corporation.

In this case a graph does help to show clearly what this criterion implies. What it requires for equity is that each person have the same budget hyperplane, *BAK* (figure 2.9). Here, for ease in representation, we assume that there is only one good, *x*, and two individuals, with an hour of 2's leisure worth twice that of 1's. As a result, the fixed budget is capable of buying twice as much of person 1's leisure ($B = 2K$) as it can purchase of individual 2's.

Now, since both persons have the same budget hyperplane the criterion would appear to treat them equally, but in fact it does not. For individual 1 has no way to consume 2's leisure time, nor vice versa. Hence, the relevant segment of the budget plane for person 1 is AB, while the corresponding budget line for individual 2 is only AK. While AB and AK permit the same range of purchases of x, AK permits 2 to buy only half the number of hours of her own leisure time that AB permits 1 to purchase. Thus, the equality of incomes means that if they choose to consume equal quantities of goods, 2 will receive only half the leisure that 1 does.

Hence, the income fairness criterion *over*compensates for differences in ability. It literally penalizes the person with superior capabilities. Thus, this criterion is one that provides additional compensation to persons handicapped in any way—even in terms of lack of talent or ability.

10   Production Fairness and Pareto Optimality

It has been proved by Pazner and Schmeidler that the first of our criteria of fairness in the presence of production, i.e., *consumption fairness*, is not, in general, compatible with Pareto optimality. That is, in some cases there exists no resource allocation-distribution that is both Pareto optimal and consumption fair. There is no need to reproduce the counterexamples by means of which they prove their results. The authors even provide a case in which there is no difficulty achieving Pareto optimality but in which no consumption-fair distribution exists.[23] This case involves two individuals, 1 and 2. 2 is less able, gets lower wages, and consumes smaller quantities of goods than 1. The problem arises if 2 loves to consume while 1 loves leisure. In Varian's words, "Efficiency will always require that agent 1 do [most of] the work and agent 2 compensates him by allowing him larger consumption. But in such a situation agent 2 will envy agent 1 because he consumes more of the goods and agent 1 will envy agent 2 because he consumes more leisure" [1974, p. 72].

An intuitive argument suffices to show that there exist Pareto optimal allocations that are *income fair* (if indifference curves and the production set have the properties usually assumed of them). For this purpose it is merely

---

23. The authors propose to reconcile the conflict between fairness and efficiency with the aid of a new criterion, which they call *egalitarian* equivalence (Pazner and Schmeidler [1978]). For a pure trade economy an allocation is said to be egalitarian equivalent if its distribution of utilities could have been achieved by equal division of any set of commodities. From this Crawford constructs a procedure involving auction of the role of divider, and permitting the chooser to select *either* one of the bundles offered by the divider *or the equal division bundle*. Crawford shows that this procedure yields an allocation that is both Pareto efficient and egalitarian equivalent in pure trade economies (see Crawford [1979A]).

necessary to adopt the competitive prices p_k, w_i used in describing the income fairness criterion, with purchasing power redistributed so that everyone has the same income (is on the same budget hyperplane). Then the free market equilibrium with this distribution will be Pareto optimal for the usual reasons, and, by construction, it must be income fair since everyone is on the same budget hyperplane, as this criterion of fairness requires.

A somewhat more complicated argument is required for the case of *contribution fairness* but the basic result holds here too: Given the normal behavior of the indifference map and the production set, it can be shown that there will be at least one Pareto optimal solution that is contribution fair.

What is the upshot of this discussion? It tells us that if we adopt as our criterion of fairness in the presence of production either the contribution fairness or the income fairness criterion, then there need be no conflict between equity and efficiency. However, if we prefer the criterion of consumption fairness, there may very well be a trade-off between the two goals that policy makers will have to take into account.

Part of these results, those relating to consumption fairness and contribution fairness, are entirely plausible. For, under contribution fairness, larger rewards to superior effort and superior ability are considered quite appropriate, so that fairness rules need give rise to no disincentive problems, and hence to no inefficiencies even in an allocation that is not imposed. On the other hand, consumption fairness does not recognize as legitimate any rewards for superior ability and so adherence to the fairness goal automatically invites inefficiency. Thus, lack of reward for effort and ability can be expected intuitively to lead to more leisure and less production of goods than may best serve consumer preferences.

What is paradoxical in this explanation is the case of income fairness, which, as we have seen, literally penalizes superior ability. How, then, is a conflict with efficiency avoided under this criterion? The answer is that its redistribution process amounts to a set of lump sum taxes or subsidies that do not affect relative prices and, hence, do not distort the trade-off between consumption and leisure for anyone, neither the person who is very able nor the person who is very unproductive. In terms of figure 2.10, what such a redistribution does is to shift the low-income budget hyperplane $B'A'K'$ of an inefficient individual upward to BAK, where it attains the income level that is the egalitarian norm. But, assuming similarity in tastes, that must be a parallel shift because the slopes before and after are both given by the

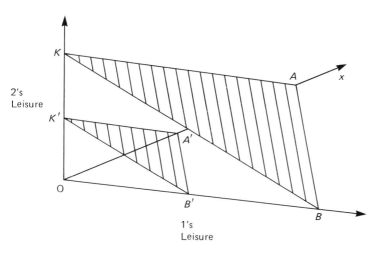

Figure 2.10

competitive equilibrium for the economy.[24] A similar downward shift will apply to the wealthy. Since, before and after, 1's budget line $K'B'$ or KB will offer the right rewards for an additional hour of labor, as given by their slopes, that person will have no motivation to provide an inefficient quantity of labor, and the same will hold for person 2. The tax or subsidy is lump sum because it is based on the person's earnings *ability* of which he cannot divest himself by supplying the wrong amount of work.[25]

11   Concluding Comment

This chapter has sought to recapitulate the pertinent portions of the literature in a manner that deliberately avoided sophistication. Wherever possible simple graphic arguments were chosen over more complex and more formal generalizations. If there was any substantive contribution in the chapter, it consisted in the examination of superequality as an alternative to superfairness and as a possible remedy for some of the latter's conceptual difficulties and for the paradoxes to which they give rise.

---

24. If the tastes of the formerly wealthy and the formerly poor do differ, the slopes will change because the competitive equilibrium will change as a result of the income redistribution. However, the results will still be efficient both before and after since marginal rates of substitution will still everywhere equal competitive price ratios.

25. It is not clear whether problems arise if in the model the individual can reduce his hourly productivity—if he can choose to slack on the job rather than cut the amount of his labor input.

Perhaps the upshot of the discussion is the wisdom of Varian's position, which considers a distribution to be fair only if it is both Pareto optimal and envy-free. Yet somehow this position still leaves one a bit uncomfortable because of its elimination of the distinction between fairness and efficiency, and of the possibility of a trade-off between the two, which is surely apt to be an important issue in reality.

The next chapter will consider some of these matters further and propose some further modifications in the analytic procedure that are necessary to increase their applicability in practice.

3

Superfairness: Incremental, Partial, and Sequential

Having laid out the elements of superfairness theory as it emerges from the literature, I turn now to a few simpleminded extensions, several of which are needed in order to permit the theory to be applied to policy issues as they occur in reality. These moves are *not* costless. They seem unavoidably to involve a significant trade-off—applicability is purchased only at the expense of some analytical rigor and philosophical defensibility.

When a congressional committee or an agency of the executive branch of the government inquires into the fairness of, say, a change in the pricing of local and long distance telephone calls or a scheme to ration the use of gasoline and heating oil, its concerns are far too limited to permit direct use of the basic superfairness criterion. There are at least two sources of incompatibility. First, the inquiry is usually concerned *only* with the goods and services *directly* involved (local and long distance calls or gasoline and heating oil) and not with any other commodities. In contrast, the superfairness criterion considers the *full vector* of commodities held by the individuals in question and asks whether individual i envies individual j's total commodity bundle. Thus, in application we are apt to have to use what I shall call the criterion of *partial fairness*, which concerns itself only with a portion of commodity space, in contrast with the (total) superfairness criterion. We shall see, as a matter of fact, that the two criteria may yield conflicting results because of complementarity or substitutability between items included and those excluded from the partial fairness calculation or because the budget constraint means that changes in the individuals' holdings of the commodities considered by the partial fairness analysis inevitably affect their holdings of other commodities or their preferences relating to them.

There is a second modification of fairness analysis that applied issues require. In inquiring whether the proposed change in telephone pricing is in some sense fair one is not asking whether the measure will transform this manifestly unfair world into one that is totally equitable. Rather, what is in effect being asked is whether the contemplated change makes the world's arrangements a bit more just or somewhat more unjust. The superfairness criterion is far more demanding than this. It asks whether after the change is adopted matters will have altered so dramatically that Mr. Micawber will no longer have reason to envy the bundle of commodities held by Lord Rothschild. But that is, surely, an unreasonable question whose answer is clear in advance. No relatively modest change in pricing arrangement and no limited rationing scheme can reasonably be expected to rectify totally the inequities of society. No one in his right mind even considers such a target when examining our illustrative policy issues. There, rather, the pertinent concern is whether the proposed change adds to fairness or subtracts from it—whether or not it is what I shall call "incrementally superfair."

This chapter will also consider several more theoretical issues. We have seen that the set of superfair solutions can conceivably be rather substantial, leaving an extensive range of distributions, all of which pass the fairness test. Both for theoretical and practical reasons it may be desirable to narrow that range, perhaps substantially. I shall provide a procedure, involving a sequence of steps that seeks to do this. This analysis I shall refer to as "sequential superfairness." I shall also return to the superequality criterion that was introduced in the preceding chapter, both as a means to narrow the set of superfair and incrementally superfair distributions, and as a device to avoid some further behavioral peculiarities of superfairness that will be reported in this chapter.

1   Incremental Superfairness

Definition 1   A change in distribution is called *incrementally superfair* if each affected individual prefers the resulting vector of *increments* in his own consumption bundle to that of any other individual.

We shall see now that the diagrammatic construct of the preceding chapter also works for the concept of incremental fairness. Figure 3.1 contains what may be described as an incremental Edgeworth box, in which the dimensions of the box represent changes in total consumption of two commodities. Suppose one is considering a modification in telephone pricing that increases the price of local calls and lowers that of long distance calls. The price change can then be expected to result in a net decrease in the volume of local calls ($\Delta x^* < 0$) and an increase ($\Delta y^* > 0$) in those that are

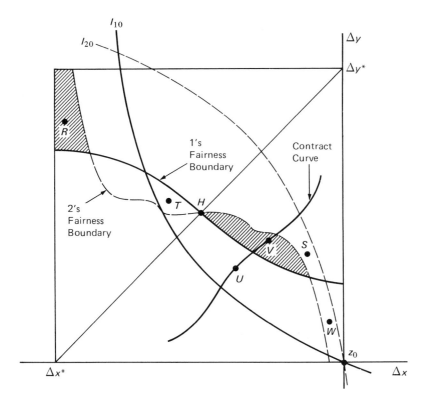

Figure 3.1

classed as long distance. As a result, the incremental Edgeworth box will lie in the northwest quadrant, above and to the left of the origin, $z_0 = (x_0, y_0)$, representing the initial consumption vector. The price change that elicits this modification in quantities consumed will presumably put the two consumers represented in the diagram at some specific point in the diagram, a point determined by the market. The question is whether the change in distribution represented by this point is at least fair to the two parties.

The diagram also shows, as in the preceding chapter, the fairness boundaries of the two individuals, and the (shaded) regions of incrementally superfair distributions. The price change in question will, then, be incrementally superfair if the new equilibrium point falls anywhere in these shaded regions.

The concept of an incrementally fair distribution is closely related to a concept that has appeared previously in the literature and that was contributed by Schmeidler and Vind [1972]. This concept, which they call "fair net trade," refers to the fairness of the increments in the holdings of two (or more) individuals that result from a process of exchange between them. Schmeidler and Vind define a net trade as any change in the holdings of any or all individuals that leaves each of them with a nonnegative quantity of each good. They say the net trade is "balanced" if the sum of the increments is zero for each good, i.e., if for every increase in quantity of good y received by one person there is an offsetting reduction in the holdings of other individuals. Finally, they call a net trade *fair* if each agent considers his net trade at least as good as the net trade of any other agent [1972, p. 637]. However, the concept of incremental superfairness is more general than that of a fair net trade since the latter refers only to a case in which total available quantities (the dimensions of the Edgeworth box) remain unchanged, while incremental superfairness applies also when there is a change in the available quantities of the commodities in question and, indeed, is concerned primarily with such changes. Indeed, a net trade is a case in which $\Delta x^* = \Delta y^* = 0$ so that the incremental Edgeworth box degenerates into a point.

2 Incremental Superfairness and the Two Pareto Criteria

In parallel with the concepts of fairness and incremental fairness, we shall make frequent use of the concepts of Pareto optimality and Pareto improvement, whose definitions hardly need to be repeated here. Returning to figure 3.1, we obtain immediately

Proposition 1   A redistribution that is incrementally fair need not be a Pareto improvement over the initial position, and a distribution that is a Pareto improvement over that position need not be incrementally fair.

The first part of this proposition is obtained from the diagram by noting that the region between I_{10} and I_{20}, the indifference curves through the initial position, z_0, represents the set of all redistributions that are Pareto improvements over z_0. We see at once that there are superfair redistributions, such as R, that, individual 1 feels, leave *both* him and 2 with an output combination that 1 considers inferior to the initial one (from the viewpoint of 1's utility function). Then this distribution is clearly not a Pareto improvement since it reduces 1's welfare. Yet it can be fair or superfair (1 sees no benefit from an exchange with 2—he does not *envy* the increments in 2's fate in comparison with his own). This can occur if the move from z_0 to R reduces the utility to individual 1 of his own holdings but reduces the utility to individual 1 of person 2's holdings even more. If 2's attitude is similar, the new position will, by definition (absence of envy), be incrementally superfair, but it will clearly not represent a Pareto improvement. It also seems quite obvious that some Pareto improvements will not be incrementally fair, if both parties benefit, but, say, in 1's opinion a disproportionate share of the benefit goes to 2 (point U is an example).

However, we also have at once

Proposition 2   Any trade that is entered into voluntarily by two utility-maximizing individuals must be both incrementally superfair and a Pareto improvement over the initial position.

Proof   It is obvious that such a voluntary exchange must be a Pareto improvement. Moreover, let Δz_1 be the bundle of items received by 1 (and given up by 2) and let Δz_2 be the bundle received by 2. If 1 envies 2's increment, i.e., if $U^1(\Delta z_2) > U^1(\Delta z_1)$, then 1 obviously would have refused the exchange and held on to Δz_2. Thus 1 cannot possibly envy 2's increment, and the same is true of 2.

It may be noted that if there are more than two people, then bilateral trade must still, of course, be a Pareto improvement, but it may no longer be incrementally superfair because the change may arouse envy in others. Besides the relation between incremental fairness and Pareto improvement the former also bears some relation to the concept of Pareto optimality. We shall see now that there is an association between Pareto optimality and the possibility of an improvement in fairness. Usually we take a proposal to qualify as a means to improve resource allocation only if it promises to move us to a point that is Pareto optimal from one that is not. Put the other way, if we were to start off from a Pareto optimal position in the first place, we do not feel entitled to describe any program for change as an improvement in resource *allocation*, even if it takes us to another Pareto optimum. It turns out that the same is true of the incremental superfairness criterion. In general, exchanges (trades) can be incrementally superfair only if they start off from an initial situation that is not Pareto optimal. That is,

Proposition 3   Any move from a Pareto optimal state that can be achieved by direct exchange, even if it brings the economy to another Pareto optimal state, can be expected to lie outside the region of strict incremental superfairness. In other words, it must provide someone with grounds to envy the incremental consumption vector accruing to some other individual.[1]

One should immediately suspect the truth of the proposition from the fact that any such move must, by the definition of a Pareto optimum, be detrimental to someone (person A). But the move can also be expected to be beneficial to someone—person B (otherwise, why should it even be considered?). In that case A can be expected[2] to envy B's incremental holdings and that means the result will not be superfair.

A rigorous proof of the proposition follows a simple line of argument. Since the change is assumed achievable by direct exchange, an initial trade of Δx_2 for Δx_1 must be feasible, with 1 giving Δx_2 to 2 and vice versa.[3] Then if the change is to be strictly incrementally superfair, by definition either individual 1 must prefer Δx_1 to Δx_2 or individual 2 must prefer Δx_2 to Δx_1, or both, and neither must have the opposite preference. But, then, the original situation could not possibly have been Pareto optimal, for starting from the initial position 1 could have given Δx_2 to 2, receiving Δx_1 from the latter in exchange, and at least one of them would have been made better off without harm to the other.

We may note, as a closely related matter, that incremental superfairness is not a useful criterion for the evaluation of any redistribution of purchasing power. This is so because, by definition, at least one of the affected parties is bound to lose out in the process unless there is some sufficiently strong source of offsetting benefits such as the altruism of the person whose holdings are reduced.[4]

Proposition 4   Any redistribution of purchasing power must be incrementally unfair unless there is such interdependence in the utilities of the individuals involved that even those whose holdings are reduced prefer the new situation.

---

1. I am indebted to Kenneth Arrow for this observation.

2. As a matter of fact, this is not certain since the increase in B's holdings may consist entirely of things B likes but that A dislikes, so even though A dislikes his own increment he may not wish to trade it for B's. That is why the preceding argument is only suggestive and does not constitute the outline of a valid proof.

3. That is, if $\Delta x_1 - \Delta x_2$ contains some negative elements, they must not exceed 2's initial consumption of these items, so that the exchange does not require an infeasible negative consumption of any good by 2, and the reverse must be assumed true for person 1.

4. On this subject, see the extensive literature based on the writings of Hochman and Rogers, e.g., their classic paper [1969].

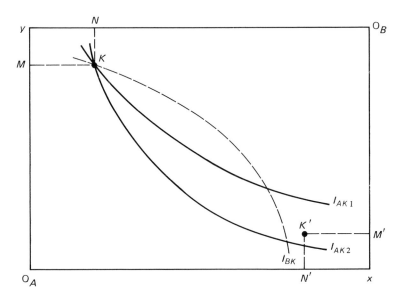

Figure 3.2

3 The Feldman-Kirman Consistency Result

One of the most disturbing results in the literature of fairness theory is a theorem provided by Feldman and Kirman [1974] in which they show that a move that is both incrementally superfair and a Pareto improvement from an initial position that is superfair can yield a new position that is unfair and can even be unfair to both parties. I shall summarize their proof by counter-example, which is entirely diagrammatic, and will then seek to suggest how this disconcerting phenomenon can arise. Because the discussion will confirm that the Feldman-Kirman phenomenon need not involve anything that is pathological, it will only strengthen the blow to the robustness of the fairness concept. For what the result suggests in the last analysis is that the fairness of a fair solution is extremely vulnerable and can be destroyed by a move that all the affected parties consider to be fair. Obviously, it also cannot fail to raise some questions about the concept of incremental fairness.

We must first deal with one preliminary matter—an alternative version of the test for superfairness in the Edgeworth diagram. In figure 3.2 let K represent any distribution of the available quantities of x and y and let K' be the symmetric image point of point K (that is, we place K' so that $K'M' = KM$ and $K'N' = KN$). Then, clearly, K' awards individual A what K

awards to individual B, and vice versa. Now, if A's indifference curve through K is like I_{AK2} and lies below K', it means that at K individual A prefers what B obtains to what A obtains for himself. Thus, if I_{AK} lies below K', then at K A envies B. However, if I_{AK} has a position like that of I_{AK1}, that is, it goes through K but lies above K', then K is fair to A, i.e., A does not envy B when the distribution is given by K.

By symmetry, if B's indifference curve I_{BK} through K lies below K', then B does not envy A when the distribution is K. Thus we have

Lemma 1   For any distribution point K, if each party's indifference curve through K lies above K' (relative to that person's origin), where K' is the symmetric image of K, then K is strictly superfair. However, if either person's indifference curve through K lies below K' relative to that person's origin, then K is unfair to that person.

Now we are ready for our main result:

Proposition 5 (Feldman-Kirman)   Starting from an initial distribution that is superfair, an incrementally superfair exchange that is advantageous to both parties can yield an endowment that is unfair to either or both of the parties involved.

Proof (by graphic example)   In figure 3.3 it is clear by lemma 1 that K is a superfair solution, since I_{AK} and I_{BK} both lie above K' relative to their origins. Now consider a move from K to L. Since that move places each individual on a higher indifference curve, it involves a trade that both parties would undertake voluntarily. So, by proposition 2, it must be incrementally superfair. Indeed, it is incrementally strictly superfair.

Finally, it should be noted that the indifference curves I_{AL} and I_{BL} through L have all the normal properties of indifference curves. Yet each of these lies below L', the symmetric image of L. Thus, by lemma 1, L is unfair to both parties.

While this geometric argument (which is taken directly from Feldman and Kirman) is entirely valid and unobjectionable, it may well leave the reader puzzled. What economic relationships can account for this curious and disquieting phenomenon? How can it come about? A concrete illustration suggests that it can arise from complementarities between the two commodities.

For this purpose let us go back to the sort of illustration with which we

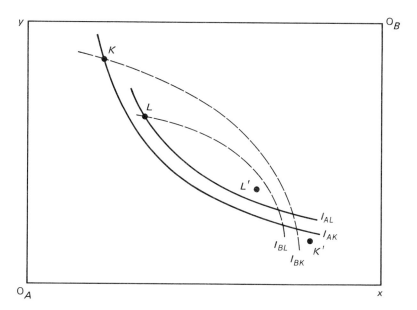

Figure 3.3

began our discussion of the fairness criterion. Let us assume we are dealing with the distribution of some quantity of nuts and some quantity of raisins between the two parties. Let *A* have the following preferences:

(i) If forced to have only raisins and no nuts or nuts and no raisins, *A* prefers the raisins.

(ii) *A* prefers any mix to either item by itself, holding, say, total weight constant.

(iii) *A* prefers a mixture made up preponderantly of nuts to one composed predominantly of raisins.

Moreover, let *B*'s preference patterns reverse these three attributes.

It may be observed, first, that there is no inconsistency in these preference patterns, which can easily arise out of complementarity of the two goods.[5] Second, it is clear by (i) that an initial allocation that gives *A* all of the raisins and *B* all of the nuts is strictly superfair. Second, by (ii) an exchange of a small amount of raisins for an equal quantity of nuts is a Pareto improvement and is, therefore, incrementally superfair. Yet, by (iii),

---

5. By this I do not, of course, mean complementarity in the Hicksian sense, which can only arise when a third good is present.

if the exchange is sufficiently small, A will end up envying B and B will envy A.

This example suggests the source of the Feldman-Kirman phenomenon —the possibility that an incrementally fair exchange will lead one or both parties to revalue the other person's holding. Thus, though the exchange increases A's valuation of his own holdings, it increases A's valuation of B's holdings even more. And that is made possible by complementarity, which can transform what (in A's eyes) is an inferior initial holding by B, call it z_B, and an inferior increment, Δz_B, into a combination, $z_B + \Delta z_B$, which is superior to $z_A + \Delta z_A$.

In this example it is striking that because the new position is unfair to *both* parties, both can gain from an exchange of all their assets, and the position resulting from the exchange will then obviously be superfair. Indeed, this observation can be generalized:

Proposition 6 Letting z_A and z_B, respectively, represent the vectors of A's and B's holdings in distribution $z = (z_A, z_B)$, if z is unfair to *both* parties, then $z' = (z_B, z_A)$ must be a Pareto improvement over z, and z' must be strictly superfair.

However, it is easy to transform the preceding examples into illustrations in which an initially superfair solution and an incrementally superfair change yield a new distribution that is fair to one of the parties but not to the other. Then there is no obvious move that will restore the superfairness of the distribution.

The preceding discussion is another reminder of the dangers of casual application of fairness theory. The Feldman-Kirman result is perhaps the most sobering of the disturbing propositions about fairness theory that are found in the literature.

Here, too, as in the preceding chapter, the problem disappears if the superfairness criterion is replaced by the more restrictive superequality criterion—Pareto superiority or Pareto equivalence to the equal division point, H. It will be recalled that in chapter 2 the paradoxes of the superfairness criterion were attributed to its failure to take account of the possibility of envy by person 1 of person 2's utility level or wealth and the range of consumption options that wealth permits to 2, even though it does rule out envy by 1 of the particular consumption bundle chosen by 2, which may reflect tastes very divergent from those of person 1.

It was also implied that the more restrictive requirement of the superequality criterion does, at least, address itself to both forms of envy. Superequality does indeed preclude consumption bundle envy because by proposition 8 of chapter 2 every distribution that is superequal must also be superfair. And it deals with the issue of wealth or utility envy at least to this extent: that every distribution that is superequal must, by definition, make every person at least as well off as he would be under equal division.

We can now see readily that if one substitutes the superequality criterion for superfairness the basic Feldman-Kirman paradox cannot arise. To see this let us begin with any superequal initial distribution, D_0. Consider any redistribution of the initial totals of the goods in question that is mutually beneficial[6] and so is Pareto superior to D_0. Then the new distribution D_1 must be Pareto superior to D_0, which in turn must be Pareto superior to H. Hence, if all preferences are transitive, D_1 must be Pareto superior to H; i.e., it must satisfy the superequality criterion.[7]

4   Partial Fairness

Despite the disturbing properties of the concept of incremental superfairness that have emerged from the analysis, the concept seems no less

---

6. Note that if a move is incrementally superequal (i.e., Pareto superior to equal division of Δy^* and Δx^*), it need not benefit both parties or even either party. Thus, suppose one starts from a position that is Pareto optimal and that Δx^* and Δy^* are both negative. Then the move must harm at least one party. Yet the Δy^* and Δx^* can be distributed equally to yield equal incremental distribution point ΔH. And from ΔH some trades will be incrementally superequal, even if they cannot restore the initial distribution. However, if $\Delta y^* > 0$ and $\Delta x^* > 0$, then an incrementally superequal move must benefit everyone. For ΔH, the incremental equal division must make each person better off and hence so must a move Pareto superior to ΔH.

7. This does not dispose completely of every paradox of the Feldman-Kirman type that may still arise when there is a change in the quantities of goods available. For suppose the change from superequal point D_0 to D_1 is incrementally superfair or even incrementally superequal. Then we cannot be sure that the new position will be superequal. That is, we do not know (and it is general not true) that D_1 must be Pareto superior to the new equal division point $H + \Delta H$. Such a conclusion requires the following strong independence assumption:

if all $U^i(y^i) \geqslant U^i(\sum y^i/m)$ and $U^i(y^i + \Delta y^i) \geqslant U^i(y^i + \sum \Delta y^i/m)$,

then $U^i(y^i + \Delta y^i) \geqslant U^i(\sum y^i/m + \sum \Delta y^i/m)$.

But we cannot be sure that complementarity or substitutability among the Δy^i and the y^i will not violate this premise. Incidentally, it is hardly necessary to set out as a separate proposition the observation that any distribution that is incrementally superequal must also necessarily be incrementally superfair, though the converse does not hold generally. The proof is identical with that of propositions 3, 4, and 8 of the preceding chapter.

defensible than that of fairness itself. While application may sometimes force us to deal with such an incremental concept (i.e., incremental super-fairness or incremental superequality), there is no need to apologize for doing so. No crude oversimplification is entailed in its use.

Matters are very different when we turn to our second major step toward application, the concept of *partial fairness*.

Definition 2 Partial superfairness (partial incremental superfairness) is defined in exactly the same way as superfairness (incremental superfairness) but encompasses only a proper subset of the commodities possessed (acquired) by the individuals in question. That is, a distribution is partially superfair in commodities 1, 2, ..., n if no individual is willing to exchange his holdings of those items for any other person's, so that no one envies any other person's holdings of those items alone.

Two considerations drive us to deal with partial superfairness, despite its analytic deficiencies, which will emerge in the next few pages. First, sometimes the applications with which we shall deal will be so complex that they will be intractable analytically unless some strong oversimplification is resorted to. That, of course, is the usual excuse for partial analysis. But our objectives here provide a second reason (perhaps, equally shaky): communicability with politicians, administrators, and others who make policy and to whom applied analysis must be transmitted effectively if it is to be of any use. My observation, for what it may be worth, is that such policy makers, understandably, usually focus their attention exclusively on the goods and services directly encompassed by a piece of legislation or some other proposal that is under consideration. A proposed environmental regulation normally gives rise to debate over the jobs that may be lost in the industries whose mode of operation will be constrained directly, and the industries that manufacture the equipment they may be driven to install. Rarely is any consideration given to the many other activities that, general equilibrium analysis tells us, will surely be affected. Such indirect effects, though they may in the aggregate affect welfare substantially, are rarely considered, particularly when the consequence for any one indirectly affected activity is small, so that no political pressures are expected from those quarters. The policy maker is apt to regard such considerations, if they are raised at all, as academic quibbles that trouble his deliberations needlessly.

Partial fairness, then, is a concept designed to accommodate the analysis to this point of view, which is, after all, not so different from that of our fellow economists when they resort to partial analysis elsewhere.

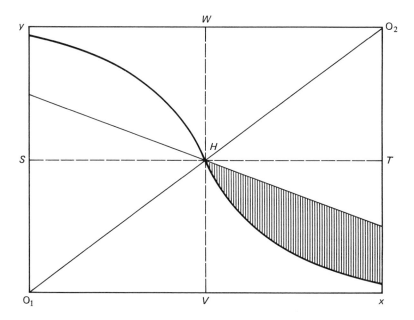

Figure 3.4

As always, such an approach has its perils. They will be illustrated next both diagrammatically and in terms of a particular application that will be pursued in some detail in a later chapter. Figure 3.4 is the standard box diagram that we have been using and it contains, as usual, the fairness boundaries, F_1 and F_2, and the shaded regions of superfair distributions. Since the diagram deals with the two commodities X and Y, a partial analysis must consider only one of these alone. We must deal with such a single-good case if we are to avoid recourse to a three-dimensional diagram.

We first need the obvious

Lemma 2   Where just a single item is to be apportioned among several individuals who are not sated in the commodity, equal division is the only fair solution, and there exists no solution that is strictly superfair.

The result is clear because any unequal division of the two items would lead the recipient of one of the smaller amounts to envy someone else. And, as usual, the equal division point is only marginally fair.

Next, returning to our figure, it follows from lemma 2 that if Y is the item to be divided, all fair solutions must be found on the horizontal line segment ST through fair division point H. Now it is clear that *every* point on ST is partially fair, just as every point on vertical line segment VW is partially fair if X is the item to be divided. Yet comparison of ST and VW with the shaded region of superfair distributions shows that with the exception of H every partially fair distribution is actually unfair and, *a fortiori*, not superequal. We conclude

Proposition 7   A distribution that satisfies a partial fairness (or partial super-equality) criterion is not necessarily fair (or superequal).

The reason, of course, is that the partial fairness (or the partial super-equality) criterion takes no account of possible inequities in the distribution of commodities outside its purview.

Later, when we examine the fairness of different rules for the rationing of scarce commodities, the issue will prove highly pertinent. For example, we shall see that if there are two such commodities to be rationed, say, beef and lamb, a standard scheme of fixed rations that assigns each consumer the same quantities—b pounds of beef and c pounds of lamb per month—is obviously partially (marginally) fair. Similarly, if each person instead is assigned a fixed number of ration coupons, which entitle him to purchase beef at r ration coupons per pound or lamb at s ration coupons per pound, we shall see that this arrangement can yield distributions of beef and lamb that are partially strictly superfair. However, that may redistribute the purchasing power unspent on beef and lamb from the poor to the rich (since the latter may undergo the larger cut in meat consumption). This consequence is ignored entirely by the partial fairness analysis that will be presented here. Yet one may very reasonably take the position that the effects of a rationing program on the overall distribution of real income (wealth) between rich and poor should materially affect any reasonable valuation of the fairness of that program.

I conclude from all this that partial fairness analysis can be quite misleading if used carelessly, but if used with caution and accompanied with adequate warnings, it may nevertheless prove to be helpful.

5   Sequential Fairness

I come, finally, to a modification of the diagrammatic fairness analysis that is probably more pertinent for theory than for application. Yet it may conceivably also prove helpful for the latter—for example, in dealing with the advantages that may accrue to the cutter in the cut and choose process

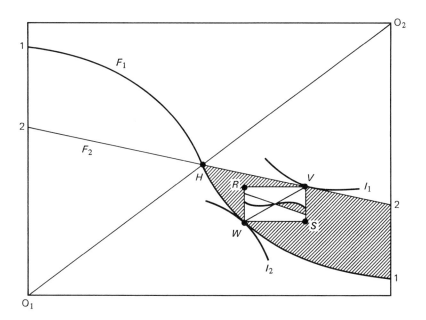

Figure 3.5

of fair division (see section 7 of the preceding chapter). If, as has been suggested (see, for example, Crawford [1977, pp. 241, 246], the divide and choose approach may prove helpful in applied problems of fair division such as those that arise in cases of divorce, the sequential approach to the determination of fair divisions may facilitate use of the approach.

While all distributions represented by points within a superfair region are superfair, some are more superfair than others. This is clearly envisaged in diagrammatic terms. In figure 3.5 let the shaded area be a region of superfair distributions with F_1 and F_2 being 1's and 2's fairness boundaries, respectively. Consider point V, the tangent point between F_2 and 1's indifference curve I_1, the highest of 1's indifference curves that can be attained within the region of superfair distributions. Then it is clear that any distribution represented by a point just below and to the left of V is (marginally but strictly) superfair. The same is true of any point just above and to the right of W, the point of tangency of F_1 with 2's indifference curve I_2. But the former offers individual 1 much more than is in his view necessary to give him a fair share while it offers virtually no such surplus to 2; the reverse is obviously true of point W. Clearly, in some sense, W is "superfairer" to 2 and V is "superfairer" to 1. In that sense, an intermediate point seems "more superfair," the interests of both parties considered, than is either a point near W or one near V.

The wide range of candidate distributions that is the source of the problem is, of course, narrowed somewhat, and perhaps even considerably, if one substitutes the superequality of fairness for the superfairness test. For, as we know (proposition 8 of chapter 2), the region of points Pareto superior to H is a proper subset of the superfair distribution points. Yet it can still involve a very substantial set of points that vary considerably in terms of the extent to which they favor one individual or another. Thus, even if one adopts the superequality criterion, the issue of a fair procedure to narrow the range of distributions initially judged to be fair remains very relevant.

The example of the cutting of a nonhomogeneous cake should bring out the source of the issue. Suppose one-quarter of the cake is covered with chocolate chunks and the opposite quarter with raisins, with the remainder of the cake having neither. Suppose that chocolate-lover 1 is indifferent between the quarter of the cake having the chocolate and the remaining three-quarters of the cake, and that the reverse is true of raisin-lover 2. Then any division of the cake that gives 1 the chocolate-covered quarter and a bit more is strictly superfair, and the same is true of any division of the cake that gives 2 the raisined quarter and a bit more, since in neither case will either of the parties wish to exchange with the other. But it would seem that a fairer and better distribution yet would result if the cake were cut in half with the half containing all the chocolate and no raisins going to 1 and the remainder going to 2. Such a solution is, however, arbitrary. It returns us to the problems of interpersonal comparison with which one can deal in practice in a rough and ready manner, but that is quite unsatisfactory as a basis for analysis. What if 1 likes chocolate more than 2 likes raisins? Indeed, what does that mean and how does one measure the difference in intensity of feeling? And what is the implication for the fairest of superfair divisions of the cake? The entire approach is obviously unsatisfactory analytically, though, I repeat, not always insoluble in practice.

We can, however, do something to narrow the issue analytically. Perhaps the search for any one distribution that is fairest of all is ultimately a quest for a phantom—there is no perfectly just price and no perfectly fair distribution. Then, the best we can hope for is to rule out those distributions that are in some respect demonstrably *un*fair. From this point of view, the fact that we are left with a range of choices is not in itself unsatisfactory. What is unsatisfactory is the possibility that the region of superfair distributions as so far traced out may be discomfortingly large, and permit discomforting asymmetries in terms of the preferences of the individuals. However, there is a simple iterative replication of our superfairness analysis that may enable us to narrow that range of choice as much as we like, at least in principle.

The procedure is readily illustrated with the aid of figure 3.5. Consider the rectangle $RVSW$ whose northeast corner is V, individual 1's most desired superfair distribution, and whose southwest corner, W, is the superfair distribution most preferred by 2. Any point inside that box represents a redistribution of the surplus, between maximal satisfaction to 1 with just marginal fairness to 2 at the one extreme, and the opposite situation at the other. But the choice among the distributions in rectangle $RVSW$ may itself be treated as an issue of fair division, and it can in its turn be analyzed with the aid of the instruments described here.

Thus, we can consider $RVSW$ to be an interior Edgeworth box containing the indifference curves of 1 and 2 over the redistributions represented by points in the box. We can use our previous construction to trace out regions of superfair distributions within that box. If individual 1's optimal superfair point lies above and to the right of W, the optimal superfair point of 2, as is not unlikely, then by the negative slope of the fairness boundaries all of subbox $RVSW$ will lie inside the shaded region of superfairness, and so the (shaded) superfair distributions within the interior Edgeworth box must obviously also lie within the original superfairness region. Thus, the second stage of such a superfairness analysis will have narrowed the range of solutions that we consider most meritorious on equity grounds. If this narrowing is considered insufficient, the process can be repeated, carrying the sequential fairness analysis through as many rounds as we desire.

Once again, the cake-cutting example helps to explain the sequential superfairness calculation. Suppose we assign to 1 the quarter-cake covered with chocolate that is most important to him, and assign to 2 the quarter covered with raisins that is most important to her. That guarantees fairness to each party, since there is no slice of the remainder that either prefers to what he or she receives. Let us, therefore, examine what has so far been assigned to neither of them and consider it the surplus still to be divided between them (with *any* division of the surplus being "fair" by our criterrion). But if the surplus in turn is divided by 1 cutting and 2 choosing, or vice versa, that will be a superfair division, representing the second stage of our superfairness algorithm.[8]

---

8. Philpotts [1983] also shows that a distribution arrived at by the iterative process just described can be inferior to a distribution D_u that violates the superfairness criterion and that is unfair to all the individuals involved. That, however, is not true if one uses super-

The iterative process I have just described can, in principle, narrow the region of superfair distribution, and may reduce it considerably at each step, as is suggested by figure 3.5. Indeed, by repeating it a substantial number of times with the successive Edgeworth subboxes each nested within its predecessor in the manner just described, we would appear to approach a limit point.[9]

It is easy to devise an analogous algorithm for an exchange process involving m persons and n commodities. Any such algorithm is designed to reduce the region of superfair solutions sequentially, at each step removing some subsets of points that are "less superfair" than those that remain. It should be clear that such a process will not be unique. The following is an example of such a procedure:

Step 1 (initial solution) Calculate the market exchange solution that would result if all m individuals were given equal incomes, i.e., if the initial point were H and all voluntary exchanges were permitted. We have already seen that the resulting distribution $y^h = (y^1, \ldots, y^m)$ must be Pareto optimal and superfair. Here y^i is the vector of quantities of the n goods accruing to individual i. Because it is arrived at by free exchange from the equal division point H, obviously y^h must also be Pareto superior or equivalent to H.

Step 2 (boundary solution for i*)* For each individual, i, calculate the minimum value of the parameter $1 \leq k_i \leq 1$ such that individual i is indifferent between $k_i y^i$ and the vector y^*/m he would receive at the equal division point H for the vector, y^*, of total available quantities; i.e., one solves the problem

$$\min k_i$$

subject to $U^i(k_i y^i) \geq U^i(y^*/m)$, $0 \leq k_i \leq 1$.

Next, let the amount given up by individual i in the move from y^i to $k_i y^i$ be divided among all the individuals in any way, say, proportionately to their holdings at y^h, so that now person r, instead of y^r, receives vy^r, where vector $v = (v_1, \ldots, v_n) \geq (1, \ldots, 1)$ satisfies

---

equality rather than superfairness as the pertinent criterion and employs the iterative process that is described next. For that iterative process, as will be seen, at each stage yields only distributions D_p that are Pareto superior to H. Hence, if D_u is Pareto superior to D_p it must also be Pareto superior to H. Thus D_u must be superequal and, consequently, it must also be strictly superfair.

9. The limit-point result was suggested to me by James Mirrlees.

$$\sum_{r \ne i} (v - 1)y^r = (1 - k_i)y^i.$$

This gives us a new distribution $y(k_i) = (vy^1, \ldots, vy^{i-1}, k_iy^i, vy^{i+1}, \ldots, vy^m)$, which is clearly superior for all persons other than i to the distribution y^h obtained in step 1 and therefore is Pareto superior to the equal division point H.

By proposition 8 of chapter 2, $y(k_i)$ must then be strictly superfair in the two-person case, and EDR strictly superfair in the m-person case (see proposition 4 of chapter 2).

Step 3 (totals to be redistributed; next iteration) Let y_j^* be the total quantity of commodity j available. We know that in the initial distribution, y^h,

$$\sum_{w=1}^{m} y_{wj}^h = y_j^*,$$

where y_{wj}^h is the quantity of good j received by person w. Therefore,

$$y_j^{**} \equiv y_j^* - \sum_{w=1}^{m} k_w y_{wj}^h \ge 0, \qquad \text{since} \quad k_w \le 1. \tag{3.1}$$

Then repeat the previous steps, this time distributing the nonnegative residual quantities, y_j^{**}, rather than the initial quantities, y_j^*, among the m individuals. This process can be repeated as many times as we desire. In principle, it can be repeated indefinitely until it reaches a Mirrlees limit point.

The process has a straightforward intuitive explanation. Step 1 is designed, simply, to give us an initial solution that is feasible and superfair. Step 2 is designed to give us the corners of the second Edgeworth box that is nested in the initial superfair region, S (it is actually nested within the proper subregion of S of superequality—of points Pareto superior to H). This step is carried out in such a way that by (3.1) a nonnegative quantity, y_j^{**}, of each commodity is left over for redistribution, these quantities to be redistributed at the next stage with the aid of the smaller Edgeworth box. The dimensions of this box are given by these quantities. It is the non-negativity of the y_j^{**} that permits the calculations to be repeated in the next iteration.

We conclude from all this

Proposition 8 Where the set of superfair distributions constitutes a region that does not consist merely of a single point there exists at least one

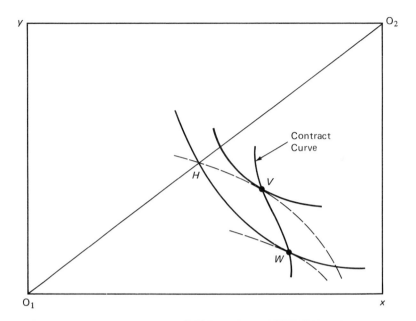

Figure 3.6

iterative process that converges to a single limit point.[10] Each stage, t, of the procedure yields a set of points, S_t, that is a proper subset of S_{t-1}, the set obtained in the preceding stage, and all points in S_t are Pareto superior to the equal division point, H_{t-1}, of the preceding stage, and hence they are all Pareto superior to the original point of equal division, H.

---

10. I do not know whether all such iterative processes converge to the same limit point, or whether such a limit point will always be a Pareto optimum. In some cases one can use an alternative iterative process that is certain to yield a Pareto optimal limit, but the method does not always work. In terms of figure 3.5 let the shaded region be, not the set of superfair distribution points, but the narrower set of *superequal* points. Then its boundaries must also be indifference curves, and points W and V of tangency between those boundaries must be the end points of the contract curve in the region and so must always be *efficient* points. Proceeding as before, we would always be sure that the nested smaller Edgeworth boxes always contain a segment of the contract curve and so the limit must be a Pareto optimum if the contract curve has a positive slope throughout, as in the textbook drawings. But as figure 3.6 shows, this need not always be so. With W to the right of V the process yields a nested subbox of "negative dimensions." That is, if individual 1 is given the quantity of x corresponding to W and 2 were given the quantity of x corresponding to V, the available quantity of x would be more than exhausted and so there would be a negative amount of x to be distributed at the next round of the process.

6   Concluding Comment

This, surely, is not the end of the story, for formal fairness analysis is only in its infancy. Our discussion has sought to introduce some modifications that adapt the theory somewhat toward use in dealing with policy issues. Incremental superfairness, incremental superequality, and the sequential extension of the two approaches all raise questions that are so far unanswered. Yet each of these has at least the beginnings of a theoretical foundation. This cannot be said of partial fairness, which is at best an unavoidable evil and, at worst, a source of results that can be seriously misleading in both their theoretical and policy implications.

This completes my discussion of general theoretical principles. I turn now to a number of particular areas of policy in which fairness issues have played a prominent role in discussions by politicians and administrators. My task will be to see how far I can get in applying the general principles to these subjects and in deriving further illumination through this process. I can say in advance that the performance that follows is mixed. I think that it provides at least a little progress in each area examined. But in no one of them does it constitute an all-illuminating *tour de force*. In short, the material that follows seems to qualify as a progress report but one that leaves more than a little room for further study.

Appendix: Notes on the History of Fairness Theory[11]

The writings on fairness theory seem to have exceeded the normal quota of misattributions. It may therefore be useful to offer a few notes on the literature and its history.

If one imputes its origins to discussions of the divide and choose procedure, then the beginnings may be virtually impossible to trace. The modern literature on the subject (see, for example, Steinhaus [1948], Kuhn [1967], and Crawford [1977]) does offer some of the pertinent references.

Tinbergen, according to Kolm [1972, p. 18], asserts that the Dutch physicist Ehrenfest proposed the concept of superfairness perhaps in the early 1950s, though my attempts to trace this source have so far failed. In any event, subsequent writing on the subject does not derive from Ehrenfest's work. All of it appears to have its roots in Foley's writings.

In 1966, Duncan Foley completed his dissertation at Yale University and

---

11. I am deeply grateful to Duncan Foley, David Schmeidler, and Hal Varian, on whose recollections this appendix is based.

it was published in 1967. A brief section laid out the basic concepts of the fairness analysis but did not carry the discussion much further. Herbert Scarf and James Tobin were the principal advisors. Foley reports that he was led to think of the criterion after seeing a movie in which Bob Dylan graphically emphasized the importance of fairness issues.

Menachem Yaari happened to be at Yale University when Foley wrote his dissertation there but the two never discussed the subject together. Yet, along with Karl Vind, Yaari was among the first to pick up on the concept. On his return to Israel he was joined in 1968–1969 by David Schmeidler in a formal investigation of the subject and they produced in 1969 the fundamental paper from which much of the subsequent literature grew, though it was never actually published. I shall return to that paper presently.

In 1969 Schmeidler spent a period visiting Louvain at the invitation of Jacques Drèze. There, he met Serge-Christophe Kolm, who also attended a lecture on fairness theory by Schmeidler. Presumably, Alan Kirman, then at the University of Louvain, was also present. From this contact there emerged Kolm's pathbreaking monograph [1972], which laid out the entire diagrammatic apparatus that is used in this book. (It was all independently reinvented by me—hélas! seven or eight years later.) That book also provided a number of interesting extensions of the fairness concept that have, however, not attracted the attention they deserve. Out of the Louvain contact there also must have emerged the very perspicacious piece by Feldman and Kirman [1974], which seems to have been the first place in which the paradoxes of the fairness concept surfaced. This paper also proposed some ways in which one can hope to measure the degree of envy engendered by a distribution among some groups of individuals.

Before the appearance of the Feldman-Kirman piece, Schmeidler and Vind had published their noted [1972] paper, which discussed the fairness of exchanges (trades) and provided some of the basic theorems that underlie the subject, for example, the proposition (already enunciated in a few brief sentences by Foley and proved in Schmeidler and Yaari [1971?]) that in the absence of satiety, a Walrasian equilibrium with all individuals' incomes equal must be superfair as well as Pareto optimal.

Meanwhile, another branch of activity in fairness analysis had emerged in California. In 1970–1971 Yaari visited Stanford and presented some of the material in his and Schmeidler's 1971(?) paper. Specifically, Schmeidler and Yaari had sought to determine whether allocations that are both fair and Pareto optimal may exist under conditions more general than the convex preferences sufficient for competitive exchange equilibria. They thought that they had proved that fair allocations would exist with only monotonic preferences, and Yaari gave a seminar expounding their argument at Stanford. Afterward, David Gale pointed out that a step in their argument was wrong. At that point it was unclear whether the theorem was false or whether another proof might be possible.

Hal Varian was present at the seminar and his interest was aroused by the discussion.[12] As Varian puts it,

Being an ambitious graduate student, I started to look for a counterexample. In a few days—with the help of my thesis advisor [Daniel McFadden]—I came up with the example in my paper. I believe that Schmeidler, Yaari, and Gale also independently came up with other similar counterexamples, but I'm not really sure.

By then Schmeidler and Yaari had given up and had turned their attention to other things. I took another look at their proof (which I thought was very ingenious, albeit wrong) and tried to see what could be salvaged.

The result was the existence Theorem 2.5 described in my [1974] paper. The major trick used there was the one used by Schmeidler and Yaari, as I indicate in footnote 7. Basically, Theorem 2.5 uses monotonicity plus an extra assumption about the shape of the Pareto set that rules out the counterexample given in my paper.

Varian also launched into an investigation of the role of production in fairness theory. Reports of this work reached Schmeidler, who had been carrying out further research on fairness theory with Elisha Pazner at Tel Aviv since 1971. Pazner and Schmeidler were the first to recognize that distributions that are simultaneously fair and Pareto optimal may not exist in the presence of production. They also formulated one of the basic concepts of fairness in production (income fairness) while Varian provided another (wealth fairness).

Since the mid-1970s the literature has proliferated, and it is hardly possible and certainly unprofitable to attempt an extensive survey here. An excellent overview by Thompson and Varian [1985] has recently made its appearance and the reader can hope for no better guide to the more recent literature.

Since this book is devoted to applications of the theory I shall end by quoting Thompson and Varian's brief survey of that portion of the literature [1985, pp. 33–34] (omitting their kind reference to this book):

There have been several attempts to apply the concepts described above to practical policy issues ... Crawford [1977, 1979A, 1980] and Crawford and

---

12. It is ironic that earlier Foley had been Varian's advisor when the latter was an undergraduate, but they had never discussed the fairness concept.

Heller [1979] considered a number of fair division schemes that can be used as arbitration devices .... It has often seemed to us that there would be many opportunities in the legal profession for applying such schemes.

Brock and Scheinkman [1977] analyzed the implications of the non-envy criterion for analyzing questions of intergenerational equity, while Sobel [1979] considered the equitable division of a good whose supply is random. Svensson [1980] examined some related concepts concerning fair wage structures. Austinsmith [1979] and Gaertner [1982] studied issues concerning the fair allocation of rights.

Several authors considered related symmetry notions in the evaluation of income distributions. Allingham [1977], Archibald and Donaldson [1979], Kolm [1972], and Ulph [1978] are representative pieces.

4   On Rationing of Scarce Commodities

Rationing of goods during wartime or other periods of scarcity,[1] of all public acts, is surely undertaken primarily as a matter of equity rather than efficiency. Yet even here economists have persisted in focusing primarily on the latter, ranking different rationing procedures on the basis of their expected effects upon resource allocation rather than their implications for distributive justice.

As an exercise designed to illustrate the applicability of superfairness analysis to concrete issues I shall discuss what the theory tells us about the equity of the various rationing methods. Specifically, I shall deal with four rationing procedures: (1) *fixed rations*, which assign to each individual a predetermined amount of each rationed item; (2) *pure points rationing*, in which individuals are each assigned fixed numbers of ration points (their points incomes), which they can use to "buy" the rationed commodities at a fixed (parametric) point price for each commodity—in this case points but *no* money are paid for the rationed commodity; (3) *points and money rationing*, with sale of points prohibited—here each rationed commodity has a market-determined money price as well as a point price; and, finally, (4) *rationing with salable points*, the case in which the individual pays for goods with both points and money, and is free to purchase or sell points for money.

The literature does not seem to say much about the pure points rationing case. However, on efficiency grounds it generally considers points and money rationing to be superior to fixed rations, and considers rationing with salable points to be still better.[2]

---

1. "Scarcity" itself can only be defined as unwillingness to let prices distribute the available commodity supplies, which presumably will occur only because "rationing by the market" is considered unfair.

2. Of course, economists have previously recognized that a fairness issue is involved here. See, for example, Tobin's classic survey [1952].

In this chapter I shall show that

(a) Fixed rationing is always (partially) fair but never strictly superfair (and, therefore, never strictly superequal).

(b) Pure points rationing is always (partially) superequal and, therefore, superfair (though not necessarily strictly superequal or superfair). This is true even if the points prices are chosen arbitrarily and do not clear the market, in the (unlikely) event that total quantities demanded do not exceed the available supplies.

(c) With points *and* money rationing any market-clearing equilibrium solution will be partially superequal and superfair. However, it is easy to construct cases in which no market-clearing set of points prices exists.

(d) In general, the equilibrium under rationing with salable points need not be fair, much less strictly superfair or superequal.

(e) Thus, there will be cases in which the equilibrium with salable ration points will be inferior in terms of the partial superfairness criterion to the case where sale of points is prohibited, even if the former arrangement is superior in terms of resource allocation, something that is itself not as clear as usually assumed.

In this chapter the analysis will be carried out almost entirely with the aid of two-dimensional diagrams, and so it deals only with the case of two persons and two goods. However, it seems clear that similar results hold for cases involving many goods and many persons.

In general, rationing is instituted for one or both of two purposes: equitable distribution of goods in short supply and alleviation or elimination of excess demands that produce inflationary pressure. This chapter deals primarily with the first of these purposes, but in later sections the relation between rationing and excess demand will be examined.

1   Fixed Rations

The analysis of the fixed rations case is, basically, trivial and it is discussed here primarily as an introduction to the rest of the analysis.

In rationing beef and lamb each of the n consumers is given $(1/n)$th of the available quantity of beef and $(1/n)$th of the available quantity of lamb. In terms of the Edgeworth diagram used in superfairness analysis (figure 4.1a), we end up at midpoint, H, of (either) diagonal. As we have seen, all fairness boundaries must always go through H. Consequently,

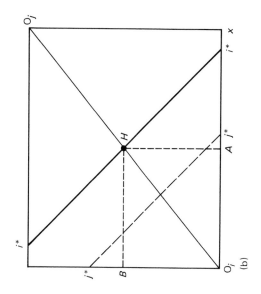

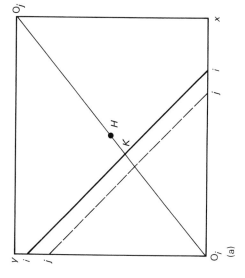

Figure 4.1

Proposition 1 A system of universal and fixed rationing with equal amounts of each rationed good to each person must be (marginally) fair to all parties in terms of the partial superfairness criterion that considers only the rationed items. It is, clearly, also partially superequal.

This conclusion is, of course, as trivial as the underlying argument. What it amounts to is the statement that, since with fixed rations everyone receives the same commodity bundle, there is no reason for anyone to prefer the bundle received by someone else. But that is just what the Foley criterion of fairness amounts to.

A complication arises when consumers are required to pay money for the rationed commodity bundles, rather than everyone simply being handed a pro rata share. For, in that case, some consumers may not be able to afford the proffered ration. In theory, in that case, markets will not clear and prices will drop. The purchasing power of each person's money will rise just until the least affluent person can afford his entire ration, since with any smaller price decrease some quantities of the rationed products will still go begging. In equilibrium, then, everyone will end up with the quantities to which the rationing rules entitle that person.

The price change is illustrated by a comparison of figures 4.1a and 4.1b. In figure 4.1a line ii is the budget line of individual i whose origin is the lower-left corner of the box. Since ii lies below H, person i must forgo some of what his ration entitles him to. However, curve jj, the budget line of person j, with upper-right origin O_j, also lies below H. That is, jj is farther from j's origin than point H. Therefore j can afford to purchase her entire ration and more.[3]

Assume, for simplicity, that the prices of both commodities fall proportionately. Let K be the intersection of ii with diagonal O_iO_j. Then prices will have to fall so that the ratio of the old prices to the new prices is O_iH/O_iK. In that case, i's budget line will undergo a parallel outward shift to i^*i^* in figure 4.1b, so that this new budget line just goes through point H. But this fall in prices will also shift jj away from O_j by the same proportion, O_iH/O_iK, to line j^*j^* in figure 4.1b.

---

3. Note that the relative position of the two price lines constitutes an inflationary gap. Since j's budget line lies closer to i's origin than i's price line does, then at the prices depicted, the two individuals have more than enough money to buy the available quantities of the two goods depicted in the Edgeworth box. Only if the two price lines coincide will there be neither an inflationary nor a deflationary gap since, by construction of the box diagram, a common point just exhausts the available quantities. More will be said about such gaps in sections 5 and 6 of this chapter.

Will the result be fair? It will be if the set of rationed commodities includes all goods in the economy. Individual i will just be able to purchase H, and with fixed rations i's feasible region will be the rectangle O_iAHB. If i's indifference curves have the normal properties and these are the only commodities on which money can ever be spent, H will be i's optimal point. While j will now have even more excess purchasing power than before relative to what is necessary to purchase H, the rationing arrangement (assuming it is effective) will not permit more than H to be purchased. Thus, the market mechanism will assure us that both individuals end up with the same quantity, H, and this, as we have seen in proposition 1, is (just barely) fair.

2 Fixed Rationing of a Subset of Commodities

The fixed rations solution will, of course, always satisfy the partial fairness criterion where, as is usually true, only a limited set of items is rationed. However, what can we say about fairness, not in the partial sense, if the economy also offers some unrationed commodities, either other goods now, or the same (or other) goods in the future? In that case the process will assure equal consumption of X and Y, the goods shown in figure 4.1, but it may well increase disparity in the consumption of the other goods. Specifically, with incomes and total quantities of the goods fixed, if rationing reduces the equilibrium prices of the rationed items, it must raise the average prices (weighted by quantities purchased) of the unrationed items (including securities and other vehicles for saving), for otherwise the community must end up below its budget line, i.e., with some income unaccounted for. As before, prices for the rationed goods must fall in order to induce purchase of their full rations by those who would not otherwise have been able to do so. Let us, for convenience, refer to this group as "the poor" and the other as "the rich." Then, if the poor persons' demand for rationed commodities happens to have an aggregate elasticity greater than that of the rich, it follows that they will end up spending more of their fixed budgets on rationed goods, and so less money must be left in the hands of poor people for the unrationed goods whose prices will have risen. Since the total quantity of the unrationed goods is fixed in our exchange problem, it follows that the poor will then end up with a smaller quantity of the unrationed goods and the rich with a larger quantity of those goods than they would have in the absence of rationing.

The new equilibrium is represented in figure 4.2, a box diagram in which X is an *un*rationed good and Y is rationed. The horizontal line, hh, which

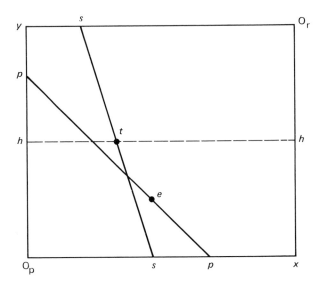

Figure 4.2

bisects the box, is the locus of points at which both parties purchase their share of the rationed commodity. Let pp be the equilibrium price line in the absence of rationing, with equilibrium point e at which poor consumers obtain less than half the available Y. Under rationing, if the market for Y is to clear, the price of Y must fall sufficiently to induce the poor to purchase O_ph and, as we have seen, the price of X must simultaneously rise. Consequently, the price line must become steeper. The equilibrium price line ss will be one on which the equilibrium point, t, also lies on hh. If ss happens to go through the nonrationing equilibrium point, e, or to lie below (to the left) of e, then t must lie to the left of e because of the negative slope of the price line. This means that with rationing the rich persons (whose origin is O_r) must end up with more of the unrationed good, X, than they obtain in the absence of rationing.

This result is, thus, necessarily unfair if neither group is sated in X, since both groups receive equal quantities of the rationed item but the poor get less of the unrationed item. But that conclusion is really obvious. The question that is more to the point is whether the change is incrementally fair. That is, given the *change* in possession of X and Y by each group, does either group prefer the other's incremental holding to its own? We cannot be sure in general, but there is a special case in which we can judge. If the new price line happens to go through the nonrationing equilibrium point, e (so that ss is a rotation of pp through e), then each group's incremental consumption must involve a zero change in total expenditure when the old and new purchases are both evaluated at the new prices. This means that each group has available to it the other group's incremental bundle of X and Y at the same (zero additional) cost as its own. Each group thereby *reveals* that it prefers its own incremental bundle to that (voluntarily) chosen by the other. Thus, in this case we conclude that the fixed rationing of a subset of available commodities must be incrementally superfair, which is as much as one can hope of a partial rationing scheme, so far as equity is concerned. One can generalize this result slightly in

Proposition 2   If all relationships are continuous, and the equilibrium budget relationship under a partial rationing scheme intersects a sufficiently small neighborhood of the point that represents the equilibrium in the absence of rationing, i.e., if the total expenditure at both equilibrium points is sufficiently close at the postrationing prices, then the rationing arrangement will be incrementally superfair.

The noteworthy feature of this result is its implication that partial rationing (i.e., rationing that excludes some commodities) may in this respect be superior to universal fixed rationing, which in general will *not* be incrementally fair since it takes away from the consumption of one group (the formerly rich) and increases the consumption of the other. Thus the rich will clearly prefer the incremental consumption of the poor to their own.

The possibility of incremental superfairness under partial rationing is to be ascribed to its preservation of a free market in some goods, which, in effect, permits the parties to trade, with the possibility that each party will obtain in the process something it prefers to what is obtained by the other party.

We note, finally, that in reality it is hard to conceive of a situation in which fixed rationing is not partial. Even if every commodity in the economy is covered, unless the rationing arrangement is expected to endure forever it automatically becomes a partial rationing scheme. Universal fixed rationing means that the larger money stocks of the wealthy are effectively destroyed, for money is robbed of all purchasing power. But if a program of rationing is temporary, the expenditures that the rich are forced to forgo when under its sway will simply add to the purchasing power in their hands when rationing comes to an end.[4]

---

4. This all follows immediately from the Hicksian way of looking at an intertemporal general equilibrium in which future purchases are simply treated as different commodities from current purchases, with prices all simply expressed in terms of discounted present value. This shows at once that the qualitative effects upon the equilibrium will be the same if some current purchases are unrationed or if this is true of some or all future purchases.

3   Pure Points Rationing with Market-Clearing Points Prices

We turn next to the case of pure points rationing, under which each individual is assigned the same number of ration points as is given to any other person, and is permitted to use them to buy whatever quantities of the rationed commodities he prefers at points prices fixed by the public authorities *without any supplementary payment of money.*

It is now trivial to show

Proposition 3   If the points prices chosen clear the market, then the resulting distribution of the rationed commodities must be (partially) superequal and, therefore, partially superfair. Moreover, if market prices of all other commodities are not subject to the control of any individual and also clear their markets, the resulting equilibrium must be Pareto optimal.

Pareto optimality follows because, in the circumstances assumed, the resulting exchange equilibrium must be a competitive equilibrium with supplies all equal to demands and (points) prices all parametric.

The superfairness follows from the usual Schmeidler-Yaari argument. The points rationing scheme simply amounts to the establishment of an artificial price line i^*i^* that goes through the point of equal distribution, H (figure 4.1b). This artificial price line is just a substitute for the market price line. The only basic difference between the two is that the market price line would presumably not have contained the equal distribution point, H. Now, since points budget line i^*i^* goes through H, it must offer identical purchase opportunities to both parties—since they have identical points incomes and face identical points prices. But unless they end up at point H, any equilibrium point on i^*i^* will give *different* bundles of goods to the two parties. Since each has had the option of purchasing without increased points expenditure either the equal division combination corresponding to point H or the combination that goes to the other party but has not chosen to do so, each reveals a preference for his own commodity bundle as against either the equal division bundle or the other person's. Therefore, on the usual premise of revealed preference theory, the distribution must be both superequal and superfair, indeed, *strictly* superequal and superfair. This completes the proof of proposition 3.

4   Points Rationing That Does Not Clear the Market

The two key assumptions underlying our result are (1) that the points prices clear the markets and (2) that only points and no money are required

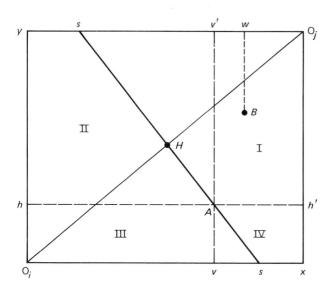

Figure 4.3

for purchases. In the next section we shall deal with the more realistic case in which money as well as points are required to buy goods. First, however, we may note briefly what will result if, as seems likely, the authorities happen to pick points prices that do not clear the market.

Graphically, this means that the two persons will not select the same position on the points budget line. The resulting solution, if it were feasible, would still be superfair for the same reason that applied in the market-clearing case. But it cannot be feasible unless some (possibly only one) of the participants decide not to use up all their points (thus remaining inside their budget lines).[5] Because of the negative slope of the points budget line, if two different positions on that line are selected by the two parties, the total demand for one of the goods must exceed the available supply while the demand for the other good must fall short of the available supply. This is shown in figure 4.3, in which ss is the points budget line. Suppose that individual 1 selects point A on that budget line. Through A draw a horizontal line hh', and also a vertical line vv'. These divide the Edgeworth box into four quadrants, labeled I, II, III, and IV going counterclockwise from the northeast quadrant, I. Suppose first that individual j were to choose any point, such as B, in quadrant I (thus, not spending all her points). It is

---

5. It is not easy to see why anyone would do this since in this case no money is needed to buy the goods and points have no other use. Individuals may be sated in the good before its supplies are exhausted, but then it is hard to imagine why rationing would occur.

clear that there would be an excess supply of both X and Y. For with individual i demanding $O_i v$ of X and individual j demanding $O_j \omega$ of the same item the two would not add up to the available supply of X given by the length of the Edgeworth box, and the same holds for good Y. Similarly, if j were to select any point in quadrant II there would be an excess demand for X but an excess supply of Y. The opposite holds if j's choice were to fall in quadrant IV. Only if j's demand fell in quadrant III could there be an excess demand for both items. But that is clearly impossible since quadrant III falls entirely below the points price line, so that j simply does not have the points to get her there. Finally, we note that because of the negative slope of the points price line it must fall entirely in quadrants II and IV. Thus, if j selects any point on the price line other than A, there must be excess demand for exactly one of the two goods, as was asserted before.

What will, in fact, happen in this case? The excess demand for the one commodity will, of course, mean shortages of that item, with its distribution settled by queuing or some other more or less arbitrary means. One possible consequence is that the authorities will recognize that the points prices they have selected are unsatisfactory, and they will raise the points price of the item whose demand exceeds the available supply. Ultimately, in this way, they may reach the points prices that clear the market, and our earlier analysis will then apply. Alternatively, or at least in the short run, points prices will not clear the market and then i's and j's consumption positions in the box diagram will not coincide. But then j's consumption must always be represented by a point to the northeast of i's, since they cannot possibly consume more than the available supplies.

That such a result is inefficient is obvious. But it is also clear that there is no reason to expect it to be fair, let alone superfair. Since under the circumstances the amounts of the two commodities with which the two individuals end up is indeterminate, we simply have no basis for prejudging its fairness. In other words,

Proposition 4 Pure points rationing, unless it establishes market-clearing points prices, may not yield results that are fair or that can even be expected to be more equitable than the distribution that would occur in the absence of rationing.

5 Points Rationing with Money Prices for Goods

In reality, points rationing has always involved the payment of money as well as points in exchange for goods. Each rationed commodity has its money price, determined by market forces, as well as its points price

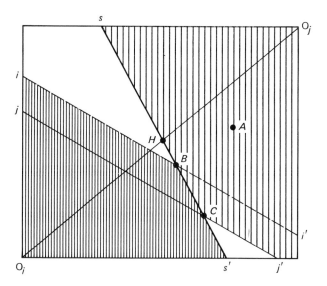

Figure 4.4

determined by the authorities. As has long been recognized, this makes the individual consumer's decision problem one involving maximization of utility subject to *two* linear constrants: the money budget inequality and the points budget inequality, with the feasible region being a convex polyhedron.

Since the analysis is most pertinent to a case involving inflationary pressure, it is useful to assume that the two parties represented in our Edgeworth box have, between them, more than enough money to purchase the available quantities of the two outputs. This means that individuals i and j's price lines will not coincide. They will have the same slopes since, in the absence of price discrimination, they will face the same relative prices. However, with i the individual whose origin is the lower left-hand corner of the box, i's budget line, ii', will lie above and to the right of j's (figure 4.4), meaning that the two together can, at current prices, afford to buy more than the available quantities of the two goods. Notice that the two together cannot afford to end up at a point such as A that lies above ii'. It is true that j has the money to pay for the quantities of X and Y assigned to her by that point (because it lies nearer to her origin than her budget line). But since A lies above i's budget line he cannot afford to get to it. For exactly the same reason no point below j's budget line is financially feasible. That is, the two parties can only afford to get to points lying on or between their budget lines ii' and jj'.

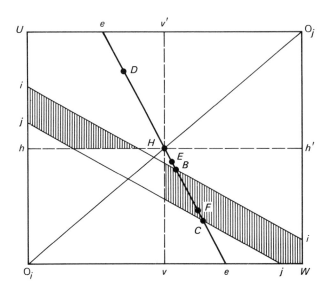

Figure 4.5

We can now see easily what happens if the authorities decide to impose points rationing. As we know, this amounts to the introduction of a new points budget line, ss', which cuts through point H of equal division. An equilibrium point must now satisfy both the monetary and the budget constraints. That is, it must lie on ss' and, as we have just seen, on or between the two monetary budget lines ii' and jj'. This leaves us with only the line segment BC of ss' that lies between ii' and jj'. No other point in the diagram is consistent with the constraints.

This can be seen in a slightly different way. The region that is feasible for i consists of all points that lie below *both* his money and his points budget line, and will therefore be the shaded region whose northeast boundary is iBs'. Similarly, j's feasible region must lie above and to the right of the southwest boundary sCj'. The only positions common to the two feasible regions and, hence, feasible for both parties are those lying on line segment BC, as just noted.

But this is true only at the relative points prices whose ratio is equal to the slope of price line ss'. If the authorities select other points prices, the points price line will rotate through H. The feasible price lines will range from a vertical price line, vv', along which the points price of Y divided by the points price of X equals zero, to horizontal price line hh', along which the reciprocal of that price ratio is zero (figure 4.5).

As the points budget line rotates counterclockwise from vv' to hh' in figure 4.5, the feasible line segment BC (from figure 4.4) covers the two shaded regions in figure 4.5 lying between money budget lines ii and jj. That is, only points in this shaded region can conceivably be attained under points rationing. But this is not the end of the story. Such a point can be attained only if two conditions are satisfied: (a) if the points prices selected are those that clear the market, and (b) the equilibrium point on the corresponding points budget line happens to fall in one of the two shaded regions in figure 4.5. That is, suppose ee in figure 4.5 is the points budget line that clears the market. If a position such as D or E on that line is the points equilibrium, the arrangement will not work because individual i will lack an amount of money sufficient to get to the purchases he would like to make with the ration points in his possession. Only if the equilibrium happens to fall at a location such as F on line segment BC on ee will the points rationing clear the market. It will then work most admirably. As we shall now see, it will clear the market, it will eliminate all inflationary pressure (if all goods are included in the ration scheme), it will be Pareto optimal, and it will be superfair and superequal. We know it will clear the market because it places both persons at a common position in the Edgeworth box. We know it will stop the inflation, at least in the prices of the two rationed commodities, since neither individual will have any ration points left over to bid for more and so each will be left with a useless amount of money in excess supply. In effect, both person's money constraint becomes ineffective, with the points budget line the only effective constraint. The only (marginal) exception occurs if the equilibrium point happens to fall at either B or C, the end points of the feasible line segment, and here one person will still have an excess stock of money while the other person's money will just suffice for that individual's purchase, so that even in these exceptional cases inflationary pressure will also be eliminated. Finally, we know that the solution will be Pareto optimal, superequal, and superfair, because with money no longer an effective constraint upon either party the equilibrium is tantamount to a market-clearing equilibrium under pure points rationing to which proposition 3 applies.

Under what conditions will such a felicitous result emerge? There are two alternative ways in which we give the answer: (i) Draw the two individuals' offer curves through H. If those offer curves happen to intersect in one of the shaded regions in figure 4.5, then that intersection will be the desired equilibrium position attainable under points rationing. But if those offer curves happen to intersect only at a position such as D or E outside the shaded region, no such equilibrium will be attainable under points rationing. The reason is clear. For the usual reasons, points rationing then will only attain an equilibrium at the intersection of the offer curves through the pivot, H, of the points budget lines. (ii) There is an alternative way to describe the conditions for the existence of an equilibrium that is attainable through points rationing. Such an equilibrium will occur if and only if (a) the contract curve intersects one of the two attainable shaded regions in figure 4.5 and if, in addition, (b) there exists some position on the attainable segment of the contract curve at which the line that is the common tangent of the two indifference curves through that position happens to go through position H of equal distribution. For if this so, then this common tangent to these two indifference curves must obviously be our desired points budget line whose intersection with the contract curve is its market-clearing equilibrium. From all this we conclude

Proposition 5   Points rationing with money prices will, in general, not be able to produce a market-clearing equilibrium. However, when it does, that solution will eliminate upward pressures upon the prices of the rationed commodities, and it will be Pareto optimal, superequal, and superfair.

6   Unsuppressed Inflation and Points Rationing

The cases in which market-clearing equilibrium does not exist under points rationing are *not* ascribable to the attempt to suppress inflation and its artificial separation of the budget lines. On the contrary, if before the imposition of rationing, inflation had been permitted to run its course and mop up the excess purchasing power, the regions of attainable solution points, the shaded regions in figure 4.5, would have been narrowed to line segments. Rising prices would have shifted i's money budget line downward and j's money budget line upward until the two coincided. If prices of both products were to rise proportionately, the new common budget line must lie between the initial budget lines ii and jj.[6]

But the shift in the money price lines will not change the position of the offer curves through H since those offer curves depend only upon the (real) incomes at H. Hence, if the intersection of those offer curves did not lie in either of the shaded regions in figure 4.5, it certainly will not lie on the new

---

6. If the prices of both commodities rise proportionately, we know precisely where that common price line will lie. The shift in each person's price line resulting from inflation will be proportionate to his income—the more money he has available, the larger the absolute loss in purchasing power he will suffer. Thus, as prices rise, each person's price line will shift toward his origin *proportionately to its initial distance from that origin.* This will continue until the two price lines meet. This result is intuitively obvious and it is easy to prove.

common price line, which includes only part of that region, and (with relative prices unchanged) lies entirely within it. Indeed, it is more than possible that if the intersection of the offer curves through H lies in the shaded region, it will *not* lie on the common money price line yielded by inflation. We conclude the following:

Proposition 6   The elimination of excess money supplies through proportionately rising money prices will, in general, not increase the likelihood that a market-clearing equilibrium can be attained via points rationing.

7   Rationing with Salability of Points

We come, next, to a variant of points rationing that has recommended itself more strongly to many economists. The idea is to create, along with points rationing, an organized market in which points can be bought and sold at a price that equates their supply and demand. It is argued that the result must be Pareto optimal and that it must constitute a Pareto improvement over the equilibrium that occurs when ration coupons are not salable since all trades of ration points for money must be voluntary and so, as usual, there must be mutual gains from the trade.

   We shall note first that this argument is not necessarily valid; that is, we shall see that it is false under rather plausible assumptions. Second, we shall show that even where the argument *is* valid the resulting equilibrium may well be inferior to the unsalable points equilibrium on the fairness criterion. We may observe that the gains from trade argument for the Pareto superiority of salability of points is valid only if such sales do not generate a detrimental externality in the form of what may be described as a loss of the feeling of fairness in the system. Suppose that most people consider it unfair for the wealthy to be able to get more than their "fair share" of rationed goods. Given the opportunity, a large majority of the public might choose to vote to prevent everyone (including themselves) from participating in such sales. Yet once such sales become legal, so that the wealthy will be able to get additional points on the market, an opponent of the arrangement gains nothing by withholding his own surplus points from the market. Certainly he obtains gains from such trades, if legal trades will take place in any event. But his gains may be greater still if the market for points is eliminated altogether. The problem is that other persons' sales of ration points create detrimental externalities by offending (nearly) everyone's sense of fairness. Here, as usual, the market is unable to cope with the externalities problems, and the resulting gains from trade, like the

Pareto optimality of the resulting free market solution, can be purely illusory.[7]

Before we can use our fairness criterion to examine the fairness of the equilibrium under salability of points we must first characterize that equilibrium. When points can be bought and sold freely the two constraints that characterize normal points rationing are effectively reduced to a single constraint. For then money and ration points simply become two different forms of purchasing power that can be transformed into one another at the current market price of points. One can see this clearly by writing out the relevant constraints.

Since we can easily generalize our argument, let there be n commodities and q individuals and let

x_{ab} = the quantity of commodity A obtained by individual B,

x_a = the quantity of commodity A available to the economy,

p_a = the market price of A,

c_a = the number of ration points required to buy a unit of A,

m_b = B's money income,

z = the number of ration points issued per person,

z_b = the number of points bought (sold) by B, and

p_z = the market price of a ration point.

Then individual B's money and points constraints are, respectively,

$$\sum_a p_a x_{ab} + p_z z_b = m_b \qquad (b = 1, \ldots, q), \tag{4.1}$$

$$\sum_a c_a x_{ab} = z + z_b. \tag{4.2}$$

Multiplying the ration points constraints (4.2) by p_z and adding the result to money constraint (4.1) we obtain the one effective constraint for individual B,

$$\sum_a (p_a + p_z c_a) x_{ab} = p_z z + m_b \qquad (b = 1, \ldots, q), \tag{4.3}$$

where, following Becker, we may describe $p_z z + m_b$ as individual B's full income; i.e., it represents m_b, the money available to him directly as well as the money value of the points issued to him, $p_z z$. This full income can be

---

7. Note the analogy to the argument of Titmuss [1971] against a market for blood. This argument also occurs in Baumol [1952, 2nd ed., pp. 130–134, 205].

disbursed among the available goods in any way the individual desires. Each unit of good A he buys costs him p_a in money and c_a in ration points, each worth p_z dollars on the market. Thus each unit of A effectively costs $p_a + p_z c_a$ (the "full price" of A). For any two goods X and Y, the slope of the individual's money price line (4.1) is obviously $-p_x/p_y$, that of the points constraint line (4.2) is $-c_x/c_y$, and that of the full income line with salable ration points is

$$-(p_x + p_z c_x)/(p_y + p_z c_y). \tag{4.4}$$

Clearly (4.4) will lie between the slope of the money price line and the points budget line. It will equal the former when the price of points, p_z, is zero, and will approach the latter as p_z approaches infinity. Similarly, for any two individuals R and S, relative purchasing power will obviously change from m_r/m_s to

$$(m_r + p_z z)/(m_s + p_z z). \tag{4.5}$$

We may conclude at once

Proposition 7 Salability of points amounts to a partial equalization of the real incomes of the individuals. The greater the money value of $p_z z$, the points issued per person, relative to the available money incomes, the greater the equalization that will occur.

However, so long as the number of ration points issued and their market price both remain finite, as is normally to be expected, a regime of rationing via salable points will amount only to a partial equalization of incomes, as indicated by (4.5), along with a modification of relative prices toward the ratios decided upon by the authorities, in accordance with (4.4). We have seen from (4.5) that the greater the total money value of the ration points issued, the nearer the solution will be to that under pure points rationing, since the less the share the initial endowments of money income will have in the individual consumer's full income. However, there will generally be a maximal value of the ration points, which cannot achieve full income equality, and which corresponds to the issue of some finite ("intermediate") number of points. For, obviously, the issue of a sufficient number of ration points to make them absolutely redundant will drive their price and, hence, their total market value to zero.

How, then, do we evaluate the outcome of pure points rationing with a market in ration coupons? Assuming away the externalities problem raised at the beginning of this section, the result will obviously be Pareto optimal since it involves free exchange at the nondiscriminatory and fixed "full" prices, $p_a + p_z c_a$. But will the result be fair?

We have seen that under points rationing equilibrium can only occur somewhere on the contract locus and at a point that lies in a region of superequal and superfair distributions. In the complete absence of rationing of any sort, if the market is competitive, the solution will also lie somewhere on the contract locus, but, in general, this equilibrium need not be fair. With salability of ration points and in the absence of externality problems, we know from (4.5) that the distribution of real income will be intermediate between that under pure points rationing and that under the free market solution without rationing, both of which lie on the contract curve if markets are competitive. Consequently, if over the relevant range the contract locus is everywhere single valued and continuous in every variable, the solution S_s under salability of ration points will be intermediate between the superfair solution S_p under pure points rationing and the solution S_c yielded by a competitive market without rationing. But we know that with sufficient inequality S_c must lie outside the region of superfairness, since this is true of each individual's origin. Obviously, then, the salable ration points solution, S_s, which will also be somewhere on the contract curve, can be expected to lie closer to the superfairness region than S_c. But, like S_c, S_s may not lie within it.[8]

---

8. One can prove by counterexample that the white market solution, S_s, need not be superfair. For simplicity, consider a perfectly symmetrical two-good–two-person case with $x^* = y^* = k$ the (same) available quantities of the two goods, and the two persons having the identical utility functions $u^i = x_i y_i$, $i = 1, 2$. Then the fairness boundaries must satisfy

$$U^i(x_i, y_i) = U^i(k - x_i, k - y_i)$$

or

$$x_i y_i = (k - x_i)(k - y_i),$$

that is (multiplying out and simplifying)

$$x_1 + y_1 = k \quad \text{and} \quad k - x_1 + k - y_1 = k,$$

for individuals 1 and 2, respectively. These two boundaries clearly coincide. Therefore, the entire superfairness region is the straight line $x + y = k$. By symmetry, the contract curve must be the $45°$ line $y = x$. Thus, there is only one free market equilibrium point that is superfair: the midpoint, H. Here, if income is divided unequally to *any* degree between the two persons, they must end up at some point on the contract locus other than H, for at H their real incomes *must* be equal. Moreover, since by proposition 7 the issue of ration points with a free market in the coupons only equalizes income partially, it follows that the resulting equilibrium point will also not be superfair.

Proposition 8   Under rationing with resalability of points the solution may be fair but need not be so. It can be expected to lie closer to a region of superequal or one of superfair solutions than the free market solution without rationing.

8   Concluding Remarks

While this chapter has dealt with many issues related to a variety of forms of rationing, its primary purpose has not been to provide another analysis of rationing. Rather, its goal has been to show that the fairness criterion is operational—that it can be applied to concrete problems and that with its aid one can derive results that are not all obvious in advance. Of course, rationing was selected for that purpose because, of all economic equity issues, it seems to lend itself most readily to this sort of approach.

Something else that emerges is the impression that the views of non-economists on the subject of rationing, at least sometimes, have a more solid basis than some of the discussions in our literature would seem to imply. For example, salability of ration points does not turn out to be the unmixed blessing we sometimes suggest it to be, and the "common man" is shown to have reason for suspecting its fairness.

5   Compensation of Victims of Externalities and Pricing for Conservation

There is, perhaps, no more dramatic example of the conflict between the requirements of fairness and efficiency than that which arises from the economist's standard prescription for the control of externalities: Pigouvian taxes and subsidies. The fairness issue that is widely recognized to stem from this arrangement involves the possibility that the taxes will be regressive. Here, however, the evidence is mixed,[1] and the hypothesis that Pigouvian taxes will cause a substantial decrease in the progressiveness of the tax system is hardly overwhelming. The direct clash between equity and efficiency arises, rather, from another quarter, which is not widely recognized: the fact that economic efficiency is, in general, precluded by *any* compensation payments to the victims of externalities.[2] That is to say, if the pertinent elasticities are not zero, any compensation payment will elicit behavior on the part of the victims of externalities that is incompatible with achievement of Pareto optimality. The source of the difficulties, as we shall see, is directly analogous to the problem of moral hazard in insurance.

The problem posed for fairness by this conclusion is obvious. If a smoke-

---

1. See, for example, Freeman [1972] and Dorfman and Snow [1975, pp. 101–115].

2. Here, I naturally exclude "lump-sum" payments that, by definition, do not interfere with efficiency. It seems clear that such taxes are virtually inconceivable in reality and one can even make a theoretical case for the view that they are, in principle, impossible. Of course, they are a legitimate and useful analytic device, but it is not helpful in the discussion of the material of this chapter. Yet, it must be admitted that the case of externalities sometimes comes as close as any to permitting lump-sum payments. If external damage falls entirely upon the value of land near the source of the damage, then compensation can, clearly, be paid to the landowner without causing any misallocation of resources. But in that case the externality itself is, arguably, purely pecuniary and will have led to no inefficiencies. On the other hand, if the externality affects more than land value and influences some decision, compensation will also affect it and so it will no longer be lump-sum.

emitting factory moves into a residential neighborhood whose inhabitants had no reason to expect it when they first selected the site for their homes, and afterward both doctor bills and laundry expenses increase significantly, virtually anyone will agree that fairness requires some sort of compensation of the victims.[3] This is readily confirmed in terms of either the Pareto-improvement or superfairness criteria of equity. Yet, we have just noted that any such payment must reduce economic welfare. A trade-off is then forced upon society, which must balance off any gain in fairness against its cost in terms of efficiency.

In this chapter it will also be shown that (i) if full Pigouvian taxes are charged for emissions and it nevertheless pays polluting firms to open for business, superfairness requires *over*compensation of victims, i.e., payment of amounts exceeding that which just makes them indifferent between the presence and absence of the polluter, but no such fair solution may be feasible; (ii) the magnitude of the distortion in behavior of the victims from its Pareto optimal pattern will in competitive equilibrium increase with the amount of compensation they are offered, but it may not increase monotonically; (iii) the magnitude of the (second-best) Pigouvian tax on emissions may well increase with the level of compensation of victims. Unfortunately, aside from its negative slope, it does not seem possible to provide a general characterization of the shape of the trade-off frontier between fairness and efficiency and that, in turn, precludes substantial conclusions about the qualitative properties of the optimum.

I shall end the chapter with a brief discussion of another application of fairness theory—the use of prices as a means to induce conservation of very scarce resources.

1 Incompatibility of Compensation and Pareto Optimality

In this section the reason compensation of victims is inconsistent with Pareto optimality will first be explained intuitively. Then, a formal proof of the proposition will be provided.

The source of the conflict between compensation and efficiency is easy to explain by analogy. The well-known moral hazard problem in burglary insurance is that protection against loss makes it rational for policyholders

---

3. Posner has, however, questioned this conclusion. He points out that any land purchaser is faced by some probability, however small, that a polluter will someday open nearby. That probability is already included in the price of the land, reflecting the market's valuation of those odds. If the buyer purchases voluntarily he implicitly accepts the terms of this gamble *ex ante* and has no grounds for complaint if it happens to turn out badly. See Posner [1980].

to reduce their outlays on protection against burglary. The less they stand to lose as a result of their insurance coverage, the less it pays them to spend on locks, burglar alarms, etc. Indeed, with full coverage against loss, it pays to spend absolutely nothing on measures to discourage thieves. Thus, insurance, which is designed to cover the risks inherent in a given state of nature (the probability of being burglarized when precautions against burglary are optimal), leads the potential victims to react in a way that alters the state of nature and yields an equilibrium in which the resources devoted to the discouragement of theft are less than optimal

In the same way, compensation for the damage caused by pollution discourages efforts by victims to protect themselves from its effects. Thus, suppose a factory opens for business and emits pollution at location A, and that in the absence of compensation a neighbor of the emitting factory would be induced to move to cleaner location B. If he is offered full compensation for any damage he sustains by remaining at A, one can expect that individual to remain at that location that (aside from the effects of the pollution) he has been revealed by his earlier choice to prefer. In this way, the compensation payment (a mere transfer) induces victims to reduce their outlays on measures to decrease the pollution damage they suffer; i.e., it lures them into subjecting themselves to pollution damage (a real social cost). Thus, the payment alters the "state of nature," and the resources devoted to reduction of the damage caused by the emissions will be less than optimal.

Inadequate self-protective outlays by the victims of externalities are not the only efficiency cost of compensation payments. Other decision variables are likely to be affected as well. For example, compensation payments may lead to excessive outputs of products damaged by the externalities. In a smoke-beset community the high real cost of laundry operations may make it optimal for individuals to have their clothes washed rather less often than they would have otherwise. Compensation may prevent this. After the payments to the laundries, competition may force laundry prices down to a level appropriate for a less polluted community and this may in turn induce consumers to adopt standards of fastidiousness higher than those consistent with Pareto optimality. Compensation may also induce excessive entry into the laundry industry. In short, compensation payments may distort many decisions in the economy and not only the outlays by victims to protect themselves from the consequences of the externality.[4]

_____

4. The same is, of course, true of the moral hazard distortions induced by burglary insurance. The availability of insurance may, for example, induce consumers to buy larger quantities of jewelry than is consistent with Pareto optimality.

These intuitive arguments are readily confirmed by formal analysis. For comprehensibility, the general equilibrium model employed in the following discussion is highly simplified.[5] It assumes that competition is perfect and universal, and that the cost of negotiation of any voluntary agreement between the victims and the polluters on the lines suggested by Coase [1960] is prohibitive and rules out any such arrangement for the control of externalities.

In addition, I assume that there is only one scarce resource (labor) and that the externality (smoke) only affects the cost of production of neighboring laundries, rather than causing disutility to consumers. We now prove

Proposition 1 Any (non-lump-sum) compensation of the victims of externalities is inconsistent with economic efficiency and, therefore, with Pareto optimality.

Proof Let us use the following notation:

y_1 and y_2 = the outputs of electricity and laundry, the economy's two consumer products,

a_1 = the magnitude of the polluter's smoke suppression (abatement) activity,

a_2 = the magnitude of victim's damage reduction activity (e.g., outlay on air conditioning),

y_3 = unused labor (leisure),

$C^1(y_1, a_1)$ and $C^2(y_2, a_2, s)$ = the respective real (labor) cost functions of electricity and laundry, and

$s = S(y_1, a_1)$ = the quantity of smoke emitted.

Efficiency, and, hence, Pareto optimality, then requires us to

maximize y_1

subject to $y_2 \geqslant k_2$ (constant),

$$y_3 \geqslant k_3,$$

$$s = S(y_1, a_1)$$

and the labor requirement constraint

$$C^1(\cdot) + C^2(\cdot) + y_3 = R.$$

---

5. For a more sophisticated construct yielding the same conclusions, see Baumol and Oates [1975].

The Lagrangian is

$$L = \sum_{i=1}^{3} \lambda_i(y_i - k_i) + \beta[s - S(\cdot)] + \gamma[R - C^1(\cdot) - C^2(\cdot) - y_3].$$

Writing

$C_y^i = \partial C^i/\partial y_i$, etc.,

we obtain among our first-order conditions (assuming the values of the pertinent variables are all nonzero)

$$\partial L/\partial y_1 = \lambda_1 - \beta S_y - \gamma C_y^1 = 0, \tag{5.1a}$$

$$\partial L/\partial y_2 = \lambda_2 - \gamma C_y^2 = 0, \tag{5.1b}$$

$$\partial L/\partial a_1 = - \beta S_a - \gamma C_a^1 = 0, \tag{5.1c}$$

$$\partial L/\partial a_2 = - \gamma C_a^2 = 0, \tag{5.1d}$$

$$\partial L/\partial s = \beta - \gamma C_s^2 = 0. \tag{5.1e}$$

Let us see now what prices, emissions tax rate, and level of compensation of the victims are required to induce everyone to behave in a manner consistent with satisfaction of the economic efficiency requirements (5.1). We take labor as the numeraire and set the wage rate equal to unity.

The electricity generator's decision model requires him to maximize his profit[6]

$$\pi^1 = P_1 y_1 - C^1(y_1, a_1) - ts,$$

subject to the smoke emission constraint

$$s = S(y_1, a_1),$$

where t is the tax rate on emissions.

Differentiating in turn with respect to y_1, a_1, and s, and letting δ be the Lagrange multiplier, we obtain the first-order conditions [numbering them to match the corresponding conditions in (5.1)]

$$P_1 - C_y^1 - \delta S_y = 0, \tag{5.2a}$$

$$- C_a^1 - \delta S_a = 0, \tag{5.2c}$$

$$- t + \delta = 0. \tag{5.2e}$$

---

6. Here, to save on subscripts, the discussion proceeds as though there were only one electricity generator and one laundry, though this conflicts with the perfect competition premise. As is readily demonstrated, nothing of substance is altered by this simplification.

Similarly, the laundry's profit maximization model is

$$\pi^2 = P_2 y_2 - C^2(y_2, a_2, s) + wD(y_2, a_2, s), \tag{5.3}$$

where $wD(\cdot)$ is the compensation to the laundry for smoke damage, $D(\cdot)$. Since the quantity s is outside the laundry's control, to obtain its first-order conditions we differentiate only with respect to y_2 and a_2 to obtain

$$P_2 - C_y^2 + wD_y = 0, \tag{5.2b}$$

$$-C_a^2 + wD_a = 0. \tag{5.2d}$$

Comparison of the behavioral conditions (5.2) for the firms with the corresponding Pareto optimality requirements (5.1) shows that if the solution is unique, we must have

$$\lambda_1 = P_1, \qquad \lambda_2 = P_2, \qquad \gamma = 1, \qquad C_s^2 = \beta = \delta = t, \qquad w = 0, \tag{5.4}$$

for which values (5.1a) $\equiv$ (5.2a), ..., (5.1e) $\equiv$ (5.2e).

Thus, (5.4) yields the prices, tax, and compensation rates required to elicit Pareto optimal behavior and shows, in particular, that the emissions tax on smoke must, indeed, equal its marginal social damage, C_s^2, and that w, the compensation rate for victims, must equal Zero.

More directly, since by comparison of (5.1a) with (5.2a), $\gamma = 1$, the zero compensation result $w = 0$ follows directly from (5.1d) and (5.2d). At any nonzero value of w the damage reduction activity will not be carried to its optimal level at which[7] $C_a^2 = 0$.

This completes our proof of the inconsistency of economic efficiency and (any) non-lump-sum compensation of externalities.[8]

---

7. Condition (5.1d) requiring $\gamma C_a^2 = 0$ may at first glance seem peculiar. It simply represents the premise that a_2, the activity that reduces the damaging effect of pollution, incurs some cost for the victims (it has nonzero marginal labor cost) but it also reduces the cost imposed on the victim by the emissions. An optimal solution requires the marginal cost of this protective activity to equal its marginal (cost-saving) benefit, at which point its *net* marginal cost, C_a^2, must be zero.

8. The proof is in fact not quite complete because it is possible to compensate the victims in a way that leads each firm individually to make its decisions in a manner consistent with Pareto optimality and yet in which inefficiency occurs in the form of an excessive number of firms. Thus, suppose the damage function is defined as

$$D^*(y_2, a_2, s) = \pi^{2*} - [p_2 y_2 - C^2(y_2, a_2, s)],$$

where we may define π^{2*} as the maximum profit firm 2 could have earned in the complete absence of smoke emissions (or it can be any other constant). Then we may interpret $D^*(\cdot)$ as the profits firm 2 must forgo as a result of the emissions. But now the first-order conditions for firm 2 become, by (5.3),

2   Compensation, Victim Abatement Efforts, and Pigouvian Taxes

Suppose, next, that despite the reduction in welfare, it is decided to pay some compensation, presumably on grounds of fairness to the victims. That is, suppose it is decided to set $w > 0$ in (5.3). It is reasonable to conjecture that this will reduce a_2, the victim's damage abatement effort. Indeed, one can surmise that the value of a_2 will fall monotonically with w because a rise in w reduces the marginal return to abatement activity. In the large, this conjecture turns out to be correct, but over small intervals it transpires that there may be cases in which $\partial a_2/\partial w > 0$. That is,

Proposition 2   While an increase in the compensation of the victims of externalities from zero to some positive amount can generally be expected to reduce victims' abatement outlays, the relation need not be monotonic.

Proof   Let us assume that with zero compensation for smoke the optimal abatement outlay by the victim is $a_2^* > 0$, while, by definition, when smoke damage is zero $a_2 = 0$.

Now, under *full* compensation ($w = 1$), by definition,

$$(1 - w)(p_2 - C_y^2) = 0, \tag{5.2b}$$

$$(1 - w)C_a^2 = 0, \tag{5.2d}$$

which are perfectly compatible with the efficiency requirements (5.1) so long as $w \neq 1$. Intuitively, the reason this occurs is that when the damage compensation described in this footnote is added to firm 2's profit function, its marginal profit from abatement, $\partial \pi^2/\partial a_2$, is reduced at every value of a_2 except the optimal value where $C_a^2 = (1 - w)C_a^2 = 0$. Put in another way, if we depict $\pi^2(y_2, a_2)$ graphically in (π^2, y_2, a_2) space, the addition of wD^* shifts the three-dimensional graph of $\pi^2(\cdot)$, but does not change the value of (y_2, a_2) at which $\pi^2(\cdot)$ attains its maximum. Yet, it is easy to show that the net result must be inconsistent with Pareto optimality. To see this, it must be recalled that for the entire analysis to be applicable as it stands we must be dealing with a case of universal perfect competition. The net benefit of laundry production by an additional firm must be $p_2 y_2 - C^2(\cdot)$. But with *any* positive compensation paid, competitive equilibrium requires

$$p_2 y_2 - C^2(\cdot) + wD(\cdot) = 0, \qquad \text{i.e.,} \qquad p_2 y_2 - C^2(\cdot) < 0,$$

so that society would benefit, i.e., some persons could be made better off, *ceteris paribus*, if at least one laundry were closed. The point, of course, is that the payment of wD must be considered to constitute a subsidy to the firm and, under perfect competition, it must induce entry. If the number of laundries is optimal when $w = 0$, it must be excessive when $w > 0$. This can all be formalized in terms of a Pareto optimization model in which n, the number of laundries, is introduced as an explicit choice variable.

I am indebted to David Dollar and Charles Wilson for assistance on these points.

$$\pi^2(y_2, a_2, s) \equiv \pi^2(y_2, a_2, 0), \tag{5.5}$$

with a zero compensation payment corresponding to the right-hand side since with zero smoke emission the damage is zero $[D(y_2, a_2, 0) = 0]$. Hence, by (5.5), under full compensation the profit-maximizing values, y_2^0 and a_2^0, to the laundry will be the same as those in the absence of pollution, i.e., we must have $a_2^0 = 0$.

In sum, a_2 will fall from $a_2^* > 0$ when $w = 0$ to $a_2^0 = 0$ when $w = 1$. Consequently, if the relationships are continuous, for the interval $w = [0, 1]$ the derivative $\partial a_2 / \partial w$ must "predominantly" be negative.

However, we can go further than this, using the standard mathematics of comparative statics. For simplicity, rewrite the first-order conditions for maximization of (5.3) as

$$\pi_y^2 = 0, \qquad \pi_a^2 = 0.$$

Then, total differentiation yields

$$\begin{aligned}
\pi_{yy}^2 \, dy_2 + \pi_{ya}^2 \, da_2 &= -D_y \, dw, \\
\pi_{ay}^2 \, dy_2 + \pi_{aa}^2 \, da_2 &= -D_a \, dw.
\end{aligned} \tag{5.6}$$

Thus, we obtain

$$\frac{\partial a_2}{\partial w} = \begin{vmatrix} \pi_{yy}^2 & -D_y \\ \pi_{ay}^2 & -D_a \end{vmatrix} \bigg/ \Delta = (D_y \pi_{ay}^2 - D_a \pi_{yy}^2)/\Delta, \tag{5.7}$$

where Δ is the determinant of (5.6) and is positive by the second-order maximum conditions for (5.3). We may assume $D_a < 0$ (increased abatement effort reduces smoke damage), $D_y > 0$ (increased laundry output increases the damage caused by a given amount of smoke), and $\pi_{yy}^2 < 0$ (diminishing marginal profit returns). But we cannot be certain of the sign of π_{ay}^2. If $\pi_{ay}^2 \leqslant 0$ (increased output does not increase the marginal profit yield of abatement), then it is easy to verify that the sum of the terms on the right-hand side of (5.7) must be negative and $\partial a / \partial w$ must be negative everywhere. But if a_2 and y_2 are profit complements[9] so that $\pi_{ay}^2 > 0$, the results become ambiguous. That is because a rise in w can make it profitable to increase y_2, which, in turn, raises the marginal profit yield of a_2. Such a relationship surely is not impossible—an outlay on better air conditioning

---

9. Here we cannot rely on the simplicity of the model taking y_2 and a_2 to be the two outputs of firm 2, and argue that complementarity is impossible in a two-commodity model. After all, our analysis is intended to apply to a firm with any number of outputs and no more than a single consumers' good is included just for the sake of expository simplicity.

may plausibly be expected to provide a higher (marginal) profit to a busier laundry. But if this effect is sufficiently large, it may yield an interval in which $\partial a_2/\partial w > 0$. This completes our discussion of proposition 2.

The effect upon the value of the Pigouvian tax rate, t, of the selection of a compensation rate $w^* > 0$ can also be inferred intuitively, but a rigorous and general characterization does not seem possible. Since the value of w does not appear directly in our original Pareto optimization model, its role can only be described by proxy via a relationship between the compensation rate and the abatement outlay,

$$a_2 = a_2^* = A^2(w^*), \tag{5.8}$$

which can be added directly to our Pareto optimality model by substitution of this relationship for condition (5.1d), or by direct addition of (5.8) to the original model in the form of a supplementary constraint. In this case, it is also easy to show by differentiation of the resulting Lagrangian that (5.1d) is the only condition whose *form* is affected by the restriction upon the value of w. That is to say, it follows that the resulting second-best optimum, while it can be expected to involve changes in the values of the variables, will still satisfy conditions (5.1a)–(5.1c) and (5.1e). Moreover, the model describing the behavior of the polluter will not be affected.

From this we deduce by comparison of (5.1a) with (5.2a) and (5.1e) with (5.2e) that the second-best solution must still satisfy $t = C_s^2$. In other words, even in the second-best solution the Pigouvian tax must remain equal to marginal social damage. Yet the magnitude of that tax cannot be expected to remain the same as that in the "first-best" solution because the change in w from $w = 0$ to $w = w^*$ can be expected to affect the marginal damage figure, C_s^2

Unfortunately, we do not seem to be able to predict the nature of that change with any degree of certainty. Intuition may suggest that $\partial^2 C^2/\partial s\,\partial w \equiv C_{sw}^2 > 0$, i.e., that increased compensation raises marginal social damage by reducing abatement effort, a_2, so that the higher the compensation of victims, the larger will be the second-best Pigouvian tax $t = C_s^2$. Indeed, we can, if we wish, adopt $C_{sw}^2 > 0$ as a premise and settle the issue by assumption. But there are at least two reasons for hesitation.

First, as we have seen, there may exist intervals (ω', ω'') in which $\partial a_2/\partial w > 0$ so that in such a region an imposed rise in w may reduce smoke damage. Second, while an increase in a_2, by the very nature of abatement activity, should decrease *total* damage, i.e., $\partial[C^2(y_2, a_2, s) - C^2(y_2, a_2, 0)]/\partial a_2 < 0$, it does not follow that a rise in w should reduce the *marginal* damage from an additional puff of smoke; that is, we cannot be confident that $C_{sa}^2 < 0$.

Thus, while we may still suspect that $\partial t/\partial w = C_{sw}^2 > 0$, there are two reasons why we cannot be sure that this will be so. Hence, it is plausible but by no means certain that the second-best Pigouvian tax will increase with increased compensation of the externality's victims.

3   Strict Incremental Superfairness and Overcompensation of Victims

Though *any* compensation of victims is inefficient, I shall show now that strict incremental superfairness requires more than this. *If it is possible*, it requires not merely $w > 0$, but $w > 1$. (I shall refer to this as *overcompensation* of the victims, meaning that the victims of externalities have to be paid even *more* than the amount at which they evaluate the damage they suffer.)

A simple extension of our scenario will make the point. Assume that the laundry opened for business before anyone had considered building an electricity generation plant nearby. Those who proposed to construct that plant are given permission to do so, but with the understanding that they will have to pay the (first-best) optimal effluent charges upon any pollution they emit. Assume also that with this understanding (which is adhered to), the generator is nevertheless built and put into operation.

The point of all this is that the introduction of the generating station under these conditions *must* bring with it a net increase in welfare (producers' and consumers' surpluses). For with all the externalities internalized, if entry is profitable, the result follows at once.

The increase in welfare means that at least one person in the economy is better off than before. But, then, strict incremental superfairness (absence of envy) requires that the owners of the laundry not just to be as well off as before (a zero increment in their welfare). Rather, they must have some share in the net benefits and that can only happen if they are *over*compensated for the net damage they would otherwise suffer from the advent of the electricity producer.

This would appear to be all that has to be said to show that overcompensation is *always* necessary for strict superfairness under a system of Pigouvian charges, but there is a complication. For, as we have seen, the very payment of compensation leads to inefficiency, and so necessarily erodes the benefits flowing from the establishment of the power station to some unknown degree. Should it transpire that because of the compensation payment to the victims economic efficiency is no greater than it was before the generating station was built, then a fair solution with voluntary entry of the generator of the externality will not be possible. For since its entry is voluntary, it must yield a net gain to the entrant. But then, absence of envy requires some gain to everyone, and not just to the victim of the externality. This is, however, impossible if the community's overall welfare has not increased. Thus we have

Proposition 3   If full compensation of victims is consistent with net welfare gains from the introduction of the generator of the externality, then fairness requires overcompensation of the victims. Otherwise, no fair arrangement will be consistent with voluntary entry of that externality generator.

4   The Trade-Off between Fairness and Efficiency

It is important to reemphasize that no one proposes to impose fairness as an inviolable requirement. What has been shown here is that its attainment is not costless and so it is perfectly rational to consider just how much efficiency one is willing to sacrifice for the purpose. With a social welfare function that values both efficiency and fairness some compromise is likely to be the optimal solution, with neither maximal efficiency nor superfairness actually achieved.

Figure 5.1 shows the situation. The horizontal axis indicates the value of w, the share of full compensation paid to victims. Thus, $w = 1$ is the full compensation point, and anything to its left represents undercompensation. Point f, the fairness boundary, lies in the region of overcompensation (though its position will vary with the point on the frontier selected by society). The vertical axis is some measure of efficiency, such as the sum of consumers' and producers' surpluses. Regrettably, as proposition 2 tells us, we do not know the shape of the trade-off frontier, which may conceivably be concave like BB, but may also be convex or irregular, like AA. We can be sure only that the slope of the frontier is generally negative though it may even have positively sloping segments if $\partial a_2 / \partial w > 0$ anywhere, i.e., if in some interval a rise in compensation stimulates abatement effort.

If the relationships are continuous and there is an interior solution, the optimal solution will, of course, lie at the point where the frontier is tangent to an indifference curve of the social welfare function (point M). Here, obviously, neither maximal efficiency (OA) nor superfairness (OF) is attained.

Convex frontier BB illustrates two phenomena: first, that superfairness

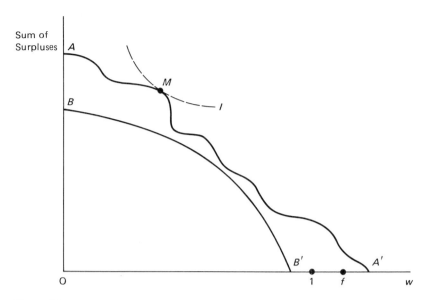

Figure 5.1

may not even be possible (since the entire frontier lies to the left of the full compensation point) and, second, that convexity of the frontier favors a considerable degree of fairness (a relatively high compensation rate) since at the left-hand end the low slope of BB means that little efficiency is sacrificed by a considerable increase in the value of w.

This is perfectly analogous to the optimal compromise with the moral hazard that is elicited by insurance against burglary. This compromise does not rule out the socially valuable service supplied by the insurance firms, but it does preclude full coverage and thereby provides some incentive for policyholders to devote effort to protect their property from theft. The retention of some incentive for the victims of pollution to undertake a degree of abatement activity, which entails some undercompensation, is the analogue in our discussion.

All of this, however, risks the fallacy of composition. Insurance makes sense in a society where burglary victims are rare. But suppose burglary were so widespread that virtually everyone could expect to be burglarized, sooner or later, and that the losses were fairly even and predictable. Then insurance would generally become irrational because each policyholder could expect to be repaid, over time, just about what he had put into it (or, rather, this amount reduced by the insurance firm's costs and profits). Thus, policyholders would realize little in return for their outlays but efficiency would nevertheless be impaired by the moral hazard effect. Then the trade-off's benefits would all but disappear, with society receiving little in return for the moral hazard that the provision of insurance entails. Insurance is worthwhile only if the events against which it protects are rare and very costly so that the policyholder cannot afford to protect himself, and in the event he is paid, that payment is likely to amount to considerably more than he put into it.

In our externalities problem similar considerations arise. Externalities are certainly a widespread phenomenon. Everyone suffers from them to some degree. Suppose their damage is roughly similar to all members of society. Then, equal compensation (transfer) payments to everyone must in reality amount to compensation payments to no one.[10] However, the apparent compensation payments will still constitute a disincentive to abatement outlays since such an abatement outlay will reduce the payment to which the victim who undertakes it is entitled. In such a case, clearly, compensation of victims makes no sense and is apt to harm every individual. For it will reduce the overall real welfare output of the economy, while the merry-go-round of compensation payments provides benefits to no one and, hence, can provide no offset for those welfare losses.

In such a world, compensation of victims for the sake of fairness makes no sense, first, because it incurs a social cost without any compensating benefit, and second, given the relatively even distribution of external damage in the aggregate, because even without any compensation, matters are relatively fair. In that case it may be rational to impose a sort of deductibility feature on any compensation arrangement, precluding compensation for small amounts of damage and providing it only to the victims of (more or less) catastrophic externality effects.

5 Pricing and Resource Conservation

Let me turn now to a second issue related to environmental matters— the use of increased prices of resources threatened with exhaustion as a means to promote their conservation, dealing in particular with the special problems raised by differences in elasticity of demand by different customer groups. It will be shown that the combined short and long run effects of a program of conservation through pricing may well tend to be

---

10. Indeed, transactions costs mean that at least some persons must lose out in the course of the transfer process.

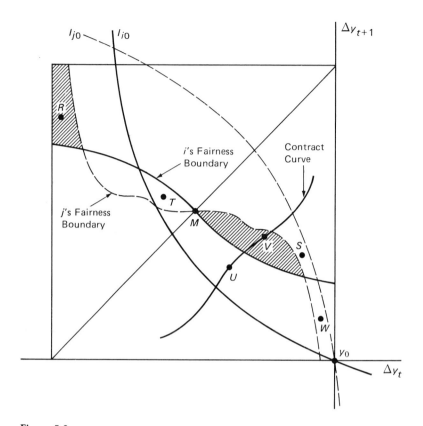

Figure 5.2

superfair or nearly so. This is by no means guaranteed, but some presumption for this striking conclusion is nevertheless there.

Figure 5.2 is an incremental Edgeworth box, in which the dimensions of the box represent the changes in total consumption of, say, petroleum resulting from a rise in current price. Since the price change, if successful in its goal, results in a net decrease in consumption of oil in period t and an increase in period $t + 1$, the box will lie in the northwest quadrant, above and to the left of the origin, y_0, representing the initial consumption vector.

Now. let $y_0 I_{i_o}$ and $y_0 I_{j_0}$, respectively, be i's and j's indifference curves through the initial point, y_0. Obviously, the region between these curves constitutes the region of Pareto improvements—cases in which neither party is made worse off by the price change.

What may we plausibly expect to happen in the case of the price changes we are considering, i.e., a rise in current price relative to future price of oil? Will the results tend to be an unfair distribution of benefits between rich and poor? One cannot say in general since that depends on their relative responses to the price changes. But I shall argue that on the criterion of superfairness there is some reason to hope that unfairness will generally not result. This is so despite the fact that it is hard to say whether we can usually expect the petroleum demands of the poor or of the rich to be the more price elastic. One may, for example, suspect that because the wealthy can afford to pay relatively little attention to a price rise, their demands will be the more price inelastic. On the other hand, one may surmise that use of gasoline by the poor is more preponderantly devoted to journeys to work and other largely unavoidable trips, while the rich do proportionately much more pleasure driving, so that on this view it is the poor whose oil demand is the more inelastic.

Fortunately for our main result, it does not matter which of these views is correct, or if one or both groups are heterogeneous, so long as relative elasticities of individuals remain roughly the same in the two periods and over the relevant range. If one income group has a highly inelastic demand, its position after the price change will remain very close to the initial position, y_0. That is, both y_t and y_{t+1} for that group will, by definition, remain fairly close to the coordinates of the initial (planned) consumption point, y_0. The opposite will clearly be true of the group with the more elastic demand, so that the latter group's solution point (the symmetric image of the former group's solution point) will lie near the upper left-hand corner of the Edgeworth box (the two solution points having the usual equilibrium property that they must exhaust the available quantities so that either point will also indicate the solution for the other group, given the total shift in consumption from period t to $t + 1$).

Now, all of this means that whichever hypothesis about the relative price elasticity of poor customers is correct, the solution point will tend to fall near the negatively sloping diagonal of the Edgeworth box—the shaded regions where superfair solutions tend to lie. Of course, this *by itself* is not enough to lend a presumption that the equilibrium will approximate incremental superfairness. After all, if the solution is, say, T in figure 5.2, it lies near the diagonal in question but nowhere near a superfair region. However, we do have one other pertinent piece of information. Assuming that there is no price discrimination, i.e., that rich and poor pay the same price in a given period, then it is clear that the equilibrium must lie on the contract curve, i.e., it must be Pareto optimal. Now, a slight modification of the Schmeidler-Yaari argument (proposition 9 of chapter 2), but starting from an initial position with an equal distribution of Δy_t and Δy_{t+1}, instead of y_t and y_{t+1}, shows that the contract curve must have at least one point in common with the zone of incrementally superfair distributions. With our equilibrium point, say, point U or point V, lying on the contract curve and near the negatively sloping diagonal of the Edgeworth box we have the

Conjecture If the poor have either constantly more or constantly less elastic demands for the product conserved by a rise in its current price, there is reason to presume that the resulting change in intertemporal consumption patterns will approximate incremental fairness.

A simple intuitive argument can be used to explain the rationale of this conjecture. The point is that a rise in price of petroleum today and a fall in its price tomorrow will cut consumption today but provide a compensatory rise in consumption tomorrow. Someone whose demand is inelastic will neither cut back consumption very much today nor expand it very much tomorrow, while the opposite will be true of someone whose demand is elastic. For this reason we can, perhaps, expect rough justice in the resulting intertemporal shift, with those giving up a greater amount now receiving greater compensation later.

Thus, at least by this interpretation, there is some reason to expect the price mechanism to perform reasonably well here in terms of fairness as well as efficiency.

6　Industry Pricing and Paretian Fairness

An arena in which fairness issues have played a prime role in the discussion of public policy has been pricing by business firms, particularly those that are subject to government regulation or that attract the attention of the antitrust authorities. Here, too, there has been a direct clash between the orientation of economists and that of others involved. Economists feel, with good reason, that they have a good deal to contribute on pricing policy, but virtually all of it is addressed to allocative efficiency. Yet the bulk of the discussions of the subject by others can be interpreted to take equity as their primary focus.

This chapter will describe the nature of the primary fairness issues that have been raised in discussions of regulation and antitrust policy. It will also show how economists have dealt with such equity matters when they could not avoid taking some position on the subject. It will be seen that the bulk of those discussions have taken Pareto superiority as their criterion of equity and in the process have tended to conclude that in this arena the requirements of fairness and efficiency are identical.

As is well known, many regulators have relied as a criterion of fairness upon an accounting procedure known as the full allocation of costs, which most economists have considered reprehensible. As a possible substitute some sophisticated observers have proposed a game theoretic approach, using the Shapley value or some related construct as its criterion of fairness in pricing. In the next chapter, I shall argue that despite the analytical virtues of the Shapley value concept it is unsuitable as a guide to equity in price determination.

I shall turn, finally, to the superfairness criterion, discussing what impedes its adoption as a general guide to equity in price setting, and shall show how it can be adapted to deal with some of the issues that arise here. Some evidence will, incidentally, be offered to indicate that the courts' view of fairness seems, at least sometimes, to come closer to that underlying the superfairness criterion than to that of the Paretian standard.

1   Two Basic Issues in Fairness in Pricing

Of course, the very concept of monopoly gives rise to visions of prices that are excessive and, consequently, unfair. This is a subject to which I shall return later. But, curiously, until recently at least, this pricing issue has occupied no more than second place in the attention of regulators and antitrust authorities, where it has barely arisen at all. Much more prominent a place has been assumed by the range of subjects subsumed under the term "cross-subsidy."

Cross-subsidy becomes a pertinent possibility when a multiproduct firm sells some products for which there are competing suppliers but enjoys effective monopoly in the sale of other(s) of the outputs it sells. A cross-subsidy is then said to be provided from the monopoly products to the firm's competitive products if the firm offers the latter at prices so low that they cannot be justified in terms of costs. It is taken to make up the resulting deficiency in earnings by charging excessive prices for its monopoly products. In these circumstances it is said that a cross-subsidy is being provided by the consumers of the firm's monopoly products to the purchasers of its competitive products. The alleged objective of the exercise from the viewpoint of the suspect firm is, clearly, to permit it to underprice its competitors, even when the low relative prices cannot be defended in terms of costs, and presumably then to drive those competitors from the field.

For a firm that is unregulated and whose objective is maximization of profits this cross-subsidy story makes no sense. If the price, p_m, of monopoly product m is already set so as to maximize the profit contribution the enterprise derives from the sale of this product, despite the appearance of competitors for some other its products, c, the company can derive no financial benefits by raising p_m. Indeed, such a price rise can be expected to *reduce* the earnings the company derives from m, since that is the necessary implication of any departure from a profit-maximizing price.[1]

---

1. Matters are, of course, complicated somewhat if products c and m are not independent in demand or in production. Entry of competitors for c may affect both its price and output and that will influence the profit-maximizing price of m. In particular, if c and m are complements in demand and competition decreases p_c, then the demand curve for m will shift upward and the profit-maximizing value of p_m is apt to rise. It is also true that even if c and m are not complements, it may conceivably pay our unregulated firm to engage in predatory behavior by selling c at a price below whatever cost is considered pertinent. But then the company cannot help to make up from its resulting losses on c by raising the price of m. Hence, while there may be predation, there is no cross-subsidy by buyers of the monopoly product.

However, government regulation of prices that, as usual, imposes some sort of overall ceiling on company profits, affects this conclusion substantially. If the regulated firm's profit-maximizing price vector, p^0, yields profits that violate the ceiling, then the company may find itself forced to adopt a value of p_m that is lower, and perhaps substantially lower, than p_m^0. Such a firm then may have an untapped source of profits to which it can turn if earnings from other portions of its product line fall, regardless of the reason. This means that if such a regulated firm should want to engage in cross-subsidy, the possibility cannot be ruled out a priori. It has been argued that there are other reasons that may make this unlikely, but they do not concern us here.

Should a cross-subsidy occur in such circumstances, there are two distinct groups each of which may well feel that the results are unfair to it. The first group is made up of the customers of the monopoly service who may feel they have been overcharged in order to permit the customers of competitive services to benefit at their expense.

Yet while much is likely to be said about the unfairness to customer groups against whose interests a cross-subsidy is claimed to discriminate, these customers rarely speak up on their own behalf. It is much more common for their case to be made by other firms—the competitors of the regulated enterprise. These competitors can be expected to claim that a cross-subsidy is unfair not only to particular customer groups but also to themselves as victims of unfair competitive measures by the enterprise against which the charges are raised. There is, then, a double issue of fairness raised by the phenomenon of cross-subsidy—fairness in the comparative treatment of different customer groups and fairness in the competitive position of the affected enterprises. The question is whether there exists any rule that distinguishes between the prices that are "fair" and those that are "unfair" to the two groups. Economic analysis, as we shall see, has a good deal to say on the subject.

2   The Approach of Incremental Analysis

When a firm produces an output vector $y = (y_1, \ldots, y_n)$, then

Definition 1   The *incremental cost* (*IC*) *of an entire product*, call it product 1, given the output y_2^*, ..., y_n^* of each other product, is defined as $C(y_1^*, y_2^*, \ldots, y_n^*) - C(0, y_2^*, \ldots, y_n^*)$, where y_i^* is the quantity of product i supplied by the firm and $C(\cdot)$ is its total cost function.

Now it was argued[2] long ago that if total profits of an enterprise are effectively constrained by regulation, then if the price, p_1^*, that the firm charges for product 1 yields a total revenue (TR) from the sale of that product that exceeds the incremental cost of product 1, the buyers of products 2, ..., n must as a group be better off when product 1 is sold at price p_1^* than they would be if 1 were withdrawn from the product line.

The reason is straightforward. If the constraint on profits is *effective*, so that even without the sale of 1 the company's total profit would reach its ceiling, then the addition of 1 to the product line must, *ceteris paribus*, cause company profits to exceed their ceiling if TR_i, the revenue flowing from the added product, exceeds IC_i. Regulation will then force the firm to reduce the profit contribution it derives from the sale of its other products, presumably through a reduction in some or all of their prices.

It is at least implied that then the price p_1^* is not unfair to the buyers of goods 2, ..., n since those buyers gain from the sale of item 1 at that price. This is obviously a Pareto (or at least a Kaldor-Hicks) improvement criterion. The customers of product 1 must be made better off by the supply of the item at price p_1^* because they purchase it voluntarily. Since the buyers of other company products must also gain as a group, then all buyers of the company's outputs are potential gainers and no customer need lose out in the process.

This, then, is the argument that there is equity among customer groups when prices satisfy the incremental cost criterion. But defenders of this standard also imply that it simultaneously precludes unfairness to competitors of the enterprise in question.

The criterion accomplishes this second feat by virtue of its preclusion of cross-subsidy. It is held that any price that passes the incremental cost test is automatically free of any taint of cross-subsidy by virtue of the nature of the subsidy concept. After all, a subsidy of individual or group, A, by another person or group, B, means that B voluntarily or involuntarily sacrifices something that is then transferred to A. But if both parties gain because commodity 1 is offered at price p_1^*, no one can conceivably be said to have sacrificed anything as a result, and this offering therefore cannot possibly entail a cross-subsidy by any reasonable interpretation of the term.

---

2. See, for example, Hadley [1886, chapter 6]; Alexander [1887, pp. 2–5, 10–11]; and Acworth [1891, chapter 3, pp. 57–60]. See also the discussion by Lewis [1949, pp. 20–21]. It should be made clear at once that I am among those who have espoused the incremental cost criterion (and still do). But here my purpose is to examine its place in the analysis of fairness, not to argue its virtues.

But if product 1 neither requires nor receives a subsidy, competitors have no grounds on which to complain that price p_1^* entails unfairness in competition. The firm that provides service 1 receives no help in this part of its activities from buyers of its other goods and service 1's revenues cover all of the costs incurred as a result of the provision of the service. A firm can surely find it desirable to undertake a service on such terms even if doing so does not eliminate any competitor, and so it cannot in any sense be deemed to be "predatory" or unfair to competitors.

It should be noted here that while a Pareto improvement argument has just implicitly been used to judge the fairness of p_i to consumers of other company products, j, the same is not true of the logic of the discussion of the fairness of p_i to the company's competitors. After all, it is most unlikely that the company's offering of i will benefit other suppliers of i, so that this will constitute no Pareto improvement for all affected firms.

To summarize, the incremental cost criterion is held by its proponents to deal at one blow with the requirements of fairness of treatment of both the parties in question—the customers of the firm's other products as well as its competitors.

3   Some Complications

Further investigation of the incremental cost test has raised problems that require some degree of complication of the criterion without weakening its reliance on the Pareto improvement approach, and without weakening its logic.

The first problem to be noted is combinatorial. It is possible for the prices of each of several competitive products individually to satisfy the incremental cost criterion and yet for several or even all of the firm's competitive products to fail it as a group. In that case the fairness arguments described in the preceding section do not hold up. To avoid this difficulty, the criterion must be extended to require the revenue of each service individually *and* for any combination of such services to yield revenues that at least equal the corresponding incremental costs.

An example will indicate the nature of the difficulty. Suppose products R and S each require for their supply a piece of equipment that costs $10 million, a cost that is completely fixed in the sense that once installed the equipment can process as large a quantity of R or of S, or of any combination of the two, as may be desired. Moreover, assume that the equipment is useless for any other purpose. Now the $10 million is obviously no part of IC_S, the incremental cost of S if any of product R is also supplied, since the equipment with its limitless capacity must be installed in any event in order to permit the nonzero output of R. Similarly, that item is also[3] excluded from IC_R. Yet it is clear that the $10 million *is* part of IC_{R+S}, the incremental cost of R and S together. Had the firm decided against production of both R and S, the money simply would not have been spent. If the total revenues from the sale of R and S are insufficient to provide $10 million over and above the incremental costs of R and S individually, the company will suffer a reduction in profit from the decision to supply them.[4] Thus, the proper criterion for absence of cross-subsidy requires not only that the revenue of each product individually cover its incremental cost, but that the same be true of each and every *combination* of the company's outputs.

---

3. Here the temporal order in which the products made their appearance is sometimes considered pertinent but that is a misapprehension. Once some of each product is in fact being supplied, the possibility that one of them may have been marketed earlier than another is an irrelevant bit of ancient history. *Either* product by itself now requires the equipment so that, *other things remaining equal,* supply of the other adds nothing to the equipment's cost.

4. These observations bring out another point—the role of fixed cost in incremental costs. Some fixed costs *do* enter into incremental costs, even though marginal analysis is a special case of incremental analysis and the former must, by definition, automatically drop fixed costs from its calculation. The fixed component that enters the incremental cost of a particular product never includes any of the cost fixed for the firm as a whole, e.g., the president's salary, but it does include what have been referred to as the "product-specific" fixed costs. Those are the costs that must be incurred before any of some particular output, i, can be produced, and that the firm could avoid if that product were not provided, but that do not change with the magnitude of that output. The product-specific costs for good i whose output is y_i may be written as

$$F_i = \delta F_i^* \quad \text{(constant)},$$

where $\delta = 0$ if $y_i = 0$ and $\delta = 1$ otherwise. Since F_i^* constitutes part of the increase in the firm's total cost that results when it enters the production of i, it must be included in the incremental cost of i by the definition of that concept.

In the legal literature relating to the subject we are discussing, the *average variable cost* of product i has been used as a related concept, but its definition has not always been clear, because it is not generally obvious whether those who use the term intend it to include the product-specific fixed cost. If they do, then the concept is, of course, identical with average incremental cost (AIC), the incremental cost of i divided by the output of i, that is

$$AIC_1 = [C(y_1, y_2, \ldots, y_n) - C(0, y_2, \ldots, y_n)]/y_1.$$

The average variable cost concept has received a great deal of attention as a result of the work of Professors Areeda and Turner, about which more will be said later. In a letter to me (November 13, 1981) Professor Areeda indicates that he does include the product-specific fixed costs in his definition of average variable cost, so that for him $AVC_i \equiv AIC_i$.

A second modification that may be required in this criterion relates to the size of the output increment that it encompasses. As described so far, it deals with the increment between the given (current?) output of some product, i, as compared with the decision to discontinue its supply altogether. But what about the cost of smaller increments in output? Indeed, what about the limiting case in which the change in output considered approaches zero, so that the average incremental cost becomes the product's marginal cost? It is easy to see that a product's total revenue may exceed the incremental cost of the entire output of that item and yet the item's price may be less than its marginal cost. This is certainly possible whenever the average incremental cost of the item is a rising function of its output. The question, then, is whether some sort of fairness consideration requires price to exceed marginal cost as well as average incremental cost for every relevant quantity increment. Later, we shall consider this issue again, noting first that marginal cost rather than incremental cost is taken as the preferred standard of the Areeda-Turner pricing test, and observing also that there is a fairness criterion, "anonymous equity," which requires price to equal or exceed both of these costs. We shall show also that, at least in theory, under perfect contestability (of which perfect competition is a special case), the requirements of anonymous equity must always be satisfied in equilibrium.

There is a third way in which it has been proposed that the incremental cost test of cross-subsidy in pricing may usefully be supplemented. This requires the investigator to take into account the cross-elasticities among the firm's own products in determining whether the incremental revenues of product i are sufficient to cover its incremental costs. Thus, suppose i's incremental cost is $5 million per year, that its revenue is $7 million, but that i is a substitute for another product, j, supplied by the same company and that the availability of i reduces the value of j sold by $3 million. Then what may be called the *gross* incremental revenue of i, $7 million, clearly exceeds i's incremental cost. However, its *net* incremental revenue, $4 million, does not. This possibility has given rise to what has been named the *burden test*:

Definition 2   A price, p_i, for product i constitutes no *burden* upon the consumers of other products supplied by the same firm if at that price the product's incremental cost is equaled or exceeded by its net incremental revenue (i.e., its revenue after subtraction of revenue losses on other products, j, resulting from the cross elasticity of demand between i and j).

The burden test tends to be (but is not necessarily) a more stringent criterion than the incremental cost test if i is not a gross complement of any of the firm's other products and is a gross substitute for some of them, because in that case i's net incremental revenue will clearly be less than its gross incremental revenue.[5]

There has been some argument over the appropriate choice between the two criteria. On its face, the burden test would appear to be the right criterion. After all, when i is added to the firm's product line it actually contributes to company revenues not a figure equal to its own earnings but that minus any associated reduction in the company's other revenues. To credit i with an incremental revenue equal to $p_i y_i$ would then seem to be a distortion of the facts.

Yet others, including Professor Areeda, have rejected this view, on two grounds. First they point out that the production of j by the same firm that supplies i must be considered fortuitous for this purpose. If i were produced by one firm, A, while j were produced by another firm, B, and the introduction of i were to reduce the volume sold and/or the price of j, the resulting loss in B's revenues would not be deducted from $p_i y_i$ in determining whether p_i is unacceptably low. Thus, there is no reason to do so if j is produced by firm A itself rather than by B.

Second, it is argued in defense of the incremental cost criterion that if firm C is a competitor of A in the production of i but C does not produce j, then any loss in revenues from j ascribable to the introduction of product i does not harm C and so is not relevant to the issue of the fairness to competitors[6] of p_i.

---

5. It may seem strange, then, in the case of substitutability between i and j that the burden test can ever be less stringent than the incremental cost test. However, while in this case cross-elasticity reduces j's revenue (by amount ΔTR_j) it also reduces its output and, hence, its incremental cost. Thus, if $|\Delta TR_j| > |\Delta IC_j|$, the burden test is, indeed, more demanding, but the opposite must be true if this inequality is reversed. We shall return to the role of ΔIC_j later.

6. It is appropriate to quote Professor Areeda in full: "Should the defendant's revenue from product X be reduced by the net revenues lost by the defendant on substitute product Y as a result of its price reduction on X? No. First, no such adjustment would be made if the two products were made entirely by different firms. Second, the health of rival X producers is ordinarily unaffected by the decline in Y sales. (If all or most producers make both products, one might consider both products together the relevant product line, but rivalry would not be impaired so long as the product line as a whole remains profitable.) With each product considered separately, so long as the price cut does not push the price of X below its marginal cost and so long as the diminished volume of Y does not result in costs above the price of Y, the Areeda-Turner rule would not be violated" (letter of November 13, 1981). The discussion refers, of course, to a charge of predatory pricing in an antitrust case.

A resolution of the dispute may involve the difference between the two fairness issues with which we are concerned: fairness among customer groups and fairness to competitors. I shall argue now that a strong claim can be made for the burden test as the appropriate criterion for intercustomer fairness while the same can be said for the incremental cost test in relation to fairness to competitors.

The Pareto improvement criterion as used to judge equity among customer groups clearly requires a comparison of the *net* IR of i with its IC; i.e., it requires the burden test. For suppose the introduction of i yields a gross IR > IC but a net IR < IC. Then the introduction of i must, *ceteris paribus*, decrease company profits. Hence, if $p_j < p_j^0$ because of a regulatory profit constraint (where p_j^0 is the profit maximizing price of j), it can pay the firm to raise p_j and then the customers of j will be harmed by the introduction of i. Only the burden test can be relied upon to preclude this possibility.

On the other hand, as we have seen, fairness in dealing with competitors cannot be judged in Paretian terms, since one cannot reasonably require p_i in any sense to *benefit* the competitors of the firm in question. A different standard is called for here, and while we have not spelled it out, at least up to this point, it clearly does not require our firm to offer any of its competitors any advantages over the situation in which it would find itself if our enterprise were a single-product firm. This is the Areeda argument, and it would seem to favor use of the incremental cost test over the burden test in antitrust proceedings in which there is an allegation that the defendant has engaged in predatory and, hence, unfair competitive practices.

Yet there remains at least one caveat. To bring out the point, we must distinguish between gross and net incremental *costs* (GIC and NIC) just as we have distinguished between the two types of incremental revenue. Thus, GIC_i refers to the increase in the firm's total cost that would result from the introduction of product i if *all* other outputs were held constant. Now, the burden test, quite appropriately, compares NIC_i with NIR_i. But what about the incremental cost test? To follow the line of Professor Areeda's argument, consider two firms, A and A', of which the former produces both i and j while the latter produces only i, with all other things being the same. Thus, for both of them GIC_i will be the same. But if the introduction of i reduces the amount of j A can sell by an amount that cuts its total cost by k dollars, then for A, $NIC_i = GIC_i - k$, while for A', $NIC_i = GIC_i$. Thus, by Professor Areeda's argument, if the price of firm A is to be tested for predation on terms comparable to those that apply to A', then it is true that an incremental cost test is appropriate, but it should consist of the requirement $GIR_i \geq GIC_i$, not $GIR_i \geq NIC_i$. In other words, in carrying out the incremental cost test some care must be taken to make certain the firm's incremental cost figure for i contains no deduction for the associated decrease in production of j. Such an inappropriate deduction will, for example, have occurred automatically if IC_i is calculated by subtracting from actual total cost (when y_i of i is produced) the total cost that the firm would experience if y_i were reduced to zero and all other outputs were to adjust themselves to the resulting responses in market demands.

4   Stand Alone Cost as Obverse of Compensatory Pricing

It is convenient to use the term "compensatory prices" to refer to prices that satisfy some agreed upon form of the criteria that have so far been described. The fairness requirement that prices be compensatory focuses its attention upon the customer groups that are candidate *recipients* of cross-subsidies. The assertion that prices are compensatory can be taken to mean that these customer groups are paying enough to cover all of the costs caused by providing commodities to them. In saying this we refer only indirectly to the other customer groups who constitute the potential *sources* of a cross-subsidy—those who would have to pay for it if there were such a subsidy. Of course, the object of an intercustomer fairness calculation is presumably to protect the interests of the latter group—the potential payers who would be the victims of unfairness, rather than to inhibit the flow of benefits to the potential recipients of any subsidy. It is therefore perhaps somewhat unsatisfying to work with a fairness criterion expressed exclusively in terms of the circumstances faced by the potential subsidy recipients—rather than by those who would bear the burden.

   We shall describe next a widely used criterion of fairness in pricing formulated in terms of the potential payers of cross-subsidy. It seems reasonable to expect that the implications of this alternative criterion will not conflict significantly with those of the incremental cost test since they both deal with the same issue, merely approaching the analysis from different directions. We shall see that this is indeed so, and that, under the assumption that the firm earns only normal profits overall, the two criteria are perfectly equivalent. Nevertheless, the second criterion, the stand alone cost[7] test, turns out to be important for other purposes as well.

Definition 3   The *stand alone cost* of serving any buyer or group of buyers whose bundle of purchases is the vector, y, is the total cost that would be

---

7. The term seems to have been contributed by Faulhaber and Zajac [1976].

incurred if the suppliers of y were to produce it without simultaneously producing any other items or any additional quantities of any of the commodities included in y.

In other words, the stand alone cost of y is the amount it would cost to produce any *combination* of goods y if its production were deprived of all further economies of scale and of all economies of scope—the cost savings that derive from complementarities with the production of other commodities in the suppliers' product lines.

The stand alone cost criterion then states that no group of buyers of any commodity or combination of commodities supplied by some firm should be required to pay more for their purchases than the stand alone cost of those purchases. The logic of this criterion, of course, is that any group that receives the vector y in return for a payment, $p_y y$, that is no greater than its stand alone cost must not be harmed and may be benefiting from the fact that the supplier is serving other customers in addition to themselves. If the criterion is satisfied, those customers have no incentive to disassociate themselves from the other customer groups served by the firm. Since the criterion is required to hold for each and every customer group of the firm, including the group composed of its entire body of customers, the stand alone cost test provides buyers the same protection against excessive pricing that is offered them by the forces of competition. That is, competition forces a reduction in the prices of any combination of goods if and only if they can be supplied more cheaply by an entrant, that is, if and only if the prices exceed the corresponding stand alone costs.

The stand alone cost criterion is equivalent to the game theoretic concept of an imputation that lies in the core of a "cost-sharing game," requiring each subset of members of a coalition to receive as a result of their membership a payoff at least as large as they could obtain for themselves if they were to leave the coalition and fend entirely for themselves.

The stand alone cost concept immediately offers us a significant application to fairness in utility pricing going beyond what can easily be done with incremental costs directly. The beginning of this chapter mentioned a problem of fairness in pricing that, despite its importance, has not been discussed very extensively in the literature. This is the issue of an appropriate *maximum* for the prices charged by a firm with monopoly power. It is curious that much of the literature, following the courts and the regulatory agencies, has devoted itself to discussing when prices should be judged excessively and unfairly low though, as Adam Smith long ago suggested, common sense would appear to require us rather to assign priority to the prevention of prices that are excessively high. Probably part of the reason so little has been said on the latter subject is that it has proved so difficult to arrive at a criterion that is fully satisfying and fully persuasive.[8]

A number of economists have turned to stand alone costs as a defensible ceiling upon pricing by a monopolist. They have, in effect, pointed out that prices that violate the test conflict with the Pareto improvement criterion in the following sense: such prices charged by a supplier who produces whatever combination of products and whatever output quantities he finds most profitable leave the buyer worse off than he would be if served by a competitor forced to operate under the very inhibiting constraint that he produce exactly the output demanded by that one buyer, no more and no less, and serving no other customers. Thus, if the customer is forced to buy at a price above stand alone cost (say, because a patent precludes anyone else from offering the product), he will certainly be a loser relative to what it would cost him to fend entirely for himself in obtaining the item. One can also assert the obverse of this proposition: If the price charged by a firm with many customers is lower than the stand alone cost of supplying any one of them, or any subgroup, then every customer must have gained by being supplied together, and the firm must also have gained since it supplies its entire set of customers voluntarily.[9]

When this concept has been proposed before regulatory agencies some concern has been expressed about problems in the calculation of stand alone cost. After all, if no firm in an industry has ever specialized in the production of just one of its outputs, let alone served one of its customers in isolation, how can one hope to obtain any reliable estimate of the cost that would be incurred in this unlikely situation? As it turns out, no such calculation is necessary if it can be shown that every customer group is paying at least its incremental cost, and the firm as a whole is earning no more than the cost of its capital, i.e., no more than a normal profit. For we have

Proposition 1 If a firm's total revenue is exactly equal to its total cost, and any customer group, A, spends any amount $p_a y_a$ for its vector of purchases,

---

8. There is, of course, another reason that is also pointed out by Smith, who described it as ". . . the interested sophistry of merchants and manufacturers." Inefficient competitors who turn to the courts and regulatory agencies for protection from competition that threatens to be all too effective have much to gain by persuading others that their rivals' prices are "unfairly" low and, hence, predatory. However, often there are no comparably organized groups who stand to gain by demonstrating that a supplier's prices are unacceptably high.
9. For further discussion of the Paretian implications of the stand alone cost ceiling, see Faulhaber and Zajac [1979].

y_a, that exceeds (or equals) the incremental cost of y_a, then the firm's remaining customers, B, must pay less (no more) than the stand alone cost $C(0, y_b)$ of supplying their vector of purchases, y_b.

Proof   The premise that A pays more than its incremental cost can be written

$$p_a y_a \geqslant C(y_a, y_b) - C(0, y_b). \tag{6.1}$$

The normal profit requirement asserts that

$$p_a y_a + p_b y_b = C(y_a, y_b). \tag{6.2}$$

Subtracting (6.1) from (6.2) we obtain immediately

$$p_b y_b \leqslant C(0, y_b). \tag{6.3}$$

We also have

Proposition 2 (converse of proposition 1)   If the firm earns only normal profits and a customer group pays for its purchases no more than its stand alone cost, then the prices charged to the firm's remaining customers must satisfy the incremental cost test.

The proof is immediate, requiring only reversal of the steps in the proof of proposition 1.

Since the same argument can be applied seriatim to any pair of subsets of group B it follows that propositions 1 and 2 can be generalized to

Proposition 3   If a firm earns normal profits and its prices involve no cross-subsidies, as defined by the incremental cost criterion,[10] then none of its customers will be charged more than the stand alone cost of serving them, and conversely.

The intuitive reason for the relationship between the incremental cost criterion and the stand alone cost criterion is straightforward. Suppose group B were to pay more than the stand alone cost of its purchases,

---

10. That is, the cross-subsidy criterion involved is the incremental cost test rather than the burden test. This is seen in (6.1), where the values of the elements of the vector y_b are the same in both terms of the right-hand side, so that there is no adjustment for effects on the quantities of y_b demanded of the elimination of the supply of y_a. Such an adjustment is precluded by the nature of the stand alone cost test, which investigates what it would cost to supply group B in isolation *with the same vector of outputs, y_b,* that it obtains now.

including the cost of the requisite capital. Then the firm must thereby be earning more than normal profits on the activities devoted to serving group B. In that case the company must either earn abnormal profits overall or it must get rid of its excess profit by incurring an offsetting loss in serving customer group A; i.e., it must then provide a cross-subsidy to A. Thus, if cross-subsidies and abnormal total profits are both precluded, then B cannot possibly be paying more than its stand alone cost.

5 Generalization: Anonymous Equity

Up to this point fairness among different sets of consumers of a given firm has been discussed in terms of buyers of different sets of commodities, particularly the buyers of goods sold monopolistically by the company versus the buyers of items offered simultaneously by other suppliers. But cross-subsidies need not always arise only in this way. There can be cross-subsidy of one group of buyers of a given good by other purchasers of the same good—as when rural or elderly or inner city consumers of a product are served at prices below incremental costs. There may even be cross-subsidy of purchases of a given good by other purchases by the same consumers, or some part of the purchase of a given consumer may provide (receive) such a subsidy. Willig [1979] has proposed an extended criterion of fairness that blinds itself to the identity of the person or group receiving or paying the subsidy. He refers to this criterion as "anonymous equity." He defines this as "... the absence of [all] cross subsidy: that every consumer and group of consumers expend enough for their consumed services to cover at least the incremental costs of provision of those services." As defined here by Willig, this still refers to transfers between one customer or customer group to another. Faulhaber and Levinson [1981], however, have extended and formalized the concept by defining the price vector p to be *anonymously equitable* if the firm earns normal profits and for the vectors p and q

$$p \cdot q \leqslant C(q) \qquad \text{for all} \quad q \leqslant Q(p), \tag{6.4}$$

where $Q(p)$ is the corresponding demand function of the firm.

It should be noted that there are two differences from Willig's definition: First, Faulhaber and Levinson prefer to proceed on the basis of stand alone cost, $C(q)$, rather than absence of cross-subsidy. However, this, as we know, is inessential and Faulhaber and Levinson immediately remind us of their equivalence. But there is a second difference, which is substantive. In Faulhaber and Levinson's definition there is no reference to customer groups but only to quantities of outputs. They require that no vector constituting part of the *sales* of the firm, however small or large, may be a source of a cross-subsidy. These authors express their criterion in terms of output quantities rather than customer groups because they want to preclude inequity not just to some particular sets of customers with given patterns of demands and purchases, but to *any* conceivable configuration of consumers with any conceivable set of consumer demand vectors.

One immediate implication of the extended definition of anonymous equity is

Proposition 4   Prices that satisfy the criterion of anonymous equity must equal or exceed not only average incremental costs[11] but marginal cost as well.

Faulhaber provides a formal proof of this result, but such a proof is unnecessary here. It follows immediately from proposition 2. For, by proposition 2, under anonymous equity

$$p_a > [C(y_a, y_b) - C(0, y_b)]/y_b = AIC_b. \tag{6.5}$$

Now, if we let y_b be a small quantity of a particular commodity (and some of that same good may be contained in the vector y_a) then as y_b approaches zero the limit of the right-hand side of (6.5) is obviously MC_b.

We conclude that the anonymous equity extension of the Pareto improvement approach to fairness among customer groups requires not only that all prices satisfy the incremental cost test, but, in addition, that they each be at least equal to the corresponding marginal cost.

6   Efficiency and Anonymous Equity

One of the attractive features of the concepts of fairness in pricing considered in this chapter is their close relationship to the pricing requirements of allocative efficiency. Indeed, one can show immediately

Proposition 5   A price vector that violates any of the requirements of anonymous equity must also violate the requirements of efficiency in the allocation of resources.

---

11. We have previously expressed the requirement under discussion as total revenue from i, $p_i y_i \geqslant IC_i$. However, this is the same as $p_i > IC_i/y_i = AIC_i$, which has the convenient attribute of ease of comparability with marginal cost.

In other words, anonymous equity is a necessary condition for Pareto optimality. The proof is straightforward. If anonymous equity is violated, there must be some output vector, y^*, that is sold by a firm, I, that is incumbent in the industry, at a price less than its incremental cost. Let D represent the difference between the price and incremental cost of firm I. This must mean that if there exists any other firm, J, whose (incremental) cost of producing y^* is below that of firm I, the difference involving a saving $S < D$, then it is obviously in the interests of society that y^* be produced by J. But, if no source of cross-subsidy is available to J, J will be unable to match I's prices for y^* and cover its total costs. Thus, any such cross-subsidy violates the pricing conditions called for by allocative efficiency because it will, potentially, preclude supply of the subsidized bundle of outputs by any firm that has efficiency advantages over the incumbent, but whose efficiency advantage is less than the cross-subsidy.

The following may be noted:

Proposition 6   The converse of proposition 5 is not valid, in general— anonymous equity is not sufficient for efficiency in resource allocation.

Proof by counterexample   Consider a case in which a firm's products are all independent in production so that $C(y) = C(\sum y_i) = \sum IC_i$ and let each product have decreasing AIC so that $MC_i < AIC_i$, and let $AIC_i = kMC_i$, $k > 1$. Then the prices

$$p_i^* = AIC_i = kMC_i \tag{6.6}$$

must satisfy $\sum p_i y_i = \sum IC_i$ and must therefore be viable financially. Moreover, for any division of $y = y^a + y^b$ the average incremental cost of y_i^b (given the production of y_i^a), call it $AIC(y_i^b)$, must be less than or equal to the average incremental cost of $y_i = y_i^a + y_i^b = AIC_i$. Hence, $p_i^* = AIC_i \geqslant AIC(y_i^b)$ so that p^* is anonymously equitable. By (6.6) the prices are proportionate to marginal costs. But if the demands for the different goods are also independent and have different price elasticities, we know the p_i^* will violate the Ramsey optimality conditions

$$(p_i - MC_i)/p_i = \lambda/E_i.$$

7   Digression: The Areeda-Turner Test of Predatory Pricing

The work of Areeda and Turner [1975] has already been referred to several times in this chapter. We are now in a position to offer a comment on the test they have devised to determine whether some price should be considered predatory and hence subject to the sanctions of the antitrust laws.

For this purpose, they have proposed that a price, p_i, be considered predatory if and only if $p_i < MC_i$, indicating, incidentally, that in their view short run marginal cost should be used for the task. They note that it may be difficult to determine the magnitude of MC_i in practice and propose, therefore, that AIC_i be permitted as a proxy for MC_i.

Their argument for the requirement $p_i \geqslant MC_i$ is a double one. First, they: point out that the standard pricing requirement for allocative efficiency is $p_i = MC_i$ so that any rule that precludes a price as low as MC_i must surely be unacceptable from the point of view of the general welfare. Second, they note that a firm may find it in its interest to charge a price in the neighborhood of marginal cost even if there is no prospect that this will harm a competitor. Consequently, any rule that precludes such pricing will prevent normal and legitimate business decisions.

The Areeda-Turner rule is perfectly compatible with everything that has been said in this chapter. Its only curious feature is its exclusive emphasis on the marginal cost criterion and its treatment of the incremental cost test as a second-best substitute that ought only be used, *faute de mieux*, when the marginal cost information, which should really be employed, is unavailable.

The analysis here has shown, on the contrary, that the incremental cost criterion has legitimate and parallel standing of its own. Certainly, it is a necessary condition for allocative efficiency, and if it does not play as central a role as marginal cost in optimal pricing, it surely must, if anything, be judged to have a more critical role in the fairness of pricing. In sum, one can criticize the Areeda-Turner choice of cost criteria for the appropriateness of prices only because it is excessively apologetic for its acceptance of incremental cost information.

8 Competition and the Fairness Criteria

Since we have seen that anonymous equity, the strongest of the Paretian fairness criteria, is a necessary condition for allocative optimality in pricing, it follows that perfect competition must in that sense guarantee fairness in pricing as well as allocative efficiency. That is hardly surprising so far as either unfairness through excessive pricing or unfairness to competing firms is concerned. After all, the essence of perfect competition is its deprivation of the firm of all power to charge a price with any taint of monopoly profit, and its elimination of any opportunity for gain through strategic behavior. The conclusion that it leads to fairness among customer groups is hardly more unexpected since no perfectly competitive firm can earn on any of its activities the excess profits needed for cross-subsidies to other activities.

But as everyone recognizes, perfect competition is a polar case, which may well be regarded as an abstraction that is rarely even approximated in reality. It is therefore worth noting that there is also a somewhat broader market form that satisfies the requirements of anonymous equity—the perfectly contestable market, which has recently been introduced into the literature (see, for example, Baumol, Panzar, and Willig [1982]).

This market form has been proposed as a generalization of perfect competition. Unlike a perfectly competitive industry, one that is perfectly contestable may contain very large firms and the total number of enterprises may well be small. That is, the number or size of the firms is not, in itself, relevant for an industry's contestability.

The crucial feature of a contestable market is its vulnerability to hit-and-run entry. Even a very transient profit opportunity need not be neglected by a potential entrant, for he can go in and, before prices change, collect his gains. He can then depart without cost, should the climate grow unattractive to him. The performance of firms, industries, and markets under perfect contestability has a number of critical attributes that follow directly from their vulnerability to hit-and-run incursions.

First, a contestable market never yields monopoly profits to anyone. In a contestable market economic profits must always be zero or negative even when that market is oligopolistic or even monopolistic. The reason is straightforward. Any economic profit means that a (possibly) transient entrant can set up business, replicate the incumbent's output at the same cost as his, undercut the incumbent's prices slightly, and still earn a profit. That is, the opportunity for costless entry and exit guarantees that an entrant who is content to accept a slightly lower profit can do so by selecting prices a bit lower than the incumbent's. In sum, in a perfectly contestable market the economic profit earned by an incumbent automatically constitutes an earnings opportunity for an entrant who will hit and, if necessary, run.

The second pertinent attribute of a contestable industry is the one that is crucial for our purposes. This attribute is the preclusion of cross-subsidy in a perfectly contestable market, that is, the preclusion of any price that is below either the corresponding marginal or average incremental cost. The reason for this is also straightforward. If any such uncompensatory price is charged by an incumbent, an entrant can simply elect to produce only the overpriced products that the incumbent is using to cover his deficit on the prices of the sales of his products that are uncompensatory; that is, the entrant can engage in what has been called "cream skimming" by critics of such behavior, and provide only the high profit products, simultaneously dropping the unprofitable (subsidized) sales from his firm's activities. By supplying only these overpriced products and dropping the unprofitable sales the entrant can, therefore, earn more than the incumbent did before entry occurred and so the entrant can certainly earn a profit. In other words, a cross-subsidy, like an inefficiency or an excessive profit, is an invitation to entry, and therefore elicits its own punishment. In a perfectly contestable industry an incumbent simply cannot afford any of these practices for any substantial period of time, for they make him vulnerable to loss of his markets, either temporarily or permanently.

It follows from all this, in the language of the contestability literature, that any set of prices that is *sustainable* under the threat of entry overhanging a perfectly contestable market must be anonymously equitable. That is, long run equilibrium in such a market is impossible if the prices do not satisfy this fairness criterion, as has been shown rigorously by Thijs ten Raa [1983].

It should be emphasized that none of the preceding analysis is to be interpreted as a Panglossian view of the market mechanism. The markets of reality are hardly more likely to be perfectly contestable than they are to be perfectly competitive. I have certainly not argued, and do not believe, that either actual or potential competition is sufficiently powerful in the imperfect world we inhabit to guarantee a universal regime of fairness even in the limited Paretian sense in which the term has been used in this chapter. What is implied by the discussion of contestable markets is that the forces of potential entry do work in favor of anonymous equity, and that reduction of impediments to entry may be desired not only because they can contribute to efficiency but also because they can work against unfairness.

9 Toward Further Concepts of Fairness in Pricing

This chapter has surveyed, albeit somewhat superficially, the implications of the Pareto improvement discussion of fairness in pricing that has dominated the economic literature. We have examined the logic of the concepts and found a happy coincidence in the requirements of fairness, those of efficiency, and the promised accomplishments of an ideally working market mechanism. However, this may well strike one as a bit too pat. There are, indeed, those who believe that there is more to fairness in pricing than what has so far been discussed. The next chapter turns to some of the directions they have taken as a substitute for or a supplement to our analysis. There, the applicability of superfairness analysis will also be considered.

7

Non-Paretian Standards
of Fairness in Pricing

The conclusion that the introduction of a product whose price satisfies the burden test can benefit all of a firm's customer groups, and hence constitute a Pareto improvement, has not satisfied all observers about the fairness of the result. Two grounds have frequently been cited for such reservations. First, it is argued that prices based on marginal or incremental cost need not really be compensatory so that, in this view, they do not really preclude cross-subsidy or unfairness to competing sellers of similar products. Second, it is suggested that even if every customer group benefits to some degree, some of these groups may benefit far more than others do. If so, even though everyone shares in them, the distribution of benefits may be unfair.

This chapter will deal only cursorily with the first of the preceding complaints since it will be argued that they are fundamentally spurious. However, the second is not so easily dismissed, if it can be dismissed at all. In our terminology, it amounts to the assertion that the introduction of a service that passes the burden test or the incremental cost test may nevertheless be incrementally unfair to different customer groups.

The chapter will discuss full allocation of costs and its game theoretic substitutes such as the core or the Shapley value. It will be shown that all of these generally violate the Ramsey requirements for allocative efficiency and that they fail for other reasons to come to grips with the issue of fairness. Finally, we shall examine the limitations that inhibit use of the superfairness approach to analysis of this problem. We shall see, however, that it is capable of shedding *some* light on the fairness of pricing practices such as we are discussing.

1 Incremental Costs and Compensatory Pricing

Various completely spurious arguments have been used to argue that the incremental cost test is no guarantee that pricing is compensatory. For example, it is implied that marginal cost is a persuasive term whose aura of technical sophistication merely conceals the fact that it systematically and deliberately omits components of costs that should be included in any legitimate cost figure. The fact that changes in fixed costs do not affect marginal costs is distorted to suggest that marginal cost is merely the same as average cost after deliberate deletion of some critical (fixed) cost components. The fact that marginal cost may either lie above or below the corresponding average cost (in the single product case in which the latter is uniquely definable), depending on the sign of the derivative of average cost with respect to output, surely shows that such contentions are completely groundless.

A more legitimate argument rests on the well-known observation that, in the presence of economies of scale, if each and every one of a firm's outputs is sold at a price precisely equal to its marginal cost, the firm's total revenue must be less than its total cost.

This does, indeed, show that a firm's prices may be uncompensatory if each price is set exactly equal to the corresponding marginal cost (or to the average incremental cost, for that matter). But as the incremental cost test was formulated in the preceding chapter such a possibility is, clearly, precluded. For, in addition to requiring that each product's price equal *or exceed* its own average incremental cost, the test demands that prices be such that each and every *combination* of products provides revenues that at least equal their combined incremental costs. In particular, the test requires this to be true of *all* of the firm's products taken as a group, and this means that any vector of prices accepted by the test must yield to the firm a total revenue at least equal to its total cost. In other words, when scale economies are present, a set of prices all precisely equal to the corresponding marginal costs is ruled out by the full incremental cost test.

In sum, the assertion that the incremental cost test is no guarantee that prices will be compensatory is simply indefensible. The test, properly defined and conducted, guarantees that every product and every combination of products will contribute revenue that at least covers the cost that its supply imposes (i.e., its incremental cost). Moreover, it guarantees that the vector of prices is compatible with financial viability of the firm as a whole.

2   Fairness in the Distribution of Benefits

As was already noted, the second reservation about the incremental cost test as a criterion of fairness is not so readily disposed of. This is the judgment that even if the appropriate form of incremental cost test guarantees that everyone will benefit from the introduction of a product, this is no assurance that all of those who participate will receive a fair share of those benefits.

If one group's gains are minuscule while another enjoys the lion's share, the result remains a Pareto improvement but one that is arguably inequitable.

This line has been taken only by the more sophisticated critics of incremental cost criteria. The Supreme Court is among these. In its noted Ingot Molds decision (*American Commercial Lines, Inc., et al.* v. *Louisville and Nashville Railroad Co. et al.*,October term, 1967, pp. 571–597), while it did not reject the railroads' defense of the criterion outright, the Court refused to place its general stamp of approval on prices that satisfy the incremental cost test. In its decision the Court addressed itself explicitly to the economists' arguments, remarking

The railroad economists point out that, because constant costs by definition are not attributable to the carriage of any particular traffic, it is to some extent arbitrary to allocate them to particular traffic. They further contend that all shippers presently utilizing a railroad's services are benefited when the railroad obtains additional traffic at a profit to it, because that profit can be used to pay a portion of the constant costs currently being charged wholly to them. The fact that charging a rate less than its fully distributed cost of carrying the traffic results in the shipper of that freight paying a disproportionally low share of the railroad's constant costs is considered to be outweighed by the overall benefit to the other shippers of having the absolute amount borne by them of the constant costs decreased by the profit earned on the traffic.... these are only a few of the questions that come to mind when we attempt to evaluate the economic arguments made in this case. We do not pretend to be able to answer them.

The basic issue can be posed in another manner, which may make the discussion of the following sections clearer. The incremental cost tests are not designed to yield a unique set of prices for the different products of the firm—a price vector that can, perhaps, be considered the "fairest" of those available. Rather, it normally leaves a wide range of choices open to the firm, only distinguishing between the set F_1 of price vectors that are fair on the incremental criterion, and the set U_1 that is unfair. But while all price vectors in F_1 are fair in this sense, some are likely to be fairer than others. The issue is whether it is possible to arrive at a unique price vector that yields the fairest, or (if the fairest is indeterminable) at least one that involves a demonstrably fair division of the Paretian benefits inherent in the set F_1. The next few sections discuss the search for such a unique and uniquely acceptable price vector.

3 Full Allocation of Costs and the Distribution of Benefits

The crudest but most direct approach that has been proposed and, indeed, widely used to determine the fair set of prices is called "full allocation" or "full distribution" of costs. This process calls for all of the company's costs (its total cost) to be divided up entirely, with each of the firm's products, i, receiving what is hoped to be its appropriate share of these costs—its fully allocated cost (FAC_i). Then, the fair price of product i is defined to be equal to FAC_i/y_i, the per unit value of its fully allocated cost (including the normal return to capital). For, then, each customer group is said to pay just the amount necessary to cover the cost properly attributable to it, and the sum of those payments must just suffice to compensate the firm for its total costs. This reasoning may seem persuasive, but for our purposes here it suffers from two fatal defects. First, there is no defensible way in which each product's share of total cost can be determined uniquely, and, second, the relationship to the notion of fairness is, in any event, specious.

I shall begin with the first of these difficulties, leaving the second to a later section, where the discussion can deal simultaneously with other proposed approaches to the determination of a uniquely fair price vector. To see why one cannot, in general, determine each product's share of total cost, one must recognize that by its nature the issue we are discussing arises only for a multiproduct firm (though it is apropos to note that virtually all if not all of the firms of reality are multiproduct enterprises). For only in such a company can the price of one product yield a cross-subsidy to another. But in such an enterprise there are almost always some outlays and, usually, significant outlays that are incurred not on behalf of any single product, but on behalf of several or even all of the company's products simultaneously.

Consider any cost component, K, whose magnitude is totally unaffected by the output of product i, or by inclusion or exclusion of i in the company's product line, all other things remaining equal. Suppose, moreover, that this is also true of another product, j, and yet that $K = 0$ if *both* $y_i = y_j = 0$, but $K > 0$ otherwise. Then there simply is no defensible way of attributing any particular portion of K to i and the remainder to j. It is true that the two products together do bear the entire responsibility for the expenditure of K. But neither i nor j can be said to have "caused" some particular portion of K.

Similarly, if we subtract from the firm's total cost, C, the sum of the incremental costs of its individual products, there is likely to be a positive residue $R = C - \sum_i IC_i > 0$. It is easy to show that such a residue will occur if (and only if) there are complementarities in the production of i and j so that the cost of simultaneous production of quantities i^* and j^* of the two items by a single firm is less than the combined cost of two specialized enterprises, one producing only i^* and the other producing j^* exclusively, i.e., if and only if there are economies of scope.

Proof   Economies of scope in products 1 and 2 are defined by

$$C(y_1, y_2) < C(y_1, 0) + C(0, y_2).\tag{7.1}$$

Then, subtracting both the right-hand and left-hand sides of (7.1) from $2C(y_1, y_2)$ we obtain

$$C(y_1, y_2) > [C(y_1, y_2) - C(y_1, 0)] + [C(y_1, y_2) - C(0, y_2)] \equiv IR_1 + IR_2.$$

The converse follows immediately by reversal of the preceding steps.

This may, clearly, be true even if the firm has no fixed costs. But there is no way to apportion among its individual products the residue, R, left after subtraction from the firm's total cost of the sum of the firm's incremental costs for all of its individual products—that is, there is, by definition, no way of showing that product i is "responsible" for any particular portion of R. Such a residue is attributable to all of the firm's products together, or to an entire subset of those products, but no particular portion is attributable to any particular *one* of its products.

This difficulty is recognized by all participants in the discussion and those who advocate an FAC approach have therefore adopted accountants' conventions, which are admittedly arbitrary, to allocate the firm's total costs among the company's products. The resulting allocations were, predictably, highly sensitive to the basis selected for the allocation. For example, the cost of track maintenance for a railroad along a given route may be allocated on the basis of the relative weights of the different goods shipped, or on the basis of relative volumes or of their relative market values (and each of these bases has at times been used). But if some of the commodities carried by that railroad are very bulky and low in weight and value, while others are very heavy and still others are very costly, it is obvious that the share of rail maintenance costs attributed to any one of the items will vary profoundly with the arbitrary choice made among the three bases for allocation (which, of course, by no means exhaust the candidate allocative conventions).

The sensitivity of the results surely should dispel any illusion that there exists any unique and defensible way of dividing all of a firm's costs among its various products in such a way that the amount assigned to product i can on any reasonable grounds be considered the portion of the firm's total cost for which i is responsible. Certainly, then, the FAC figures that emerge from any such allocation and the arbitrary choice of basis of allocation can hardly lay any claim to a standard of fairness in pricing. Even less is it possible to claim that a set of prices that corresponds to a particular full allocation of costs is the set of prices that is uniquely fairest in its relative treatment of the buyers of the firm's different products.

4 Game Theoretic Analyses of Fairness in Pricing

A more sophisticatad approach to apportionment of a company's total costs among its different products has used various concepts of game theory for the purpose. Contributors to this analysis include Shubik, Littlechild, Loehman and Whinston, Billera and Heath, and Faulhaber and Zajac.[1]

Typically, these studies have employed an axiomatic approach. That is, they start by listing a number of desiderata that an apportionment procedure must satisfy in order to be acceptable. These desiderata have generally been formal and arithmetical in character, requiring, for example, that an apportionment formula be additive and symmetric. However, economic interpretations have generally been provided for these formal axioms, as will be illustrated presently. Then, from these axioms a set of permissible apportionments has been deduced. In some cases it has been shown that there exists one and only one function that is consistent with the axioms, although, of course, the unique acceptable function that emerges varies from study to study, depending on the axioms adopted.

The resulting apportionment function usually is related to one of three game theoretic concepts: the core, the Shapley value, and the nucleolus. The *core* is the most familiar of these three concepts. It is closely related to the notion of Pareto optimality. An allocation formula, F, that lies in the core is one that apportions all of a firm's costs, attributes to each product no more than its stand alone cost, and is such that there exists no group of products that is assigned a cost greater than their combined stand alone costs.

---

1. For a survey and references, see Schotter and Schwödiauer [1980, especially pp. 488–493].

Several allocation formulas may be included in the core. Their number may be infinite or zero (the core may be empty).[2] If the set of axioms employed yields no unique formula for the allocation of cost, the exercise fails in at least one respect. For then no one cost allocation emerges with any claim to superiority over the others in terms of fairness.

The *Shapley value* (named after Lloyd Shapley, who first formulated the construct in 1953) is a function that does allocate the costs of a firm in a unique manner from some selected set of axioms. As will soon be explained more explicitly, one variant of this procedure (Loehman-Whinston) yields an allocation assigning to any buyer, b, the sum of what are described as the marginal or incremental costs *expected* to be incurred in serving that buyer. The magnitude of the marginal or incremental cost incurred by a particular buyer b is not a number predeterminable all by itself, but depends upon the magnitudes of all of the company's outputs, i.e., upon the magnitudes of the quantities provided to the firm's other buyers. Thus, instead of a single figure, MC_b or IC_b, the allocation procedure employs expected values, $E(MC_b)$ or $E(IC_b)$, which are calculated from the probability distribution generated by the full set of combinations and permutations of quantities that can be demanded by all possible subsets of those other buyers. In other words, one conducts the conceptual experiment of letting some of the firm's customers defect from it, partially or totally, and calculates the associated value of MC_b or IC_b. Considering all such possible defection patterns one then determines the corresponding expected values and that is the portion of total cost that this variant of the Shapley value approach assigns to the buyer in question.

Finally, the *nucleolus*, the third criterion for cost attribution employed by the game theorist, was constructed by Schmeidler [1969], who, as we have seen, is one of the outstanding contributors to the theory of superfairness. To define the nucleolus we first require a few preliminary concepts. A coalition, S, is defined as any set of players in a game, i.e., in our case, as

---

2. Faulhaber has shown by a remarkable and simple example that in a cost function that involves scale economies near the origin, followed by diseconomies, there may exist no allocation that lies in the core; i.e., every possible allocation of costs may unavoidably require some customer group to pay more than its stand alone cost. Thus, suppose there are three customers with identical and absolutely inelastic demands. It costs $14 to serve any one of them, $19 to satisfy the demand of any two of them, and $30 to serve all three simultaneously. Then simultaneous supply is obviously the most economical procedure. But, then, to cover costs either every buyer must be charged $10, or if some buyer, say, A, is charged $D < \$10$, then the other two buyers, B and C, must be charged together $\$30 - D > \$20$. In either case, then, B and C must pay more than their $19 stand alone cost.

any set of customers of the firm whose total costs are to be parceled out. $V(S)$ is the value of the game to coalition S—it is the stand alone cost of S—the lowest possible cost it could achieve if its purchases were supplied completely on its own. A cost assignment, $C = C(S)$, that allocates the cost C to coalition S is said to involve the complaint $e(C, S)$ by coalition S, where $e = C(S) - V(S)$, i.e., where the complaint is the excess of the cost allocated to S over S's stand alone cost. We may, incidentally, wish to consider unacceptable any allocation involving any positive complaint, i.e., any value $e(C, S) > 0$ for any S. In that case all values of $e(\cdot)$ in an acceptable allocation will be nonpositive and such an allocation will, by definition, lie in the core.

The nucleolus is then defined as that cost allocation that minimizes the maximum of the complaints of any coalition against that allocation. That is, it makes as small as possible the largest overpayment by any customer group over its own stand alone cost. If this solution lies in the core, so that there is no such overpayment by any one group, the nucleolus is the allocation that maximizes the saving relative to stand alone costs of that customer group for which the difference between allocated cost and stand alone cost is lowest. In short, the nucleolus involves a Rawlsian sharing of the savings achievable through economies of scale and scope in the total costs of the firm relative to the sum of the stand alone costs available to the firm's individual customer groups. It achieves that Rawlsian sharing by maximizing the benefits to the group of customers that gains the least in that allocation vis-à-vis its stand alone costs. It has been proved that the nucleolus always exists, that it is unique, and that it always is one of the allocations that lies in the core if the core is not empty, i.e., if there exist *any* cost allocations that involve no complaint by any customer group.

To make the nature of the game theoretic methods of cost allocation clearer I shall now describe the Loehman-Whinston approach in somewhat greater detail, omitting, however, all proofs, which are not particularly helpful for our purposes.[3]

The problem, as it is envisioned by Loehman and Whinston, involves a firm with n customers, and takes each customer, i, to have arrived at his optimal vector of quantities demanded, K_i, before the calculation begins. The problem, then, is to determine a set of charges (buyer expenditures), $e(K_i)$ (which may involve fixed prices, two-part tariffs, or some other arrangement), such that $\sum e(K_i) = C(\sum K_i)$, that is, that just suffice to cover the total cost of the enterprise. A difficulty that arises immediately is the

---

3. For the formal arguments, see Loehman and Whinston [1974].

fact that quantity demanded depends on price, i.e., that the $e(K_i)$ selected in such an approach may induce customer i to demand quantity $K_i' \neq K_i$. That is, given the pertinent demand functions, the K_i values with which the calculation starts off may be inconsistent with the charges e_i. This will be noted again later.

Loehman and Whinston adopt the following five requirements for an acceptable cost allocation rule:

1. Given the quantities demanded by all other users, if i's quantity demanded increases by ΔK_i, his charge will rise by $C(K_i - \Delta K_i) - C(K_i)$; that is, it will increase by an amount exactly equal to the incremental cost of ΔK_i. In particular, if quantity demanded goes up by one unit, i will be charged a marginal cost price for that incremental unit.

2. The total cost of providing the outputs purchased by the n customers must be covered by the charges.

3. Though the charge may not involve a uniform price per unit of output, if two customers i and j purchase the same output vectors, $K_i = K_j$, then $e(K_i) = e(K_j)$, i.e., they will be charged the same amount.

4. The charge to i is a function of only one type of datum: the incremental cost incurred by i.

5. The charge is a linearly homogeneous function of incremental costs, so that if the incremental costs incurred by user i rise by the factor V, then i's charge rises by the same factor.

These five requirements at first glance appear very attractive. Certainly they are very powerful. For Loehman and Whinston are able to show that there exists one and only one cost allocation arrangement that satisfies all five conditions.

To illustrate the solution, the authors begin with a two-customer case. If $C(K_1)$, $C(K_2)$ are their respective stand alone costs, then, the authors suggest, 1's incremental cost is $C(K_1)$ if he is the company's first customer, but it is $C(K_1 + K_2) - C(K_2)$ if customer 2 preceded him. Adopting a sort of Bayesian view of the matter, then, if we have no way of knowing whether i really was the earlier customer historically, or if we now wish to abstract from this bit of ancient history, we treat each customer as though he were equally likely to have arrived first, and obtain a mean or expected incremental cost

$$e(K_i) = \tfrac{1}{2}C(K_i) + \tfrac{1}{2}[C(K_i + K_j) - C(K_j)] \qquad (i \neq j = 1, 2). \qquad (7.2)$$

This is the charge that Loehman and Whinston propose to levy; i.e., it is the portion of total cost they propose to allocate to i. In this two-person case it is obvious that

$$e(K_1) + e(K_2) = \tfrac{1}{2}C(K_1) + \tfrac{1}{2}[C(K_1 + K_2) - C(K_2)] + \tfrac{1}{2}C(K_2)$$

$$+ \tfrac{1}{2}[C(K_1 + K_2) - C(K_1)] = C(K_1 + K_2).$$

That is, the sum of the charges precisely equals the firm's total cost, $C(K_1 + K_2)$.

The authors then generalize the formula to the case of n users. To follow its logic suppose g-1 buyers had preceded i as customers of the firm and that K_{g-1} is the vector of outputs demanded by that group. Then the incremental cost of i's arrival as an additional customer of the firm is $C(K_{g-1} + K_i) - C(K_{g-1})$. Now, to take account of the possibility of the arrival ahead of i of some other set of $g - 1$ customers (or some smaller or larger set of customers), we must consider all permutations of subsets of the set, N, of the firm's n customers, and weigh equally the corresponding incremental cost of i, to obtain as the generalization of (7.2) the expected incremental cost of K_i,

$$e(K_i) = \sum_{\substack{G \in N \\ i \in G}} \frac{(n - g)!(g - 1)!}{n!}[C(K_{G-1} + K_i) - C(K_{G-1})], \qquad (7.3)$$

where G is any subset containing both i and $g - 1$ other customers of the firm and K_{G-1} is the vector of outputs purchased by the members of G excluding individual i. The coefficient of the bracketed terms obviously corresponds to the $(g - 1)!$ orderings of the $g - 1$ individuals whose arrival precedes i's and the $(n - g)!$ possible arrangements of the $n - g$ individuals whose arrival succeeds i's.

It should be noted that (7.3) is precisely the Shapley value of the cost allocation game. As already indicated, the five axiomatic desiderata that make (7.3) the only acceptable cost allocation formula all seem quite attractive and the interpretation of the formula itself as an expected incremental cost also disposes one in its favor. Yet, we shall see that there is a good deal that can be argued on the other side.

Still, we can say a bit more in support of such a formula. First, Loehman and Whinston show that in the competitive case, or wherever else the cost function is linearly homogeneous locally, the formula (7.3) collapses into the standard formula of marginal cost pricing $P_i = MC_i$. Second, while they recognize that the arrangement is not, in general, consistent with "first-best optimality," they suggest that because (7.3) increases the charges to customer i by MC_i when his demand increases by one unit, it provides the right signals *at the margin* for efficiency in resource allocation. Finally, it may perhaps be argued that it is equitable to base the fee to each buyer upon the incremental cost of serving him and that in calculating that incremental cost the historical date at which he happened to become one of the firm's customers is an irrelevant bit of history, which should be disregarded in determining the fairness of a cost allocation. This, of course, is what (7.3) appears to do and so it would seem to be a very promising candidate for the role of the fairest of cost allocation formulas.

To evaluate these conclusions we shall now turn to the efficiency attributes of cost allocation formulas. After that we shall at last examine what can be said about their fairness. This order in the discussion is dictated by the fact that some of the comments on the fairness issue build upon observations that emerge from the efficiency calculation.

5   Cost Allocation and Efficiency

Let us start our efficiency discussion with the special case in which marginal cost pricing just covers total cost, i.e., in which the vector, y^*, of the firm's outputs that will be purchased by the market at prices $P_i = MC_i$ is such that the total cost function $C(y)$ is locally linearly homogeneous at y^*. Then there is no problem of cost allocation. The prices $P_i = MC_i$ will assign all of the firm's costs among its different customer groups and those prices will obviously meet the requirements of Pareto optimality and efficiency in the allocation of resources. No useful role would appear to be available for allocation of any costs here. But before turning to other cases several pertinent remarks may be offered on this case in which MC pricing does work.

First, it is to be noted that the proper division of costs is obtained from prices that appear, in turn, to be obtained from cost data alone. That is, one need only determine MC_i to find the requisite price of i. But this is, clearly, just an illusion. Unless all the MC_i are independent of the output vector, y, to find the appropriate magnitude of MC_i one must first discover the value of y and that can only be done with the aid of the demand function. Yet in this case it is true that no characteristic of the demand function enters *explicitly* into the pricing formula. This, as we shall see, contrasts with the cases in which MC pricing does not satisfy

$$\sum P_i y_i = \sum C_i y_i = C(y) \tag{7.4}$$

(where, as usual, we write $C_i \equiv \partial C / \partial y_i$).

Second, we may observe that some of the cost allocation formulas that have appeared in the literature [we have seen this to be true of the Loehman-Whinston formula (7.3)] automatically transform themselves into marginal cost pricing rules when (7.4) is satisfied. In other words, in this particular case those formulas are indeed consistent with efficiency in resource allocation. This is true for a number of the game theoretic allocation schemes, though it is obviously not generally true for the cost accounting methods of allocation. But, of course, where (7.4) holds all such allocation formulas become redundant, as we have already noted.

Third, in the case where (7.4) holds there is a sense in which one can relate price, marginal, and average costs as they are related in the elementary textbooks. That is so despite the fact that in the multiproduct case one cannot, in general, define the average cost for any individual product since, as we have seen, there is no meaning to the share of total cost attributable to any particular product i (that, after all, is what cost allocation is all about). Yet one can instead utilize what has been called ray average cost (RAC)—the cost of a product bundle of varying size, made up of outputs whose proportions are fixed. Here one chooses arbitrarily some such bundle, y^*, as the unit bundle, so that any other such bundle, y, must satisfy $y = ky^* = (ky_1^*, \ldots, ky_n^*) = k$. Then ray average cost is defined as $C(ky^*)/ky^*$.

We can show now that at a point $y = ky^*$ of locally constant returns to scale RAC $=$ RMC $\equiv dC/dy$. At such a point $\lim_{v \to 1} C(vy) = vC(y)$ as scalar v approaches unity from either direction. Thus in the neighborhood of such a point RAC $= C(vy)/vy = C(y)/y =$ constant. For any component y_i in input bundle, y, along a ray, $dy_i/y_i = dy/y$, so that RMC $= dC/dy = \sum C_i dy_i/dy = \sum C_i y_i/y$. Hence, if we set $P_i = C_i$, by (7.4) RMC $= \sum P_i y_i/y = C(y)/y =$ RAC, giving us the desired relationship among P_i, MC, and RAC. Specifically, in this case RAC is seen to be a weighted average of MC prices with P_i weighted by y_i/y, i's defined share in the output bundle, y, and a slight extension of the argument shows that RAC $\lessgtr$ RMC as $dRAC/dy \gtrless 0$.

Finally, it may be shown that even where (7.4) holds we may have

$$P_i y_i \leqslant IC_i,$$

so that the MC prices, while they are compensatory overall, may or may not satisfy the incremental pricing criterion. If they do not, then, of course the prices will fail the incremental cost criterion of fairness that was discussed in the preceding chapter. A trivial example, even if unrealistic, proves the point: If the firm produces two outputs and the cost function is of Cobb-Douglas form (and, hence, linearly homogeneous throughout), we have

$$C(y) = ky_1^a y_2^{(1-a)},$$

so that

$$C(y_1, 0) = C(0, y_2) = 0$$

and

$$IC_1 = C(y_1, y_2) - C(0, y_2) = C(y_1, y_2) = IC_2.$$

Therefore, if $p_i = MC_i$ for all i, so that $\sum p_i y_i = C(y_1, y_2)$, then $\sum p_i y_i < \sum IC_i = 2C(y_1, y_2)$. This problem arises for any cost function of Cobb-Douglas or translog form, no matter what the number of outputs, n. For, in any such case, $C(\cdot) = 0$ if any one $y_i = 0$ so $IC_i = C(y)$ and $\sum IC_i = nC(y)$. Hence, if $\sum p_i y_i = C(y)$, at least some $p_j y_j < IC_j$.

We turn next to the efficiency requirements for the case in which (7.4) is violated so that marginal cost pricing does not exactly cover total cost. Here it is now generally recognized that the correct (second-best) solution requires Ramsey pricing and is given by a variety of formulas. For example, for any two of the firm's n products i and j, this solution is given by

$$\frac{p_i - MC_i}{p_j - MC_j} = \frac{MR_i - MC_i}{MR_j - MC_j}, \qquad \sum p_i y_i = C(y). \tag{7.5}$$

In the special case in which the demands for all of the firm's products are independent we have the much-used inverse elasticity rule

$$\frac{(p_i - MC_i)/p_i}{(p_j - MC_j)/p_j} = \frac{E_i}{E_j}, \qquad \sum p_i y_i = C(y). \tag{7.6}$$

These well-known relationships are reproduced here for convenience in the several comments that follow about the case where $\sum p_i y_i = C_i y_i \neq C(y)$.

First, it should be clear that, in contrast with the case where MC pricing covers total cost, demand considerations enter directly and explicitly into the expressions yielding the Ramsey optimum. That is, there is no way in which Ramsey prices can be deduced from cost information alone. That is obvious in the inverse elasticity rule (7.6), but it is equally true of the more general Ramsey conditions (7.5) since

$$MR_i = p_i + \sum_j y_j \partial p_j / \partial y_i = p_i + \sum p_j y_j / y_i E_{ij},$$

where, if $i \neq j$, E_{ij} is the cross-elasticity of demand for i with respect to p_j.

Second, we note that Ramsey pricing has sometimes been described as a form of full cost allocation simply because Ramsey prices must satisfy $\sum p_i y_i = C(y)$. But that is a complete misunderstanding of the matter, involving what amounts to a play on words. *Any* exactly viable pricing arrangement can be said to be an *ex post* "allocation" of costs if we simply define $FAC_i \equiv TR_i$, because, by the nature of the case, the sum of these total revenues must cover total cost, so that then

$$\sum FAC_i \equiv \sum TR_i = C(y).$$

But this empties the term "cost allocation" of its meaning since TR_i need have no relation to any form of cost of i, and is obviously dependent on demand conditions at least as much as on cost.

The point is that an allocation of costs is a process for subdivision of the firm's total cost that, unlike the Ramsey solution, aspires to find some a priori formula, based *only* on costs and output quantities, that assigns to each product its proper share of total cost. It is then only by distortion of language that every pricing procedure that brings in enough revenue overall to cover total cost is defined, from that attribute alone, to constitute a cost allocation.

Third, it follows from the critical role of demand elasticities in the Ramsey pricing rules that no cost allocation formula that leaves out demand elasticities, including the most sophisticated of the game theoretic constructs, can yield prices generally consistent with even second-best optimality in the allocation of resources. For, assume that (by coincidence) each of the prices, p_{ai}, yielded by such an allocation happens to coincide with the corresponding Ramsey price, p_{ri}. Then a change only in elasticities of demand will change the values of the p_{ri} while leaving the p_{ai} unaffected and so thereafter $p_{ai} \neq p_{ri}$.

Finally, we digress to extend these remarks to cover two-part tariffs and other "nonlinear prices" as well as the fixed parametric price vectors with which we have dealt so far. The point is that, as has been noted, a game theoretic allocation such as that of Loehman and Whinston may sometimes call for, say, a set of two-part tariffs, i.e., a charge to customers involving fixed payments whose magnitudes do not rise with quantities bought, plus a set of relatively small user fees, rather than a set of fixed prices. As is well known, such nonlinear prices are always able to produce an allocation of resources that is at least as efficient and that is generally superior to the best obtainable through a set of fixed prices. It may appear, consequently, that some cost allocation formula, because it calls for nonlinear prices, may be systematically superior to the Ramsey rule. As will be shown, this is not so, because for every nonlinear price produced by a cost allocation procedure, there exists a corresponding Ramsey *nonlinear* price. For reasons that will be discussed in more detail in chapter 10, the latter will be at least as desirable as, and generally superior to, the former. That is, just as there are Ramsey values for a vector of parametric prices, there exist Ramsey values for the parameters of a vector of nonlinear prices that maximize welfare subject to the budget constraint $\sum p_i y_i = C(y)$.

To explain this it is first necessary to review the concept of nonlinear price and to indicate briefly the source of its superiority (noninferiority) to a parametric price. Then, the nature of a Ramsey nonlinear price will be described briefly.

A nonlinear price may take a variety of forms. As already indicated, it may be a standard two-part tariff (a $50 charge for "membership" in the customer group plus $2 per item purchased) or it may consist of a choice of payment plans (either a $200 auto rental fee per week, with unlimited "free" mileage or a $100 rental fee plus 20 cents per mile). Any such arrangement can be written in the form $p_i = p^i(y_i)$, making price a function of quantity purchased, with the function $p^i(y_i)$ describable by the values of some set of parameters. For example, in the auto rental case, if the renter plans to drive less than 500 miles ($m < 500$), it is cheaper to use the second plan, with a price per mile of $p_i = (\$100/m) + 0.20$, while for a distance exceeding 500 miles the lowest charge becomes $200/m$. Thus, the price per mile under such a scheme must satisfy the functional relationship

$$p_i = \begin{cases} a + b/m & \text{for} \quad m \leqslant m^* \\ c/m & \text{for} \quad m > m^*, \end{cases} \tag{7.7}$$

which is determined by the values of the four parameters, a, b, c, and m^*.

Such a nonlinear price will generally be able to increase the efficiency of resource allocation over what can be achieved by a fixed parametric price, p_i^*, because the former has more degrees of freedom available to it [for example, the four parameter values in (7.7)]. Thus, the nonlinear price provides a range of options unavailable under the parametric price, *but the nonlinear price is generally constructed so that, if desirable, it can replicate the parametric price.* For example, should it prove in the auto rental case that a fixed price of 25 cents per mile is optimal, the optimal solution to (7.7) simply will be $a = 0.25$, $b = c = 0$, $m^* = \infty$. In other words, a nonlinear price can do everything a parametric price can do, and opens a new range of options besides. It follows immediately that the former must always be at least as desirable as the latter.

Next, let us consider the meaning and construction of a Ramsey non-linear price. This, as before, is simply the solution to the Pareto optimality problem subject to a budget constraint, except that in this case [using (7.7) as our example again] one determines the optimal values of the four parameters, a, b, c, and m^*, rather than that of the single parameter, p_i.

Another illustration will make the issue clearer. Consider a nonlinear charge for telephone service of r cents per call plus s cents per minute of call duration. One can consider these two charges, respectively, as a per unit fee for connection and a per minute fee for transmission. Then connection and transmission can be treated as two separate (but complementary) products of the telephone company, and each of these will then have its optimal Ramsey price satisfying (7.5). If the products were independent, the relative prices would, as usual, deviate from their marginal costs in inverse proportion to their elasticities. The complementarity of connection and transmission in telephone communications precludes this simple a relationship, but obviously the nature of the Ramsey solution for a nonlinear price is no different from that for a parametric price.

The conclusion from all of this is that even if a cost allocation process yields a set of nonlinear prices, they will never be superior to the corresponding Ramsey nonlinear prices necessary for second-best optimality and they will generally be inferior to those Ramsey prices. No form of cost allocation can pretend to be compatible, generally, with efficiency in resource allocation, no matter how sophisticated its derivation.

6 Cost Allocation and Fairness

As has already been observed, the arbitrary character of the accounting procedures for full allocation of costs immediately and completely undermines any claim of maximal fairness that may be advanced on behalf of any one of them. If the allocation can be changed dramatically by replacement of one persuasive allocation criterion (say, number of ton-miles shipped) by another with no less plausibility (say, number of freight car miles traversed), it becomes difficult to attribute anything like maximal virtue to either rule of thumb or to any of the available substitutes.

Matters would appear to be different in the case of the game theoretic allocation procedures. When such a process is derived from a set of axioms that address themselves directly to fairness issues one cannot simply dismiss the pertinence of the resulting allocation rules. Yet, I shall argue, even the Loehman-Whinston axioms, which may well be the most persuasive of the available axiom sets for the allocation of costs from the viewpoint of an economist, are not really as manifest a characterization of fairness as they may at first appear.

First, it may be noted, though it has no direct bearing on the authors' axioms, that their expected incremental cost concept can easily be misunderstood to be more pertinent than it is in fact. As was stated earlier, when

n commodities are provided by a firm the fact that the company first began manufacturing product i 35 years ago while j entered its product line 12 years later is an irrelevant bit of ancient history either for efficiency or for fairness. In the case of efficiency this is obvious from the Ramsey formula that disregards all such considerations and concerns itself equally with all of the partial derivatives of today's cost function with respect to today's values of y_i and y_j. And the relevance for equity is no more persuasive— since many of today's buyers may not even have been born on the dates when i and j were first introduced. Whichever product had historical prece- dence, the relevant incremental cost of, say, product 1 is $C(y_1, y_2, \ldots, y_n)$ − $C(0, y_2, \ldots, y_n)$ because that is how much the firm can *now* reduce its expenditures if y_1 is dropped from its product line today.

Let us turn next to the Loehman-Whinston axioms. The first of these is perhaps the one that seems most acceptable, and yet that carries the most significant implications beneath its surface. This first desideratum requires that " ... if a user desires additional service (ΔK) once the demands of other users are fixed and plant capacity is set at K, then he must pay the incremental cost $[C(K - \Delta K) - C(K)]$ for his additional demands ... " [1971, p. 613]. This requirement raises problems precisely in the circumstances that the allocation procedure is designed to grapple with—when prices that cover incremental costs do not suffice to cover total costs, i.e., when $\sum IC_i < C(y)$. For in this case, compensatory prices must obviously exceed average incremental costs at least for some products, and quite plausibly for all of them. In these circumstances there seems to be no reason to consider it equitable for the customer who chooses to increase the quantity he demands to be offered a relative bargain *on his incremental purchases*. The fact that others pay prices above incremental costs while he does not always do so is precisely the sort of complaint about the incremental cost pricing test that a cost allocation is ostensibly designed to silence. Yet here that sort of difference in treatment is smuggled back in as one of the axioms designed to embody the requirements of acceptable practice.[4]

Similarly, one can raise questions about the pertinence to fairness of axiom 5, which requires that " ... if incremental costs are all multiplied by a constant, then the charge will be also" [1971, p. 613]. This requirement alone also makes the allocation procedure incompatible with the Ramsey

---

4. Loehman and Whinston explain that this axiom is designed with an eye on efficiency. "Thus, assuming plant size is optimal, the necessary efficiency condition is satisfied" [1974, p. 613]. But we have seen that in general $p_i = MC_i$ or $p_i = AIC_i$ is incompatible with the Ramsey requirements and, consequently, with the achievement of allocative efficiency.

optimality rules for efficiency. For suppose as a result of the increased prices and the consequent changes in quantities demanded, the (point) demand elasticities for the different products are affected very differently. Then Ramsey optimality will, in general, call for increases in the different prices that are *far* from proportionate even though incremental costs have risen proportionately.

Demand elasticities, then, are certainly relevant for efficiency, and so the axiom we are discussing prevents the Loehman-Whinston prices from satisfying the efficiency requirements. But it is by no means clear that elasticities are irrelevant for fairness in pricing either. On the contrary, it has often been proposed to use them in this capacity. Demand elasticity has often been defined in regulatory hearings as the proper measure of the value of (additional) product to the consumer, this value, of course, varying *inversely* with the elasticity. Thus, demands for vital medicines are said to be inelastic because they are so valuable to their buyers. The high elasticity of demand for an item with close substitutes is explained as a manifestation of the fact that availability of this product offers no great additional benefits to the consumer. But there is a well-known principle of equity in taxation that those who benefit most should bear a relatively large share of the costs. This suggests that it can be considered "fair" for customers whose demands are relatively inelastic to pay prices that are relatively high in comparison with the corresponding marginal costs, just as Ramsey pricing prescribes. This is an argument that has been used to defend the fairness of the Ramsey principle. Whether or not one accepts it either as a rough way of approaching the equity issue or as a precise quantification of fair prices, the argument certainly makes it difficult to reject out of hand the pertinence of demand elasticities to fairness.[5] Because, by its very nature, it leaves elasticities out of consideration, *any* cost allocation procedure runs into the problem that it cannot take into account the value of this parameter, which, apparently, is highly pertinent to any judgment of fairness in pricing.

In a sense, all of this discussion of fairness and allocation of costs can be characterized as quibbling over details. The point that is really central is

5. Indeed, it is curious that at least some critics have raised questions about Ramsey pricing not because it takes elasticities into account but on the ground that it disregards the true fairness implications of those elasticities. As I noted in an earlier chapter, it has been asked in some regulatory hearings whether it is just to impose high prices upon exactly those consumers who demonstrate via the inelasticity of their demand that "they have nowhere else to go," i.e., that no good substitute products are available to them.

that no such allocation process is derived from any systematic consideration of the requirements of fairness, nor can it possibly be derived in this
way because it leaves out of account all information on consumer demands
and preferences that, for example, constitute the heart of superfairness
theory.

In the last analysis, most of the allocation procedures constitute exer-
cises in arithmetic processes such as those one normally associates with
cost accounting.[6] None of this is meant as a denigration of cost accounting
or, obviously, of the rules of ordinary arithmetic. But those can hardly be
interpreted as the embodiment of fairness. I believe Professor Samuelson
once described the view that it is fair for input prices to equal the marginal
products of those inputs as the "attribution of virtue to partial derivatives."
The point is that neither the valuable appurtenances of the differential
calculus nor the very helpful rules of arithmetic can with any good
reason be accepted as proper arbiters of equity in pricing or in income
distribution.

7   Superfairness Theory and Pricing

Superfairness theory does have implications for the sort of pricing issues
we are discussing, some of them immediate. For example, it does tell us
how one can derive prices (and an income distribution) that are compatible
with both allocative efficiency and fairness in exchange. These are implicit
in some of our earlier discussion, in particular that of the existence of a
distribution that is simultaneously fair, superequal, and efficient. For this
purpose, we remember, one need merely calculate the prices that will
emerge if the available bundle of goods is initially divided equally among
all consumers and they are then permitted to trade freely. In the two-good,
two-person case these prices are given by the slope of the price line from
the midpoint, H, of the diagonal of the Edgeworth box (the point of equal
division) to the equilibrium point, E, at which there is intersection between
the corresponding offer curves of the two individuals. Point E is obviously
efficient because it involves tangency of the two persons' indifference
curves. It is also fair, since each person could have afforded to acquire the

---

6. This is true of some of the game theoretic procedures as well as the allocations provided
by accountants. For example, several of the axioms employed by Billera and Heath to
derive their allocation principle (which is also a cousin of the Shapley value) explicitly are
described as characterizations of consistency in cost accounting procedures. See, for
example, Billera and Heath [1982].

purchase of the other and chose not to do so, thus showing that each does not envy the other.

So much is true, but it does not seem to be particularly helpful for application, since in practive we are unlikely to have a way of determining the pertinent equilibrium point.

Indeed, there are several impediments to the use of superfairness theory in utility pricing. For one thing, the total incomes of the buyers of different products are apt to be highly disparate. For example, most of the entities that ship freight on a railroad are firms, while the customers for passenger service are individuals. It is therefore difficult to defend the relevance of a reference point such as H, the point of equal distribution, among the individual entities involved. Surely, fairness is not intended to justify giving all *legal persons* a comparable right to commodities—it refers to human beings not to legal entities. Moreover, it is not clear what we would mean by *envy* of an individual customer by a large corporation or vice versa, when one of them exchanges, say, a few dollars for shipment of an individual parcel while the other exchanges millions of dollars for the shipment of thousands of carloads of commodities per year.

Moreover, when the products provided to different customer groups are entirely distinct it becomes difficult to use the diagrammatic variant of fairness analysis, which would now require at least three dimensions to encompass the three pertinent quantities (money and two product quantities). While this difficulty does not prevent algebraic analysis its preclusion of the use of graphs is, at the very least, an inconvenience.

There is, however, one set of circumstances that is highly pertinent in practice, and does lend itself more readily to fairness analysis. This is the case in which two sets of customers purchase what is essentially the same commodity at different prices based, for example, on the magnitude of the purchase of each customer. Buyers of large quantities may be offered a price per unit that is relatively low and the price difference may or may not correspond to some particular measure of costs. This is true, in particular, of Ramsey prices, as we have seen. In such a case, since both consumer groups purchase the same good and give up purchasing power in exchange, a graphic analysis of fairness and incremental fairness can then be employed directly.

One other step—aggregation—is necessary to permit us to proceed. Instead of comparing the shipments of a private individual with those of a corporation, as in our illustration, we aggregate all small individual shippers into one group and all large purchasers of shipping services into another. The pertinent criterion for classification into one group or another is the criterion used in the setting of the discriminatory prices—those small customers who must pay the higher price are placed in the one group and those who benefit from the reduced price fall into the other.[7]

To simplify the situation to the utmost let us abstract from production, which, as we know, causes difficulties for superfairness analysis (though, as we saw in chapter 2, these problems are by no means insuperable). I shall assume for simplicity that our firm's production process is so lumpy that it can choose only between producing no output at all or producing an output y^* at the cost given by the constant[8] $C(y^*)$. (It can perhaps produce an amount larger than y^* but we take market demand to be insufficient for the purpose.) We divide potential purchasers of y into two groups and call them, for convenience, consumers (c) and business (b), whose demand functions are

$$y_i = D^i(p_i) \qquad (i = c, b).$$

Financial viability of the supplier and regulatory preclusion of excess profits require, as usual, $\sum p_i y_i = C(y^*)$. If consumers are the only buyers of y, then this normal profitability requirement gives us the *un*discriminatory consumer price

$$p_{cu} = C(y^*)/y_{cu}$$

and we assume that at this price the quantity of y demanded by business firms is zero. However, prices are taken to exist at which this quantity is positive, i.e., at which

$$0 < y^b = f^b(p_b), \qquad 0 < p_b < p^* < p_{cu}.$$

Thus, at such a discriminatory price to business, since firms now pay part of the given total cost, the price to consumers must be reduced to its discriminatory level

$$p_{cd} = [C(y^*) - y_b p_b]/y_{cd} < p_{cu},$$

---

7. In reality it is noteworthy that aggregation will sometimes reverse the relative sizes of the outlays and purchases of the two types of party. For example, in telecommunications, outlays on the type of long distance service that is available to individuals easily swamp total expenditures on the so-called private line services—the relatively discounted bulk services, which only can be afforded by sizable business firms and government agencies.

8. It need not be assumed that marginal or incremental costs are zero. Thus, suppose the product has a delivery cost that is unpaid on any of the good that is unused. Then we need only define p_i as a *net* price representing the net incremental contribution of a unit sold to the earnings of the firm, after subtraction of incremental cost.

with $y_{cd} \geqslant y_{cu}$ since the demand curves can be taken to be negatively sloped.

This situation is represented in figures 7.1 and 7.2. The first of these is the box diagram representing the holdings of the two groups both with and without price discrimination. The second graph is the corresponding incremental "box" diagram in which the box, as we shall see, has degenerated to a line segment.

The axes of figure 7.1 represent, respectively, holdings of y and holdings of money (M). The dimensions of the box are y^*, the total quantity of y produced, and $C(y^*)$, the amount of money the firm must raise in total from its two customer groups if it is to survive.

Since, in figure 7.1, buyers will end up with a larger quantity of y and less money than they had to begin with, the origin, which normally lies at the lower left corner of the box, now occupies its *upper* left corner. That is, from that origin customers can move to the right (more y) and downward (less money). Thus O_c, the consumer origin spending = consumption of $y = 0$) is located there. Similarly, O_b, the origin of the business customer, is at the lower right rather than its customary upper-right position. $O_c C$ and $O_b VS_b B$ are their respective price-consumption curves (i.e., their offer curves) showing the quantities of y they are willing to purchase at different prices. For example, if the consumers' price line is $O_c R$, so that p_c is the absolute value of the slope of that ray, then consumers will demand quantity $M^* r$. Note that the offer curve of the business customers has been drawn to have a horizontal segment (or, rather, a discontinuity), VO_b, indicating that at some prices business customers will withdraw from the market altogether, presumably because a more attractive substitute is available to them. For example, if p is given by the slope of $O_c R$, as before, then in the absence of price discrimination the business customers' price line is given by $O_b W$, which is parallel to $O_c R$. Since $O_b W$ intersects the business offer curve only at the origin (the business indifference curve is not tangent to $O_b W$ at any point above the horizontal line through O_b), business customers will not purchase any y (i.e., $y_b = 0$) at that price.

However, there do, obviously, exist prices at which $y_b > 0$. For example, at the price given by the slope of $O_b Q_b$ firms will purchase $O_b q_b$ and contribute revenue $q_b Q_b$. If the supplier is to earn no excess profit, that much less must then be contributed by consumer buyers of y, which will occur if they end up at point Q_c at which they demand $M^* q_c$ and they will demand this quantity if the price is given by the slope of line segment $O_c Q_c$ (not shown). However, this arrangement is incompatible with equilibrium because it involves excess demand (since $M^* q_c + O_b q_b > y^*$).

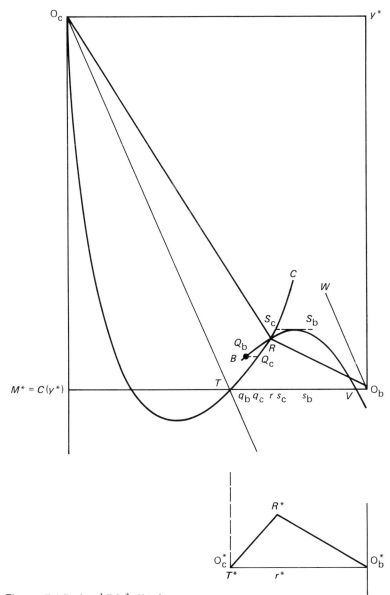

Figures 7.1 (top) and **7.2** (bottom)

Zero excess demand and zero profit occur only at point R at which the two offer curves intersect. There, consumer and business prices are given, respectively, by the slopes of O_cR and O_bR and the quantities they demand, M^*r and O_br, sum precisely to y^*. Yet, here prices are obviously discriminatory, with business buyers paying less per unit than consumer buyers do.[9]

Figure 7.2 is the degenerate box diagram, which shows the change in the position of the two buyer groups when prices change from the uniform figure given by the slope of O_cT to the discriminatory values corresponding to O_bR and O_cR. Since the total quantity of revenue to be contributed by the two parties together does not change (it must equal $C(y^*)$ under either price arrangement), the incremental total expenditure (the height of the "box" in figure 7.2) must be zero.

The incremental quantity is TO_b, the quantity of unconsumed y under the nondiscriminatory price arrangement. The new position is R^*, at which consumer money holdings are increased by r^*R^* and business money holdings fall by the same amount (recall that in this Edgeworth diagram a rise in the money holdings of business is represented by a *southward* movement). However, both consumer and business holdings of y increase (by amounts T^*r^* and $O_b^*r^*$, respectively). Thus, consumers gain both goods *and* money as a result of the entry of business customers in response to the price discrimination.[10] However, business customers end up with more y and less money than before, a change that they must always prefer, since they undertake it voluntarily, when their holdings (point O_b^*) under the nondiscriminatory price continues to be an available alternative.

The issue we must now examine is what superfairness analysis permits

---

9. Some reduction in discrimination, as measured by the difference in prices, is possible. For example, if the price to business customers is set at O_bS_b so that the revenue they provide (the height of their offer curve) is maximized, zero profit requires consumer buyers to end up at S_c. The consumer price will be lower than at R and the business price higher, but the latter will still be below the former. At these prices there will be some unsold supply, s_bs_c. However, if the constraint on the seller's profit is effective and entry does not threaten, there is no reason to expect prices to be cut. Thus, the combination of points S_b and S_c may constitute an equilibrium.

10. This qualitative pattern assumes that consumer demand is inelastic. If consumers' demand for y is elastic over the relevant range, the reduction in the price they pay will lead them to spend more on the good, and reduce the quantity of money they retain. But since revenues from business customers will have risen, this must violate the zero profit constraint upon the supplier. Only a reduction in consumer spending on y is compatible with the profit constraint, but in the elastic demand case this will require a rise in price to consumers and, hence, a fall in the quantity of y they demand.

us to say about these equilibria. I shall show the following results: (i) the discriminatory arrangement must be fair to business customers, and may or may not be fair to consumer buyers—with the likelihood of fairness to the latter increased by a rise in the marginal utility of y to consumers relative to the marginal utility of money to them, i.e., by a rise in their marginal rate of substitution of money for y; and, (ii) the change from the nondiscriminatory equilibrium may or may not be *incrementally* fair to the consumer buyers, and to the business customers; the likelihood of fairness to the former is apt to be increased by a decline in their MRS of increases in their money holdings for increases in their consumption of y, while the reverse is likely in the case of business customers.

In all this it is useful to keep in mind the disturbing result provided by Feldman and Kirman (see above, chapter 3, proposition 5), that if one starts off with a superfair allocation and then makes a change from it which is incrementally superfair, the new allocation may nevertheless prove to be unfair.

Let us now show the preceding results. Let us begin with a discussion of part (i). The discriminatory price obviously must be fair to business customers who voluntarily reject the opportunity (!) to pay the higher price charged to consumers and buy the quantity purchased by the latter. That is, the business group clearly does not envy the consumers.

The position of consumers is more complicated and a diagram is needed to permit us to analyze its fairness. In figure 7.3 points A, R, and E represent three possible positions of the discriminatory equilibrium (R is the discriminatory equilibrium of figure 7.1). I_{cH} is the (concave) indifference curve of the consumer group that goes through the equal division point, H. B_c is the consumer group's fairness boundary. Assuming that the indifference curves are convex to the origin, by propositions 3 and 4 of chapter 2, B_c must be tangent to I_{cH} at H, and B_c must everywhere be at least as close to M as I_{cH} is. Here, M is, of course, the consumers' worst position in the diagram since at that point they bear the entire cost of y^*, yet consume none of that good.

From these observations it follows that if the discriminatory equilibrium point is like E, lying above I_{cH}, then the equilibrium must be superfair (and superequal) to consumers as well as superfair to business customers. This must be so because the fairness boundary, B_c, cannot lie above I_{cH} and so it cannot lie above E. Even if the equilibrium point lies below I_{cH} it may still be fair to consumers (point R) or it may be unfair to them (point A).

We see also that the greater the absolute value of the slope of indifference curve I_{cH} the more points will be encompassed in the (shaded)

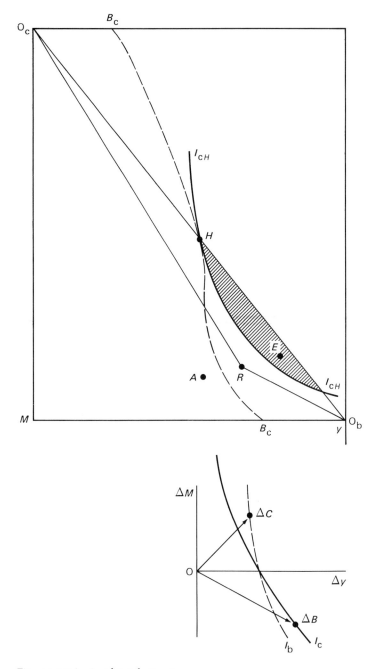

Figures 7.3 (top) and **7.4** (bottom)

region lying below diagonal O_cO_b and above I_{cH}. Since any point in this region is a possible discriminatory equilibrium and any such point is necessarily fair to consumers it follows that the steeper I_{cH} is, i.e., the larger consumers' MRS of money for y, the more likely it is that the discriminatory solution will be superfair. Intuitively, the reason is clear. If this MRS is high, it means that consumers place a high value upon the additional y they obtain after its price to them is reduced by discrimination. This is then more likely to constitute adequate compensation, making up for the price (money outlay) advantage that discrimination offers to business customers, so that consumers are then less likely to envy business customers their equilibrium arrangement.

Finally, let us examine the incremental fairness of the change (part (ii) of the conclusion with which this discussion began). Here, again, a diagram is convenient. Figure 7.4 is simply a redrawing of figure 7.2 in which, for convenience, both customer groups have been given the same origin by inversion of the axes for the business customers.

Here, point ΔC is the increment in the position of consumers involving a rise in residual money holdings ($\Delta M > 0$) and a (possibly small) rise in holdings of y ($\Delta y > 0$). Similarly, ΔB represents the change in position of business customers for whom $\Delta y > 0$ and $\Delta M < 0$.

An indifference curve for each of the two groups has been drawn in such a way that illustrates that the move from discriminatory to nondiscriminatory prices *may* be incrementally superfair. I_c, the consumers' indifference curve through point ΔB, has been drawn to lie below ΔC, meaning that consumers do not envy the business group its incremental gains. Similarly, I_b, the business group's indifference curve through ΔC, has been drawn to go below ΔB, implying no envy by business customers of the incremental benefits to consumers.

Several general conclusions follow from figure 7.4: (i) the result cannot be incrementally fair unless point ΔB lies to the right of ΔC, i.e., unless business customers' Δy is greater than that for consumers. This follows from the negative slope of indifference curve I_b and the fact that ΔB must lie below ΔC since the former is beneath the horizontal axis and the latter is above it. If ΔB were not located to the right of ΔC, *then* ΔB could not lie above the indifference curve I_b that goes through point ΔC. (ii) The flatter is indifference curve I_c and the steeper is indifference curve I_b, the more likely the change is to be incrementally superfair, i.e., the more likely ΔC is to lie above I_c and the more likely ΔB is to lie above I_b. In other words, fairness is promoted by a high MRS of business persons of ΔM for Δy and a low value of this MRS for consumers.

The intuitive reason is straightforward, even if it appears convoluted. Consumers having received a large ΔM and a small Δy will prefer this to what the business persons receive if they value ΔM highly relative to Δy, which is, of course, equivalent to a low value of their MRS of ΔM for Δy. The reverse holds for business customers.

Note, incidentally, that fairness of discriminatory pricing is made more likely by a *high* consumer MRS of M for y, while its incremental fairness is made more likely by a *low* consumer MRS of ΔM for Δy. These requirements may appear to be contradictory but they are not.

We conclude from all this that discriminatory pricing that passes the Pareto improvement criterion *may* also (but need not) be superfair and/or incrementally superfair. The outcome depends upon the magnitude of the difference in prices of the two parties, the reduction in expenditure made possible for the customer group facing the higher prices, and relative holdings of y of the different parties in the discriminatory equilibrium. It is easy to confirm that fairness is promoted by a reduction in the price differential and by an increase in the savings in expenditure made possible for consumers, and these results are intuitively obvious. Far less obvious are the qualitative preference patterns that make for superfairness and incremental superfairness, conditions that the graphic analysis has been able to draw to our attention.

This discussion may also give us a somewhat better intuitive grasp of the lack of correlation between fairness and incremental fairness. In terms of the former concept it is clearly the consumer group that seems in the most danger of mistreatment by price discrimination. For in our scenario it is the consumers who are denied access to the low price that is available to business customers. But, incrementally, the fairness bias goes the other way. Business customers get more y than before but pay for it by giving up money. Consumers get more y *and* more money than before, thus acquiring something for less than nothing.

8

Peak Pricing, Congestion, and Fairness*

This chapter examines the fairness of the classic peak pricing solution,[1] comparing it with uniformity of pricing in all periods—an issue that has disturbed observers outside our profession, but that economists have often ignored.

We offer a number of conclusions that may be surprising. (1) There are several cases, at least one of them apparently common and significant, in which, paradoxically, the optimal price in the more congested of two periods is *lower* than that in the less congested period. (2) Even in the classical model, in which required expansion of capacity is the only social cost of high peak demand, the optimal peak price may be lower than the uniform price that just permits total cost to be covered. This will be true when there are sufficient diseconomies of scale in capacity construction, or the required capacity is so expensive relative to the maximum amount peak users are willing to pay that its cost cannot be covered without a contribution by off-peak users, or where the Ramsey adjustment in prices required by the absence of constant returns is sufficiently favorable to peak users. (3) Where conclusion (2) holds, adoption of peak–off-peak prices may be a Pareto improvement over uniform pricing, but it need not be so since the price to off-peak users may actually be raised in the process. (4) In the model with disutility of congestion there seems to be a wider range of cases in which the adoption of optimal peak prices is a Pareto improvement.

Throughout the analysis of the fairness of a peak pricing arrangement we shall be comparing the following alternatives:

Arrangement a: a price that is uniform in all periods and set at such a level that total revenue equals total cost; and

---

*Dietrich Fischer is coauthor of this chapter.
1. For simplicity, we shall use the less accurate term "peak pricing" rather than the clumsier "peak–off-peak pricing."

Arrangement b: a Pareto (Ramsey) optimal set of prices that differs from period to period, depending on differences in quantities demanded, and in which the total revenue derived from all periods together just equals total cost.

1 The Possibility of Pareto Improvement in the Classical Peak Pricing Model

In the standard peak pricing model[2] the only purpose of differentiation of prices from period to period is to reduce quantity demanded in the peak period in order to decrease the quantity of equipment needed to serve traffic during that period, thereby automatically cutting cost, and reducing unused capacity during off-peak periods. Reduced peak period use does not improve service, or add to product quality in any other way—it offers exactly the same service as before, merely redistributing the time pattern of consumption in order to cut resources use. The (nearly) perfect example of this is air passenger travel, particularly where there is a shuttle arrangement under which everyone is guaranteed a seat. There, high peak demand, at least up to a point, causes little delay or discomfort to passengers and the prime reason for evening out quantities demanded at different hours is to reduce the number of airplanes needed to carry the traffic.

In such a case, there is a presumption that if one switches from uniform pricing to peak pricing, the price in the peak period will be higher than before, and since peak consumers obtain no offsetting advantages, that they will consider the change to be disadvantageous to themselves.

In the next section we shall provide some confirmation for this view. However, after that, we shall show that there are important exceptions—cases in which diseconomies of scale in provision of capacity or other

2. For classical discussions of the peak load pricing model, see, for example, Steiner [1957] and Littlechild [1970]. The standard model is a Pareto optimization construct in which capacity, k, is an endogenous variable along with y_t, quantity of use in (each) period, t. The analysis is characterized by the capacity constraints $y_t \leq K$, for all t, and an off-peak period is defined as one in which $y_t < K$. The standard (Kuhn-Tucker) analysis concludes that in any off-peak period the optimal price will equal the marginal operating cost of the facility under consideration, with absolutely no contribution toward construction cost. In a peak period, s, the optimal price, p_s, will differ from marginal operating cost by a nonnegative amount, v_s, and $\sum v_s$ for all peak periods taken together will equal the marginal cost of construction. Thus, under constant returns to scale the (first-best) Pareto optimal prices will yield total revenues exactly equal to total cost. However, when returns to scale are not constant, Ramsey pricing is required if the activity is to yield neither profit nor loss.

special circumstances mean that peak users can have their prices reduced by a departure from uniform pricing. Moreover, we shall see that in those cases sometimes everyone will benefit from the change, though that will not always be true.

2 Sufficient Conditions for Peak Pricing Not to Be a Pareto Improvement

As has just been suggested, in the classical model of peak pricing there is a widely recognized presumption that peak period prices will generally turn out to be higher than they will under uniform pricing. If this is so, the adoption of a peak pricing scheme will not be a Pareto improvement since it will harm peak users. It is therefore appropriate to examine under what conditions this is so. We shall see that in the absence of congestion costs (disutilities) the only exceptions are introduced by diseconomies of scale, by very high total costs relative to peak users' willingness to pay, or by the need to employ Ramsey prices. We shall deal with these cases separately. We shall show first, ignoring all costs other than construction costs, that peak prices will generally exceed the uniform price under constant returns to scale, provided only that under uniform pricing the volume of activity in off-peak periods is not zero. This is so because under these assumptions the cost of capacity construction must vary proportionately with the number of users in the peak period. With uniform pricing this cost burden will be shared by everyone, while under optimal peak pricing it will be borne by peak users alone.

Second, we shall show a similar result for the case of economies of scale, where Ramsey prices must be employed in an optimal solution for total costs to be covered. Clarity requires us to deal one at a time with the effects of Ramsey price adjustments and the consequences of scale economies per se. We shall therefore deal first with the scale economy effects. To avoid Ramsey complications, here we shall examine the special case in which the relevant elasticities and cross-elasticities of demand of peak and off-peak users are the same, yielding Ramsey prices exactly proportionate to the pertinent marginal costs. Later we shall consider Ramsey pricing that is not circumscribed in this way.

In most of the discussion that follows we shall ignore all operating costs and all costs other than that of construction of capacity. The analysis could readily be reformulated to eliminate this simplification, but that would only obscure the issues and the logic of the arguments.

For simplicity, we also assume that there are only two periods, one peak period and one off-peak period.

We first deal with the case of linear homogeneity and prove

Proposition 1 In the classical peak pricing model under constant returns to scale in construction, if a zero off-peak price does not violate the budget constraint, the peak price will equal the zero-profit uniform price when off-peak demand is zero under the uniform price. If the off-peak demand is not zero under the uniform price, the peak price will always be higher than the uniform price.

Proof Let

p_p and p_u represent the peak price and the uniform price, respectively,

$p = (p_p, p_o)$ be the vector of optimal peak and off-peak prices,

$y^P(p)$ and $y^o(p)$ represent the quantities demanded in the peak and off-peak periods, and

$C(y^P) =$ the cost of capacity construction.

Then, by the assumption of constant returns to scale,

$$C(y^P) = ky^P. \tag{8.1}$$

Moreover, by the zero profit requirement and (8.1),

$$p_u = ky^P(p_u)/[y^P(p_u) + y^o(p_u)] \leqslant k, \tag{8.2}$$

$$p_p = ky^P(p)/y^P(p) = k, \tag{8.3}$$

since we have the classical result $p_o = \mathrm{MC}_o = 0$ (where MC_o, the marginal off-peak cost, is 0 by our simplifying assumption). Thus,

$$p_p = k \geqslant p_u \quad \text{and} \quad p_p > p_u \quad \text{if} \quad y^o(p_u) > 0.$$

Next we turn to the case of increasing returns, for now confining ourselves to the special circumstances in which the Ramsey prices required for zero profits cause no analytical complications.

Proposition 2 If demand elasticities and cross elasticities in the peak and off-peak periods are such that Ramsey prices are proportionate to marginal costs and a zero off-peak price does not make it impossible to satisfy the budget constraint, then under increasing returns to scale in capacity construction Ramsey peak prices will always exceed the uniform price that yields zero profit.

Proof Since marginal cost for the off-peak period remains zero, by the hypothesis that Ramsey prices are proportionate to marginal costs the Ramsey off-peak price will remain zero. But now, in (8.1) unit cost k is no longer a constant. Instead, it is a decreasing function of y^p.

Again letting $p = (p_p, p_o)$, in general, $y^p(p) < y^p(p_u)$ and so we may write

$$k_p = k[y^p(p)] > k[y^p(p_u)] = k_u.$$

Then zero-profit condition (8.2) is replaced by

$$p_u \leqslant k_u,$$

while (8.3) becomes

$$p_p = k_p.$$

Thus, $p_p = k_p > k_u \geqslant p_u$.

Corollary Proposition 2 continues to hold if all other things remain as before except that the elasticity of demand in the peak period is smaller than before relative to that in the off-peak period.

Proof Under Ramsey pricing such a change never reduces the ratio of peak price to off-peak price relative to the ratio of their marginal costs.

3   Cases Where Peak Pricing Can Be a Pareto Improvement

The results of the preceding section immediately suggest conditions under which the usual presumption may be violated, that is, circumstances in which the shift from uniform to peak pricing may be able to benefit the peak user, even in the classical model in which there are no congestion costs.

Three possibilities immediately follow from our propositions:

(a) If there are diseconomies of scale in the construction of capacity and they are sufficiently strong, then a decrease in *relative off*-peak price that is able to reduce peak demand eliminates the need for the most costly portion of capacity and so it may reduce total cost by so large an amount that even the optimal *peak* price may fall below the uniform price.

(b) This may also occur when the total cost of capacity construction is so high that a zero off-peak price violates the budget constraint because maximal peak revenue is less than the corresponding construction cost. In that case, if the uniform price lies in the elastic portion of the off-peak demand curve, a reduction in off-peak price will increase the revenue contributed by that period and permit a simultaneous reduction in the peak price.

(c) If returns to scale in construction are increasing, then Ramsey optimal prices will generally exceed the corresponding marginal costs. If peak demand is highly elastic relative to off-peak demand, the peak Ramsey price will tend to be close to marginal cost and, hence, below the average cost, which equals the uniform price. However, as we shall see later, in this case the shift to peak pricing is unlikely to constitute a Pareto improvement since while the change will benefit peak users, off-peak customers can be expected to lose out because their price will then have to exceed average cost if the activity is not to lose money.

Let us, therefore, turn next to a detailed discussion of the two cases: diseconomies of scale in construction, and very high total cost of construction, in which adoption of peak pricing can constitute a Pareto improvement.

4   Pareto Improvement under Scale Diseconomies

To analyze the role of scale diseconomies it is useful to deal with the special case in which total quantity demanded in the two periods is fixed. Let us call the periods 1 and 2, to avoid prejudging which of them is the peak period, for reasons that will soon be clear. Let y_i represent quantity demanded in period i, so that $y_1 + y_2 = $ constant.

In figure 8.1a, CC' depicts the total cost, $C(y_p)$, of capacity construction as a function of y_p, where $y_p = \max(y_1, y_2)$ is quantity demanded in the peak period. It obviously satisfies $C'' > 0$ throughout and therefore involves diseconomies of scale.

Figure 8.1b shows the cross section of the total cost function above the line segment AB representing $y_1 + y_2 = b$. In the diagram the 45° ray, OR, is the boundary line between the regions in which period 1 is the peak period and that in which 2 is the peak. For at a point like W, to the left of OR, where $y_1 > y_2$, period 1 is the peak, and the opposite is true at a point such as V.

Now, on the cross-section plane $ABDE$ above AB we reproduce our total cost curve CC' from figure 8.1a and also draw in its mirror image, $C_m C_m'$, as shown. The two curves will meet at the midpoint e directly above OR. Then the cross section of the total cost surface, which we are seeking, is the heavy curve $C_m' e C'$. To see this consider any point, such as U, on the cross

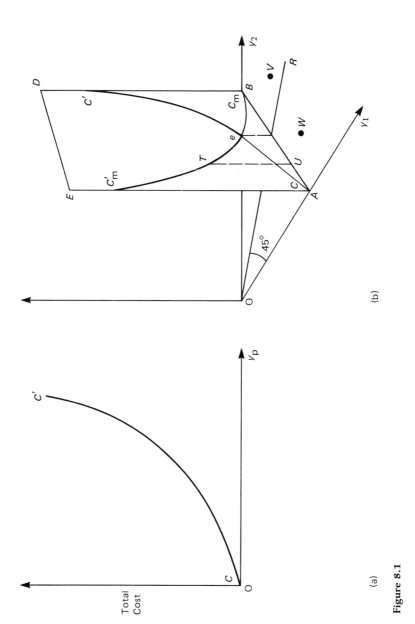

(a)

(b)

Figure 8.1

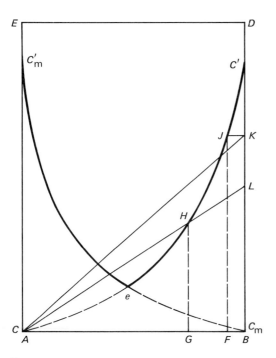

Figure 8.2

section AB. At U we have $y_1 > y_2$ so that $y_p = y_1$ and the relevant peak output must be measured leftward from point B. Hence $C_m C'_m$ is the relevant cost curve and the total cost is given by point T on eC'_m. We can now prove geometrically (and shall later show more formally)

Proposition 3   If scale diseconomies in construction are sufficiently strong and the cross-elasticity of peak demand with respect to off-peak price is sufficient, then a change from uniform to peak pricing can be a Pareto improvement.

Proof   Figure 8.2 reproduces cross-section plane $ABDE$ in two-dimensional space. Here, if the same price is charged in the two periods, let the quantity, AF, be demanded in the peak period. Under peak pricing let peak demand fall to AG with the remainder going to the off-peak period. Then, in the figure, even if the Ramsey optimal off-peak price is zero, so that the entire cost is borne by peak users, the peak price, given by the slope of AH, is less than the uniform price

$$p_u = C(y_p)/(y_1 + y_2) = BK/AB = \text{slope of } AK.$$

We see that a sufficient (but not a necessary) condition for Ramsey pricing to constitute a Pareto improvement is that the uniform price p_u be higher than the new capacity cost divided by peak demand. The peak price p_p under Ramsey pricing is never higher than the Ramsey capacity cost, GH, divided by the corresponding peak demand, AG. Thus, in terms of figure 8.2 a sufficient condition for Ramsey pricing to be a Pareto improvement over uniform pricing is that point K lie above point L.

The relation of the peak price p_p to the uniform price p_u depends on two effects of the change in price regime: (1) the effect on total capacity cost of the resulting change in peak quantity demanded; and (2) the reaction of peak quantity demanded to the change in prices. The stronger the diseconomies of scale and the more sensitive peak demand is with respect to the off-peak price, the greater will be the reduction in capacity cost, and thus the more likely it is that the peak price will be less than the uniform price.

To show the role of the degree of scale economies formally, we write

$$\frac{\partial \pi}{\partial p_o} = \frac{\partial R}{\partial p_o} - \frac{\partial C}{\partial p^o} = \frac{\partial}{\partial p_o}(p_p y_p + p_o y_o) - \frac{\partial C}{\partial p_o}$$

$$= p_p \frac{\partial y_p}{\partial p_o} + y_o + p_o \frac{\partial y_o}{\partial p_o} - \frac{\partial C}{\partial y_p}\frac{\partial y_p}{\partial p_o}$$

(here, p_p is held constant as p_o changes).

The degree of scale economies in capacity construction is given by

$$S = \left(\frac{\partial C / C}{\partial y_p / y_p}\right)^{-1}.$$

Assume that peak demand, y_p, is inelastic with respect to its own price, p_p, so that an increase in p_p increases revenue and, thus, profit. Then a reduction of p_o is a Pareto improvement if

$$\frac{\partial \pi}{\partial p_o} < 0,$$

so that a reduction of p_o increases profits and therefore requires a simultaneous reduction of p_p to restore profits to zero. This will be so if

$$p_p \frac{\partial y_p}{\partial p_o} + y_o + p_o \frac{\partial y_o}{\partial p_o} - \frac{\partial C}{\partial y_p}\frac{\partial y_p}{\partial p_o} < 0,$$

or

$$S \equiv \left(\frac{y_p}{C}\frac{\partial C}{\partial y_p}\right)^{-1} < \frac{C}{y_p}\left\{p_p + \left(y_o + p_o\frac{\partial y_o}{\partial p_o}\right)\frac{\partial p_o}{\partial y_p}\right\}^{-1} ;$$

i.e., the switch to peak pricing will be a Pareto improvement if diseconomies of scale are sufficiently strong.

5 The Case Where a Zero Off-Peak Price Loses Money

Next, we come to the possibility in the classical peak pricing model that a switch to peak pricing will be a Pareto improvement because capacity is so expensive that a Ramsey off-peak price must be positive and off-peak revenues are then greater than those under uniform prices, so that peak prices can be correspondingly lower. As we shall see now, this is not a pathological case but is, rather, a possibility that is plausible whenever capacity is sufficiently costly.

To analyze this issue we use a graphic device previously explored by Thijs ten Raa and ourselves for other purposes (see Baumol, Fischer, and ten Raa [1979]). This is the price-isoprofit locus, which shows for a multi-product firm all price combinations for the various products that yield some given level of profit—in this case, zero economic profit. Figure 8.3 shows a typical curve of this sort.

Here we see that the curve typically has a vertical point, V, and a horizontal point, H, between which the slope of the locus is negative. Along arc VH both demands are, presumably, inelastic and, in any event, a rise in either price raises total profit, π. Therefore, if p_1 is raised, to keep π constant p_2 must be decreased, giving us the negative slope of VH. At point H we reach the value of p_1 beyond which $\partial\pi/\partial p_1 < 0$ and so the effect on π of a further rise in p_1 must be offset by a *rise* in p_2. The slope of HE is therefore positive. Beyond price p_{1e} product 1 is priced out of the market completely, so that further rises in p_1 do not affect π and, hence, no offsetting variation in p_2 is required to keep π constant. Thus, EW is horizontal. The explanations of the positively sloping arc VS and of the vertical segment, ST, above S, are similar.

The welfare-maximizing Ramsey solution—the peak–off-peak prices—will always lie at a point such as p on the negatively sloping arc, VH, because otherwise it is possible to reduce one price without raising the other and without reducing profits, thus benefiting some consumers without harming anyone else.

The locus of uniform prices is, of course, the $45°$ ray, OR, so that the uniform price that yields zero profit is given by point U. Thus, our objective is to compare the uniform price point, U, with p, the peak pricing point,

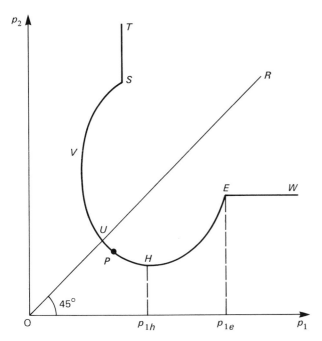

Figure 8.3

to see whether p can ever lie below and to the left of U so that p is then a Pareto improvement over U. As we shall see, this may indeed be the case, provided the cost of capacity construction, k, is sufficiently high.

To show the logic of the relationship explicitly the remainder of the graphic analysis will be based on a specific numerical example, in which we are given the demand and cost functions from which the Ramsey optimal and the uniform price solution can be determined, and the relevant price-isoreturn loci can be derived.

Let us assume that the market involves just two independent linear demand functions,

$$p_1 = 1 - y_1 \qquad \text{for period 1}$$

and

$$p_2 = a - by_2 \qquad \text{for period 2.}$$

These are depicted in figure 8.4 for the values $a = 0.75$, $b = 1.25$ (thus, $a/b = 0.6$), which will be used throughout the illustrations of this section.

Price space (figures 8.3 and 8.5) can be divided into two regions: one in which period 1 is the peak period because $y_1 > y_2$, and one in which 2 is

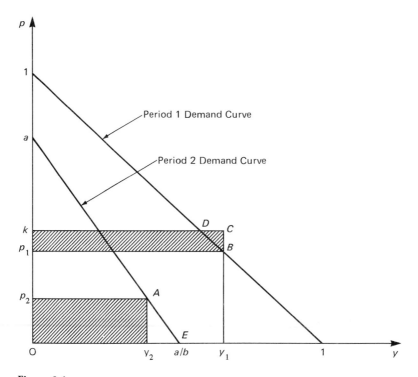

Figure 8.4

the peak period. They are separated by a line of price combinations at which $y_1 = y_2$, yielding for the borderline the equation

$$p_1 = (1 - a/b) + p_2/b,$$

or

$$p_1 = 0.4 + 0.8p_2 \qquad \text{for the given example (line } VR \text{ in figure 8.5).}$$

We continue to assume that operating costs are zero,[3] capacity costs are k per unit of peak output, and investment proceeds to the point that involves exactly zero excess capacity. Then,

$$C = k \max(y_1, y_2).$$

Let us now explain the variation in the price-isoprofit locus with various different values of average capacity costs, k. This locus is, in general, composed of two segments of different ellipses, one of which lies in region

---

3. That is, we consider only the *difference* between price and operating costs.

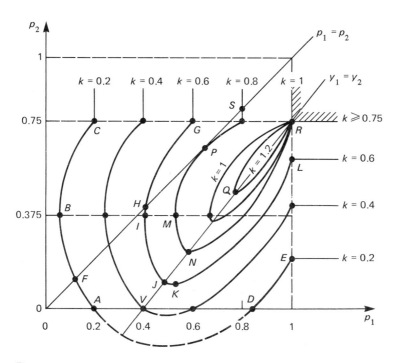

Figure 8.5

1 where $y_1 > y_2$, and the other in region 2, where $y_2 > y_1$, as we shall see now. We first consider region 1.

The condition that profit of the firm is equal to zero implies that any gain resulting from an increase of the off-peak price above zero must be exactly offset by a loss from a reduction of the peak price down from average capacity cost k. Thus, in figure 8.4 if period 2 price were to rise from zero to p_2, period 1 price must fall from k to p_1.

This implies that Oy_2Ap_2 (the profit earned during the off-peak period) and p_1BCk (peak period demand multiplied by the loss per unit produced at a price below capacity cost), the two shaded areas in figure 8.4, must be identical, i.e., that

$$p_2y_2 = (k - p_1)y_1,$$

or

$$p_2(a - p_2)/b = (k - p_1)(1 - p_1). \tag{8.4}$$

This, then, is the equation of the price-isoreturn locus in region 1.

In region 2, we have, similarly, the locus

$$p_1(1 - p_1) = (k - p_2)(a - p_2)/b. \tag{8.5}$$

Solving for p, we find for regions 1 and 2, respectively,

$$p_1 = \frac{k+1}{2} \pm \sqrt{\left(\left(\frac{k-1}{2}\right)^2 + p_2(a - p_2)/b\right)} \tag{8.4'}$$

and

$$p_1 = \tfrac{1}{2} \pm \sqrt{(\tfrac{1}{4} + (p_2 - k)(a - p_2)/b)}. \tag{8.5'}$$

In region 1, p_1 attains its minimum value where $p_2 = a/2$, i.e., where the maximum amount of revenue is gained from period 2 sales, as is to be expected. Similarly, in region 2, p_2 is lowest when $p_1 = \tfrac{1}{2}$, yielding the maximum revenue from period 1 sales. Figure 8.5 shows the price-isoprofit curves which yield zero profit for various values of average capacity cost, k.

The optimal peak-off peak price combination (i.e., that which maximizes consumers' surplus, producers' surplus being zero) is

$$(p_1, p_2) = (k, 0)$$

if that price vector lies on the isoprofit locus $\pi = 0$.[4] If at the price vector $(k, 0)$ $\pi < 0$, then the welfare-maximizing price combination is that at which[5] $y_1 = y_2$.

The feasible price combinations shown in figure 8.5 illustrate the following typical behavior: When average capacity cost is relatively small ($k \leqslant 0.4$ in this example), the welfare-maximizing price vector is $(p_1, p_2) = (k, 0)$, for example, point A for $k = 0.2$.

But from this point it is possible to trade off some efficiency in order to share some of the gain with period 1 consumers. For the peak price, p_1, can be reduced if the off-peak price, p_2, is increased, up to the value $p_2 = a/2 = 0.375$, where p_1 attains its minimum (point B). If p_2 is increased

---

4. That must be true because in this case peak demand, y_1, is greater than off-peak demand, y_2. A positive price to off-peak consumers will in that case reduce off-peak consumers' surplus by area $OEAp_2$ in figure 8.4, which is greater than Oy_2Ap_2. It will increase peak consumers' surplus by p_1BDk in figure 8.4, which is less than p_1BCk. Since, by construction, the two shaded rectangles in figure 8.4 have the same area, any increase of the off-peak price to a value greater than zero must yield a net welfare loss to consumers. Thus, the optimal prices must be $p_1 = k$, $p_2 = 0$, as we wished to show.

5. This must be true whenever construction cost is the only component of cost and there are constant returns to scale in construction. For the standard model then yields $p_t = MOC_t + V_t$, $V_t(K - y_t) = 0$, where p_t is price in period t, K is capacity, and $MOC_t = 0$ is marginal operating cost in period t. Thus, for all periods, s, for which $p_s = V_s \neq 0$ we must have $y_s = K$, i.e., outputs in all such periods must equal the same number, K.

further, then revenue earned during the off-peak period, 2, drops (since off-peak demand now enters its elastic domain), and p_1 must rise again, as occurs on arc BC. There also exists a set of price combinations (arc DE) with a very high value of p_1, where $y_2 > y_1$ and thus total capacity cost is proportionate to y_2. In that domain, both p_1 and p_2 are higher than they are at point A.

For larger values of average capacity cost ($k > 0.4166$ in this example), the price-isoprofit locus no longer cuts the horizontal axis. Thus, there is no value of p_1 for which $p_2 = 0$ satisfies $\pi \geq 0$. Therefore, it is necessary for financial feasibility that both $p_1 > 0$ and $p_2 > 0$. When $p_1 = 0$, demand in period 2 is so low that there does not exist any p_2 for which period 2 revenue can cover capacity costs. Similarly, if $p_2 = 0$, no value of p_1 can recoup costs. In this case both peak and off-peak users must make a financial contribution if the cost of capacity is to be covered. Consequently, the efficient Ramsey price will be positive, even in the off-peak period. For example, for $k = 0.6$ the off-peak price p_2 is lowest when $p_1 = 0.5$ (point K), at which peak revenue reaches its maximum. Pareto optimal price vectors lie on the arc IJK. The uniform price vector (point H) no longer lies on this arc for $k > 0.5550$.

We have already seen that if in the optimal solution (involving the optimal choice of capacity) $y_1 > y_2$ then $p_2 = 0$ must be optimal if it is consistent with $\pi \geq 0$. On the other hand, we saw that if $p_2 = 0$ is inconsistent with $\pi \geq 0$, then, as was shown in footnote 5, $y_1 = y_2$ in our model. Hence the locus of Ramsey points for different values of k must be the kinked line OVR.

Most important for our purposes is the fact that if $k > 0.75$, the uniform price, if it is feasible (point P for $k = 0.8$), is Pareto inferior to the Ramsey price vector (point N)—since N lies below and to the left of P. Thus, we have proved

Proposition 4 If the cost of construction of capacity is sufficiently high, a change from a uniform price to optimal peak pricing can be a Pareto improvement.

When average capacity cost is sufficiently high ($k > 0.8$ in this example), then a uniform price is not only Pareto inferior to price vectors on segment MN, but it implies that off-peak demand must be completely priced out of the market (for example, at point S in figure 8.5).

As average capacity cost increases further ($k \geq 1.075$ in this example), the negatively sloping set of relevant points of the price-isoreturn locus collapses into a single point (Q for $k = 1.2$). As long as $k < 1.8$, positive equal outputs in both periods are financially feasible. For $k = 1.8$, $y_1 = y_2 = 0$ (at point R in figure 8.5).

For our purposes one of the main conclusions to be drawn from this discussion is that even if there are constant returns to scale and optimal off-peak price equals zero (or, more generally, it equals marginal operating cost), a trade-off between equity and efficiency will normally be possible. That is, some welfare loss can be tolerated in exchange for a sharing of the benefits of peak pricing between peak and off-peak users (for example, the move from point A to point F in figure 8.5).

Perhaps more important for our discussion is the emergence of cases in which the optimal price vector, for example, point N, is Pareto superior to the uniform price vector, P. This possibility arises because the average cost of capacity is so high relative to the reservation price of peak users that a zero off-peak price is not feasible financially. Then the revenue contributed by off-peak users under peak pricing may exceed the amount they contribute under their (higher) uniform price, so that the optimal peak price may also be lower than the uniform price.

In sum, we have shown that in the classical peak pricing model there are at least two cases in which peak pricing can be Pareto superior to uniform pricing: that in which there are diseconomies of scale in capacity construction, and that in which average capacity cost is so high relative to peak-period reservation price that a zero off-peak price is incompatible with the budget constraint.

6   A Ramsey Congestion Model

In reality, peak period pricing is often relevant to a situation somewhat different from that most usually dealt with in the standard models, in which the only objective is to save construction cost. In the cases to which we turn next, involving heavily traveled roads or other facilities whose customers are forced to queue or to suffer other discomforts at the times when quantity demanded is greatest, a switch from uniform pricing to an arrangement with a price higher than the uniform price at the peak hour is likely to decrease the disutility (and perhaps the time cost) of congestion in the peak period. Then, peak pricing may conceivably be beneficial to the peak period consumer, even if it raises the price he pays, if this is more than offset by the resulting reduction in the disutility to him caused by peak period congestion. Let us, then, construct a peak pricing model in which congestion is explicitly taken into account.

If we divide the 24 hour day into t^* fixed periods, we can define an off-peak period, t, to be one in which an increase in consumption, dy_t, does not increase congestion, $c(y_t)$. Any other period is defined as a peak period. For simplicity, we take all (noncongestion) costs to be fixed and hence unaffected by number of consumers in any period. This does not affect the analysis in any essential way. Assume now that a fixed price, p_t, is charged per unit consumed in period t, with a budget requirement that these yield at least some fixed total revenue, B. To determine the prices that are Pareto optimal subject to this constraint, let us use the following notation:

y_{it} = (expected) travel by person i ($i = 1, \ldots, n$) in period t,

c_t = a measure of congestion (for example, delay time) in period t,

$c_t = G^t(\sum_j y_{jt})$ is the delay function, where

$$G'' = 0, \quad G'(\cdot) = 0 \text{ if } \sum_j y_{jt} < y^*, \qquad G''(\cdot) > 0 \text{ otherwise}, \qquad (8.6)$$

$u_i = U^i(y_{i1}, \ldots, y_{it}, c_1, \ldots, c_t, x_i)$ is i's utility function, where x_i is the vector of all other pertinent variables (for example, consumption of other goods),

P_t = toll charge in period t,

$R^t = \sum_i p_t y_{it}$ = total revenue in period t, and

B = required toll revenue.

Then the objective is to determine

$\max U^1(\cdot)$

subject to

$$U^i(\cdot) \geqslant k_i \qquad (i = 2, \ldots, n), \tag{8.7}$$

$$c_t = G^t(\cdot) \qquad (t = 1, \ldots, t^*), \tag{8.8}$$

$$R \equiv \sum \sum p_t y_{jt} \geqslant B. \tag{8.9}$$

We have the Lagrangian

$$L = \sum \lambda_j [U^j(\cdot) - k_j] + \sum \lambda_t [c_t - G^t(\cdot)] + \lambda(R - B).$$

Writing $U^i_{y_{it}}$ for $\delta U^i/\delta y_{it}$, etc., we obtain the following Kuhn-Tucker conditions:

$$L_{y_{it}} = \lambda_i U^i_{y_{it}} - \lambda_t G^t_{y_{it}} + \lambda R_{y_{it}} = 0 \qquad \text{for} \quad y_{it} > 0, \tag{8.10}$$

$$L_{c_t} = \sum_j \lambda_j U^j_{c_t} + \lambda_t \leqslant 0, \qquad c_t \left(\sum_j \lambda_j U^j_{c_t} + \lambda_t \right) = 0, \tag{8.11}$$

plus conditions (8.7)–(8.9) and the corresponding complementary slackness conditions. To induce consumers to behave in a manner consistent with these conditions we can set $p_t = \lambda_i U^i_{y_{it}}$, giving us, by (8.10),

$$P_t = \lambda_t G^t_{y_{it}} - \lambda R_{y_{it}}. \tag{8.12}$$

By (8.6) an off-peak period is one in which $\sum_i y_{it} < y^*$, and for such a period, by definition, marginal congestion cost $G^t_{y_{it}} = 0$, so that the first right-hand-side term in (8.12) must then be zero. Thus, for an off-peak period we shall have $p_t = -\lambda R_{y_{it}}$, which means that off-peak prices will vary proportionately with marginal revenues. For peak periods, on the other hand, $c_t > 0$, so that by (8.11) $\lambda_t = -\sum \lambda_j U^j_{c_t}$, and therefore (8.12) can be written

$$p_t = -\left(\sum_j \lambda_j U^j_{c_t}\right)G^t_{y_{it}} - \lambda R_{y_{it}}. \tag{8.13}$$

Using the dual-variable interpretation of λ_i as $\partial U^1/\partial U^i$, this can be rewritten as

$$p_t = -\sum_j \frac{\partial U^1}{\partial U^j}\frac{\partial U^j}{\partial c_t}\frac{\partial c_t}{\partial y_{it}} - \lambda R_{y_{it}}. \tag{8.14}$$

Here, the first term on the right-hand side can be interpreted as the marginal social congestion cost of an increase in y_{it}. That is, it is the disutility (measured in terms of the utility function of the arbitrarily chosen individual 1) of the increased congestion resulting from a small increase in quantity demanded by individual i in period t.

In sum, the peak period toll called for by Ramsey optimality is equal to marginal congestion cost (disutility) minus a (Ramsey) adjustment quantity strictly proportionate to marginal revenue. Here it will be noted that $-\lambda$, the factor of proportionality, is identical for all periods, peak and off-peak.

The solution corresponding to conditions (8.12) and (8.14) can be contrasted with that under uniform pricing. We obtain

Proposition 5   If there is a peak period, r, and an off-peak period, s, in which elasticities of demand (and marginal costs)[6] are equal, then the peak period's Ramsey price will be at least as high as that of the off-peak period.

---

6. Note again that for simplicity we have assumed all input costs to be fixed. If this is not so, it is easy to show that (8.12) must be replaced by

$$p_t = MC_{y_{it}} + \lambda_t G^t_{y_{it}} - \lambda(R_{y_{it}} - MC_{y_{it}}), \tag{8.12'}$$

where $MC_{y_{it}}$ is marginal (noncongestion) cost of another unit of output in period t.

Proof P_r is given directly by (8.12), while p_s satisfies (8.12) with $\lambda_s G^s_{y_{is}} = 0$. Since by the Kuhn-Tucker theorem $\lambda_r \geqslant 0$ and $G^r_{y_{ir}} > 0$, by definition of the peak period, the result follows.

Corollary If demand elasticities and marginal costs are equal for all periods at the Ramsey solution point and total output and total cost are the same under the Ramsey solution and the uniform price solution, then the average Ramsey peak price must exceed the uniform price.

Proof By Proposition 5

$$p_r \geqslant p_s \qquad \text{(for any peak period, } r, \text{ and any off-peak period, } s). \qquad (8.15)$$

But the uniform price, p_u, must satisfy

$$p_u = B/\sum\sum y_{it}(p_u),$$

[where $y_{it}(p_u)$ is the quantity of y demanded by i in period t at price p_u], while the Ramsey prices must satisfy

$$\sum\sum p_r y_{ir} + \sum\sum p_s y_{is} = B$$

or

$$\bar{p}_r \sum\sum y_{ir} + \sum\sum p_s y_{is} = B,$$

where $\bar{p}_r \equiv \sum\sum p_r y_{ir}/\sum\sum y_{ir}$ is defined as the average Ramsey peak price, and the y_{ir} and y_{is} are, respectively, the peak and off-peak outputs in the Ramsey solution. The last relationship together with (8.15) and the assumed constancy of total output yield

$$\bar{p}_r \sum\sum(y_{ir} + y_{is}) = \bar{p}_r \sum\sum y_{it}(p_u) \geqslant B = p_u \sum\sum y_{it}(p_u)$$

or

$$\bar{p}_r \geqslant p_u.$$

7 Differences in Preference for Avoidance of Congestion

The congestion version of the peak-load pricing model provides a paradoxical case which is nevertheless of substantial practical importance. The basic point that emerges has been observed before, but its interpretation as a generalized peak-load pricing issue and the observations about its relation to fairness seem not to have been offered previously. Assume that none of the affected periods have zero congestion. Then we shall show

Proposition 6   Other things being equal, efficiency may require prices in the less congested periods to be higher than those in more congested periods and this result can be fair in the sense that it constitutes a Pareto improvement over uniform pricing.

The explanation is simple and is best described by example. Assume that there are, for instance, three times a day at which a trip can occur (say, three trains per day); that a typical traveler does not prefer one to another of these times, per se; and that with equal prices that just yield a total revenue equal to the total cost of the three trains' operations, each would be equally congested, as measured, for example, by the number of travelers standing in the aisles. Suppose, moreover, that travelers differ in their marginal rates of substitution between discomfort on the train and consumption of other goods, i.e., between comfort and income. Then an incremental change in prices, raising that in one of the periods, arbitrarily chosen, reducing that in another, and leaving the third unchanged can increase total welfare. This will certainly be true if the number of passengers on the train with the unchanged fare were to remain constant, leaving that train with the same price-congestion combination as before. Because, then, the most expensive train will become the least congested, its passengers having revealed a preference for the combination of its higher fare and reduced congestion over the uniform price-congestion pattern that is still available to any one of them. The analogous conclusion follows for the train with the reduced fare, whose congestion level will have risen. With the range of choices increased and the initial price-congestion option not foreclosed, everyone must benefit, and they will benefit from prices that decrease monotonically with the degree of congestion. This completes the proof of proposition 6.

More generally,

Proposition 7   The efficient price must be higher in the less congested period if (a) congestion incurs a social cost; (b) there are several periods in which congestion will be approximately the same if their prices are equal; (c) a *ceteris paribus* rise in the price during any period reduces quantity demanded in that period, and, hence, its congestion; and (d) the subjective trade-off between congestion and income differs from person to person.

Proof   By (d) Pareto optimal prices will, generally, not be the same in all periods, and by conditions (b) and (c) the optimal price must be higher in any particular period the lower the level of its congestion.

This would seem to violate the Pigouvian requirement that price be equal to marginal social cost[7] including the marginal social damage caused by the incremental crowding when another passenger boards the train. But this is not so. The self-sorting of passengers among trains means that those on the least crowded train will be those who are particularly sensitive to crowding, or particularly rich, and to whom such incremental damage consequently has a higher marginal disutility in money terms (a higher MRS between crowding and money). If p_s is higher than p_t we can expect y_s to include only persons, i, whose $\partial U_i / \partial y_s$ (i.e., whose sensitivity to crowding) is sufficiently great so that the necessary condition for optimality is satisfied. Thus, even though congestion will be lower in s than in t, if private marginal costs in the two periods are the same, the *marginal* congestion damage and, consequently, the Pigouvian price, will be higher in s than in t.

For our purposes, the interesting conclusion to be drawn from this case is not the paradoxical appearance of the peak, off-peak prices. Rather, what is relevant (and apparently novel) is the likelihood that the adoption of peak pricing in these circumstances will constitute a Pareto improvement.

8   Pricing Reversals and Pricing Benefits to Peak Users in the Peak Pricing Model

It is not only where congestion is present that optimal prices may be lower in the more crowded period, though such cases in the standard peak pricing model seem likely to be more uncommon than in the congestion case. We shall show now

Proposition 8   Where there are scale economies in construction of capacity, the Ramsey deviation between price and marginal cost required for financial viability may lead to an optimal peak price lower than the off-peak price, with the latter higher than the uniform break-even price. Hence, even where the peak price is below the uniform price in this case, the adoption of peak pricing need not be a Pareto improvement.

Proof   Though we shall deal with a limiting case, we shall see that the

---

7. For simplicity, this assumes implicitly that constant returns to scale hold, locally, at the equilibrium point so that (social) marginal cost (Pigouvian) pricing just covers total cost. Where this is not true Pigouvian taxes must be changed into Ramsey-Pigou taxes, so that after-tax prices are Pareto optimal under the constraint that total cost must equal total revenue.

demonstrated possibility may arise under a wider range of parameter values.

We again assume for simplicity that there are no operating costs, and that total cost is given by

$$F + wy_p, \qquad w \text{ constant,}$$

where

F is the (constant) fixed cost,

y_p and y_o are the outputs under peak pricing, and

$y_{pu} > y_{ou}$ are the outputs under uniform pricing.

Assume also that $y_p + y_o = y_{pu} + y_{ou}$. Then using MC and MR to represent marginal cost and revenue, respectively, we have for the peak and off-peak periods

$$MC_p = w, \qquad MC_o = 0,$$

so that the Ramsey peak and off-peak prices must, by the usual formula, satisfy

$$p_p - w = k(MR_p - w), \qquad p_o = k\,MR_o, \qquad p_p y_p + p_o y_o = F + wy_p.$$

Suppose $MR_p \cong w$. Then $p_p \cong w$ and so

$$wy_p + p_o y_o \cong F + wy_p$$

or

$$p_o \cong F/y_o \geqslant 2F/(y_p + y_o)$$
$$= 2F/(y_{pu} + y_{ou}).$$

But the uniform break-even price must satisfy

$$p_u(y_{pu} + y_{ou}) = F + wy_{pu},$$

so that for w sufficiently small

$$p_u \cong F/(y_{pu} + y_{ou}) \leqslant p_o/2, \qquad p_p \cong w \cong 0;$$

that is, for F sufficiently large we obtain

$$p_p < p_u < p_o.$$

An example that corresponds to such a situation may be the construction by a club of a shared facility, such as a swimming pool. Suppose that at slight additional cost the pool can be built large enough to be opened up to the local community when it is not used by the swimming club. If, as is plausible, demand by the community were much more elastic than that of club members, then Ramsey pricing would assign most of the higher fixed construction costs to club members, and they would then pay more, even though at the time it was reserved for members they did not use the pool to its full capacity.

It follows that, in such cases, despite the fact that the optimal peak price is less than the uniform price, the adoption of peak pricing does not constitute a Pareto improvement, since off-peak users lose out in the process. This will be true whenever the adoption of Ramsey optimal peak pricing permits only a small reduction in total construction cost, so that any resulting price reduction to peak users must, for financial viability, be offset by an increase in payments by off-peak users.

9   Conclusions: Potential Unfairness of Peak Pricing

Having completed the formal analysis, we conclude with some informal comments on the fairness of peak pricing. We have found that the adoption of a peak pricing policy can, in a considerable variety of cases, prove to be a Pareto improvement, contrary to what seems generally to be believed on the subject. But there also is a wide range of possible cases in which the change does not constitute a Pareto improvement. What can we conclude about its fairness?

First, we may note that even in some of the cases in which the adoption of peak pricing is a Pareto improvement, many people may in practice consider it to be grossly inequitable. We have seen that where a high price is adopted for a peak period in order to produce an uncrowded enclave for those who care enough and can afford to pay the premium, everyone may well benefit. Those who live with the congestion may prefer the reduction in the price they pay and those who pay the higher price may prefer the associated protection from crowding. But such an arrangement may be considered elitist and arouse feelings of jealousy and indignation. Not everyone approves of the availability of first class accommodations on subways (as on the Paris Metro) or evenings with a specially high admission price to a museum. Whether one should regard this reaction as a dog in the manger attitude or as a desire to preserve group morale and thus to keep the social fabric intact (treating it as a public good or a beneficial externality) is not for an economist to judge. But it should be noted that such an attitude is neither necessarily perverse nor irrational. It is as defensible as universal rejection of the arrangement under which a draftee in wartime can "buy" a substitute recruit to take his place in the army, as was permitted during the Civil War. Everyone may rationally prefer a society in which such "buying" is prohibited, even those who would take advantage of the opportunity to buy a substitute draftee or to become one, if the practice were to become legal again, over their objections.[8]

Next, let us consider cases in which the adoption of peak pricing is not a Pareto improvement. In many such cases the presumption of unfairness is exacerbated by the possibility that those who lose will be members of lower income groups and that no good substitute for peak use will be available to them. Thus, consider the proposal that a high price for public transportation be instituted during the peak hours. If most travelers during this period are wage earners, and if their work hours are beyond their control, then the sufficient conditions for presumptive unfairness may, indeed, be satisfied. It is the poorer travelers who may bear the losses generated by the peak pricing program, and they may have no place else to turn.

It may be noted that, ultimately, the principle under question is Ramsey pricing itself, with its propensity to let purchasers with inelastic demands bear the bulk of the burden of unattributable costs. For inelasticity of demand *is* often ascribable to the absence of a viable alternative for the consumer in question, so that he does, indeed, have no place else to turn.

Looked at in this way, the attitudes of the Members of Parliament (as reported in an English survey) who displayed no enthusiasm for peak pricing for public transportation (see chapter 1) becomes more understandable. Economists may still prefer to give priority to the efficiency considerations. But they can hardly claim that it is irrational for others to conclude that the inequities resulting from the adoption of peak pricing are not worth the efficiency gains.

---

8. It will be recalled that the same sort of issue arose in our discussion of legalized resale of ration permits in chapter 4.

9   The Output Distribution Frontier, Taxation, and Equality Goals*

It has long been suggested that moves toward equality can have serious disincentive effects and, after a point, lead to unacceptable losses in real income.[1] I shall now offer some theoretical grounds for believing that an approximation to equality achieved via the traditional instruments— transfer payments and progressive taxation—will cause an income loss far more serious than many of us have realized. I shall show that under a set of reasonable assumptions, any attempt to guarantee *absolute equality* of incomes using only progressive income taxes and transfers for the purpose *must, at least in theory, reduce society's output to zero*! However, I do *not* conclude from this that the search for very much increased equality is quixotic. Rather, this may be taken as a criticism of the means so far used for the purpose. What is called for is an exercise in imagination and ingenuity, to find some alternative ways to go about this quest. I shall then show explicitly and examine an alternative procedure that, theoretically, can achieve *any* desired degree of equality without necessarily exacting a serious loss in output, and shall end by discussing briefly the possibility of practical approximations to such an arrangement.

---

*Like all recent work on fairness and taxation the work in this chapter, while following a very different line, can be said in an important sense to flow from Mirrlees's classic article [1971].

1. For example, the disincentive effects of income equalization are recognized throughout the works of the utilitarians of the late nineteenth and early twentieth centuries, who tempered their egalitarian arguments accordingly. Even Karl Marx, who felt that under communism distribution could ultimately proceed in accord with the maxim, "From each according to his ability, to each according to his needs," concedes that in the early stages of communism when it is "... still stamped with the birth marks of the old society from whose womb it emerges," a worker will have to be paid in accord with his contribution: "The same amount of labour which he has given to society in one form he receives back in another" [1875, pp. 17, 18].

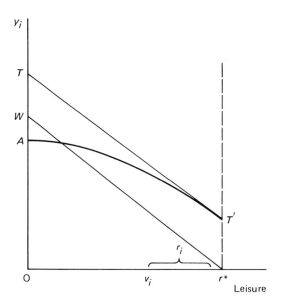

Figure 9.1

1 The High Output Cost of Equalization via Progressive Taxes and Transfers

This section will show that the use of progressive taxes and transfers to guarantee equality must threaten a startlingly great loss in the economy's output. For this purpose, we must first examine the nature of the individual's input supply choice—the trade-off between income y_i and unused input (leisure) $v_i = r_i^* = r_i$, where r_i^* is the total input quantity she has available, and r_i is the amount she actually supplies (her labor time). Figure 9.1 depicts a linear budget locus Wr^* representing individual i's trade-off between leisure v_i and income under a fixed wage rate w_i, per unit of input supplied. The equation of that locus is of course $y_i = w_i r_i^* - w_i v_i$. The second linear locus, TT', which is parallel to Wr^*, represents the result of a transfer WT to individual i, with no change in wage rate. Finally, the concave locus AT' is the result of a combined transfer plus a progressive tax on income which by definition extracts a larger percentage of y_i the higher the level of that income. This locus will, of course, differ from individual to individual, particularly if they do different types of work or differ in skill, or if they supply totally different inputs.

We can now proceed in the usual manner to see how such taxes and

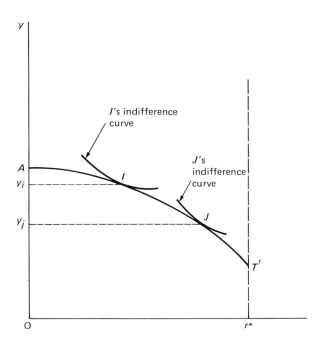

Figure 9.2

transfers affect the individual's income-leisure choice, and the degree of inequality of income distribution.[2]

The discussion assumes that, throughout the relevant range, no one is sated in either income or leisure. Consequently, it is assumed that any person's after-tax budget curve between income and retained input is nowhere positively sloping, since with no one sated in either income or retained inputs, all but the highest point on a positively sloping segment will be irrelevant.

Proposition 1   If different individuals have different budget curves between income and retained input (after transfers and taxes) or if they share a common budget curve that has a negative slope over any interval, then there exist utility functions for which the final distribution of income will be unequal.

The argument is trivial, and is illustrated in figure 9.2 with points *I* and *J*

---

2. Note that here we are seeking to approximate the issue as it is considered in reality by phrasing the analysis in terms of equality of (observable) money incomes rather than in terms of equality of subjective utilities.

the equilibria (with differing income levels y_i and y_j) of two individuals having the corresponding indifference curves. In the diagram they are assumed to face the same budget line in order to show that the problem arises even in this extreme case in which strong equalizing influences are built into the circumstances. A fortiori, the same conclusion *must* hold if their budget curves are (very) different—which is, of course, the major objection of egalitarians to current distribution arrangements.

Corollary to Proposition 1   In the large-number case[3] only a budget line that is the same for all individuals and is horizontal, that is, one that satisfies $y = k$, can guarantee equality of incomes.

Proposition 2   In an economy with a large number of persons, if individuals are not sated in incomes or retained input, and if zero input supplies yield zero output, then any system of progressive taxes and transfers that guarantees[4] equality of incomes must yield zero output in the economy.

That is, the egalitarian solution will not be feasible if any output is required for survival! The reason, of course, is that in the process of guaranteeing absolute equality, all incentive for supplying any input is removed.

Proof   Let r_i^* be the quantity of resource available to individual i, and let v_i be the amount that person retains for self-use. Then if (v_i', y) is any point on the income-retained input budget line, with $v_i' < r_i^*$, by the corollary to proposition 1, (r_i^*, y) will also lie on that budget line. But by the assumption of nonsatiety we must have, with utility function u^i, $u^i(r_i^*, y) > u^i(v_i', y)$; that is, the individual will always prefer to retain more of his in-

---

3. All the indifference curves here and in what follows will always be defined in terms of an individual's leisure and his *direct* after-tax income, assuming that the size of any transfer payment received by an individual is unaffected by the amount of labor he supplies. Any *indirect* effect of an individual's input supply on the size of the pool of total tax revenue and, through this, on the size of the transfer payment he receives, is not included. When the number m of individuals involved is small, this omission may not be justifiable since the $(1/m)$th of his tax contribution that flows back to him may not be negligible. But when the number of individuals is large, as it will be in any relevant situation in reality, this indirect effect must be negligible, and must be ignored, just as we always ignore the effect of the output of an individual supplier upon market price in a competitive industry. I am grateful to an anonymous referee for raising this issue.

4. Of course, in special situations such a guarantee is unnecessary. If, for example, everyone had equal abilities and identical utility functions, equal incomes would result without any transfer or progressive tax. A bit more will be said about such possibilities presently.

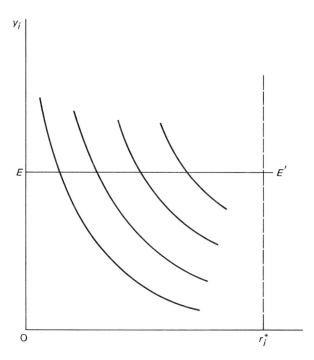

Figure 9.3

put. Consequently, that individual will always choose to supply the quantity of input $r_i = r_i^* - v_j = r_i^* - r_i^* = 0$. Since this also holds for every other individual in the economy, the economy's total output must be $y = 0$.

This is illustrated in figure 9.3, where by the nonsatiety assumption every indifference curve must have a negative slope and higher curves must be preferred to lower ones. Hence, with the horizontal budget line EE', which, by the corollary to proposition 1, is the only one that can guarantee equality of incomes under progressive taxation and transfers, the zero input supply point E' must always be optimal. This is the free-rider problem carried to its ultimate extreme.[5]

Of course, there may be special situations in which equality can be

---

5. Again note the free-rider problem (as always) is weaker in the small-numbers case. In a ten-person economy a work agreement may be reached even though payment is independent of productivity. This is, no doubt, part of the explanation of the success of the kibbutzim in Israel, where precisely that arrangement holds (see, for example, Barkai [1980]). But in the generally more relevant case of large numbers neither social pressure nor a significant marginal payoff to the individual from the contribution of his labor to the size of the total pie will serve to elicit labor from him.

achieved, using no more than taxes and transfers, without reducing output to zero. An obvious case, already noted, is that in which everyone's input supply function is identical and everyone's input of the same quality. A slightly less restrictive case is that in which input supply functions differ, but there exists a wage rate at which *everyone* supplies the same quantity of (homogeneous) input.

In an economy with many individuals such cases are extremely implausible. We may therefore postulate that *normally* there will be differences in input supply functions and input productivities sufficient to lead to the conclusion of propositions 1 and 2. That is, these differences will normally be sufficient to imply that only a uniform horizontal budget line can produce income equality via taxes and transfers, so that equality can only be achieved at the cost of reducing output to zero.

Let us make this assumption explicit—the premise that indifference curves in retained income-output space (or, equivalently, the income supply functions) of the m individuals are such that, whenever the tax schedule (AT' in figure 9.1) has a negatively sloping portion, there will be at least two individuals with different incomes. For brevity we shall refer to this as the *normal variation property*, meaning that variations in the abilities and utility functions of the members of the group are *normal*.

At this point it becomes useful to describe the trade-off between output and degree of equality employing a concept we shall call the *income distribution frontier*, which is a slight modification of the standard production-possibility locus. Our frontier represents the maximal vectors of *money incomes* that the economy can provide to the individuals who compose it. We find later that the position of this frontier will shift when there is a change in the means used to redistribute incomes.

In the two-person case, which we shall use for convenience in diagramming, this graph,[6] which may be written $y_2 = G(y_1)$, shows the maximal income available to individual 2, given the income provided to individual 1. The set of points in (y_1, y_2) space representing outputs that lie on or below and to the left of the boundary, we call the region of feasible incomes.

Proposition 3   If (i) only progressive taxes and transfers are used to redistribute incomes, (ii) the feasible region in y_i space is bounded, (iii) the derivatives of its boundary are continuous, and (iv) the normal variations

---

6. For an ingenious geometric construction that derives the boundary from two individuals' behavior and preference relations, see Wasow [1975].

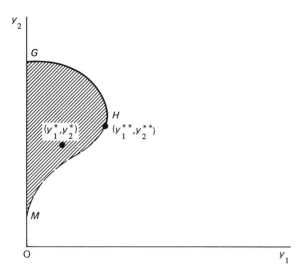

Figure 9.4

property holds, then a feasible region that contains any positive solution $y_1^* > 0$, $y_2^* > 0$ for any pair of individuals, 1, 2, must have a frontier that contains some positively sloping segment.

Proof By proposition 2 (and the normal variations property) the egalitarian solution must involve $y_1 = y_2 = 0$. Moreover, the boundary must contain a point (y_1^{**}, y_2^{**}) with $y_1^{**} \geqslant y_1^*$ and $y_2^{**} \geqslant y_2^*$. Hence, by continuity of derivatives, the segment of the frontier connecting $(y_1, y_2) = (0,0)$ and $(y_1, y_2) = (y_1^{**}, y_2^{**})$ must contain a positively sloping segment (MH in figure 9.4; shading indicates feasible region).

The reason for the positively sloping segment is not difficult to explain. With both individuals reduced to zero incomes by a tax arrangement that is absolutely egalitarian, there must in any viable community be an alternative tax arrangement that is at least slightly less egalitarian and that yields a nonzero income to each individual. This means that the move from the first to the second of these arrangements must increase the income of each individual, and hence the segment of the output distribution frontier connecting the two corresponding points will, on our continuity assumption, contain a positively sloping portion ($\Delta y_1 > 0$, $\Delta y_2 > 0$).

Corollary to Proposition 3 Using only progressive income taxes and transfers to redistribute incomes, the efficient set in (y_1, y_2) space must be discontinuous.

Proof   By proposition 2 the origin is an efficient point. Since no more than one point on a positively sloping segment of the boundary of the feasible region can be *efficient*, the result follows.

Thus, in figure 9.4, while $GHMO$ is the income distribution frontier, the efficient locus is composed of the segment GH together with the origin.

It should be noted that usually, starting from an initial point at which, say, $y_2 \geqslant y_1$, no normal system of income taxes and transfers will take us to a point at which $y_1 > y_2$. It follows that the feasible region will usually contain points on only one side of the line $y_1 = y_2$, as shown in figure 9.4.[7] That is, there is no way in which progressive taxes and transfers alone can produce an interchange in the position of the rich and the poor à la the Prince and the Pauper. The reason is that any taxes capable of producing such an interchange must constitute disincentives to labor even stronger than those necessary to yield perfect equality and so they too must disrupt the economy's productive process.

2   Digression: Goals Alternative to Perfect Equality

We can use our construction to examine the implications of some objectives other than perfect income equality under a regime of progressive taxes and transfers. We shall consider only three such goals, though others can easily be suggested:[8]

(1) Maximization of social output $y = \sum y_i$.

(2) Maximization of a social welfare function[9] $U(y_1, \ldots, y_m)$ (an "anti-poverty" welfare function), which gives weight to equalization of incomes by placing a greater value upon an increase in the income of a poor man. Thus, writing $U_i = \partial U / \partial y_i$, etc.,

---

7. For an effective analysis of a Rawlsian solution using the utility distribution frontier, depicting it as lying entirely on one side of the 45° ray, see Phelps [1973, section I]. For a simulation in utility space that contains such a frontier, showing it going through the origin at the 45° ray, see Cooter and Helpman [1974, figure I, p. 660].

8. Cooter and Helpman distinguish several other such criteria and show for each of them how the optimal position on the distribution frontier can be calculated. They include an elitist solution (maximal income to the most productive individual); the Benthamite solution, which maximizes the sum of utilities; the Nash solution, which maximizes their product; and the "democratic solution," which maximizes the income of the class of median ability. They also define an egalitarian solution that minimizes the Gini coefficient [1974, p. 658].

9. For sophisticated analyses of such optimal solutions, see, for example, Mirrlees [1971] and Wagstaff [1975].

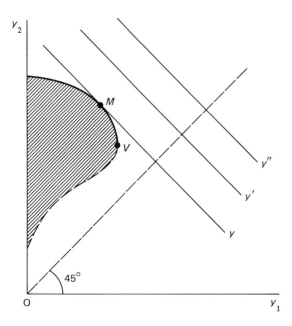

Figure 9.5

$$U_i = U_j \qquad \text{for} \quad y_i = y_j \qquad (i, j = 1, \ldots, m) \qquad\qquad (9.1)$$

and

$$U_{ii} < 0 \qquad (i = 1, \ldots, m). \qquad\qquad (9.2)$$

(3) Rawls's maximal-justice solution, which requires maximization of benefit to the individual who is in the most disadvantageous position.

The three solutions are readily depicted in figures 9.5–9.7. Figure 9.5 shows point M corresponding to y, the highest of the attainable isoincome loci $y_1 + y_2 = k$. This figure also depicts the 45° ray corresponding to absolutely equal distribution of incomes, showing that the only feasible point on this ray is the origin. Figure 9.6 depicts the point A that maximizes the welfare function[10] $U(\cdot)$, whose indifference curves I, I', and I'' are

---

10. The indifference curves I, I', and I'' of our social welfare function must have the curvature usually assumed of indifference curves. This follows by assumption (2) that the second partials U_{ii} of the welfare function are negative, if we also take the cross partials U_{ij}, $i \neq j$, all to be zero since the y_i for any individual i is independent of the earnings of any other individual. For along any indifference curve, where $U(\cdot) = k$, we have $dU = U_1\, dy_1 + U_2\, dy_2 = 0$, so that $dy_2/dy_1 = -U_1/U_2$. With $U_{21} = 0$, we then obtain $d^2y_2/dy_1^2 = -U_{11}/U_2 > 0$, giving the required curvature of the indifference curve.

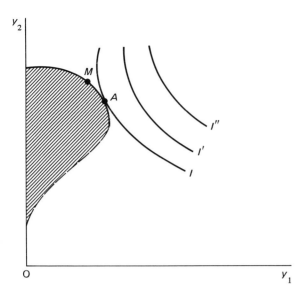

Figure 9.6

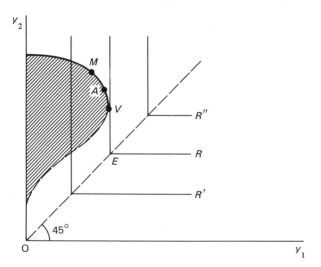

Figure 9.7

symmetric about the 45° ray because of the premise (1) that for equal incomes, $U_1 = U_2$. We would expect A to lie closer to the 45° line than M does. For the output-maximization solution (point M) requires (taking, for example, $y_2 > y_1$ as the case in the diagrams) $dy_2/dy_1 = -1$, while the welfare-maximization solution requires $dy_2/dy_1 = -U_1/U_2$, where, by (1) and (2), $|U_1/U_2| > 1$, since $y_2 > y_1$, so that *if the efficient locus is concave, A must lie closer than M to the vertical point V.*

Finally, figure 9.7, following Phelps, deals with the Rawlsian case. Rawls's criterion can be taken roughly to imply that a change is desirable if and only if it increases the income of the most impoverished individual in the community.[11] This yields a social welfare function whose indifference curves are essentially replications of the axes with the origin shifted outward along the 45° ray. For this tells us that starting from a point of equality such as E, a gain to either party *alone* is not an improvement. However, from any point (such as V) to the left of the 45° ray, where individual 1 has the lower income, any increase in 1's income alone gets us to a higher indifference curve.

Here we see that the Rawlsian solution will be given by the vertical point V on the boundary of the feasible set. It will be the most egalitarian point on the upper segment of the efficient locus, but from proposition 2 it follows that it will *not* be perfectly egalitarian when distribution is achieved by transfers and progressive taxes.

3   An Alternative Approach to Income Equalization

The main and most surprising result in our discussion so far is that with the methods of redistribution currently used, complete equalization of income would, at least in theory, bring the entire productive mechanism to a halt. One is led to surmise on a continuity assumption from this extreme case that very large output losses are also likely to accompany any attempt to get anywhere *very close* to equality.

All this is not meant to imply that equality of incomes, or some close approximation to it, is an impossible goal. Rather, it means that the methods we are currently using for the purpose, namely a combination of the progressive income tax and transfers, may simply not be up to the task,

---

11. Actually, the Rawlsian solution accepts as an improvement any change that benefits someone provided it does not harm any individual who is worse off than the beneficiary. But that is a lexicographical ordering for which, as is well known, indifference curves do not exist.

though it may be the best way to institute a more modest redistribution. I shall now describe a theoretical solution that, while it can only be approximated in practice, in pure form does make an egalitarian solution possible without exacting a high cost in terms of forgone income. The main purpose of this abstract concept is perhaps to be taken to be akin to that of an existence theorem—that is, it is intended to show that we are not necessarily wasting our time in looking for new and more heterodox means to reduce inequality without imposing an unacceptably high income loss upon society.[12]

But, as will be discussed later, there are ways in which this redistribution procedure can be approximated in practice. To describe such an alternative instrument for redistribution, let us set the policy maker free to determine a fixed wage rate w_i per unit of input supplied by an individual i, where w_i may differ from the wage rate w_j for any other individual j in any way the policy maker considers appropriate. In other words, the policy maker is given complete liberty to set *discriminatory input prices*, supplier by supplier, provided they satisfy the (inequality form of the) feasibility condition requiring total output to equal or exceed the sum of the resulting incomes.

Under such an arrangement the policy maker can achieve an egalitarian solution as follows. In figure 9.8 let $\bar{y}$ be an income level that the policy maker hopes, tentatively, to achieve for every earner. By trying alternative budget lines Wr_i^*, $W'r_i^*$, etc., with neither transfers nor progressive taxes, he generates an offer curve RR' for individual i from the points of tangency between the budget lines and i's indifference curves. The point E at which the offer curve crosses the horizontal line through target income level $\bar{y}$ gives us the required discriminatory wage rate w_i for person i, which is the absolute slope of budget line $W'r_i^*$ through point E. Then, if the corresponding input supplies satisfy the feasibility condition requiring total output to equal total income [see equation (9.3)], this is the desired solution. Otherwise, the policy maker must repeat the process trying another value of $\bar{y}$ until a feasible solution is found.

To describe the process algebraically we use the following notation:

$r_i = g^i(w_i) =$ individual i's input supply function,

---

12. As pointed out by a referee, we all know that this can be done, in theory, via lump-sum taxes, though it is hard to imagine how a tax can guarantee equality and yet be lump-sum. That is, if each person is guaranteed the same income as everyone else's (even if only in terms of expected value), we run into the problem of output loss indicated by proposition 2. With such disincentive effects, the redistribution payments by definition cannot be lump-sum.

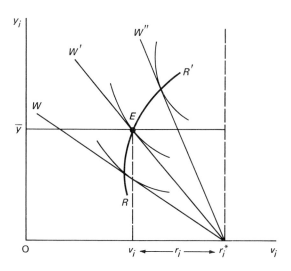

Figure 9.8

$y = f(r_1, \ldots, r_m)$ = the production function, and

y_i = individual i's income = $w_i g^i(w_i)$.

We deal, for simplicity, with a single product economy in which each of the persons supplies a single input (which may vary from individual to individual so that there can be $n \leqslant m$ different inputs). The quantity of input supplied by any one individual i varies only with the price w_i he receives per unit of input.

Algebraically, this egalitarian solution is then found by solving the condition for the feasibility of the proposed egalitarian wage $\bar{y}$,

$$m\bar{y} = \sum y_i = f(r_1, \ldots, r_m), \tag{9.3}$$

simultaneously with the $m - 1$ conditions

$y_i = y_m,$ that is,

$$w_i g^i(w_i) = w_m g^m(w_m) \qquad (i = 1, \ldots, m = 1), \tag{9.4}$$

after rewriting (9.3) as

$$\sum_{i=1}^{m} w_i g^i(w_i) = f[g^1(w_1), \ldots, g^m(w_m)]. \tag{9.3'}$$

Note that this solution yields perfect equality without tempting anyone to reduce his input supply to zero. As figure 9.8 shows, under the discriminatory price arrangement no one is *guaranteed* the income level $\bar{y}$. A person receives that income level at his assigned wage rate *only* by providing the amount of input indicated by his supply function. If, instead, he chooses to supply a zero input (point r_i^*), he receives a zero income. It is true that equality requires $w_i = \bar{y}/r_i$; that is, it requires wage rates to vary inversely with i's input supply. But our redistribution process does not proceed by adjusting i's wage rate upward each time his input supply decreases. Rather, it presumes that i's input supply function $g^i(w_i)$ is known to the policy maker and that he uses it to solve for that wage rate at which (9.4) will be satisfied by i's known and predictable wage response; that is, the policy maker solves the set of m simultaneous equations given by (9.4) and (9.3'), obtaining the m wage rates $w_1^e, \ldots, w_m^e$. The members of the economy are then left to themselves to adjust to these wage rates, which, we are assured by conditions (9.3') and (9.4), will *automatically* yield the equal income distribution that is desired.

Thus, unlike the case in which transfers and progressive taxes are used to redistribute incomes, the discriminatory wage arrangement need not yield a possibility locus that goes through the origin, or even near it, even if the variations in input supplies and abilities are "normal," as is proved in the appendix.[13] The frontier may even be concave throughout, as one might have expected on first examining the subject.[14]

4   The Role of the Utility of Leisure

The concreteness of the analysis as described up to this point has been achieved at the cost of what can be interpreted as an illegitimate oversimplification. For though we have claimed to be dealing with a single output economy, in fact a second output, leisure (input retained by suppliers for

---

13. Of course, the discriminatory wage arrangement must affect the prices of final goods and the allocation of resources, though we have no idea of the likely magnitude and direction of these effects. The shape and position of the possibility locus will therefore also be affected.

14. A comparison of figures 9.9 and 9.10 (in the appendix) indicates what happens under a policy of discriminatory wage rates to the solutions examined in figures 9.5–9.7. The Rawlsian solution (V) is now identical with the egalitarian solution (E). The antipoverty solution (A) will lie between E and the output-maximizing solution (M), since under A a relatively large gain to one individual with only a small loss to the other will be preferred to complete equality at the expense of a lower total output. But output under A will still be lower than under M, because the social welfare function will generally not consider the last extractable iota of gain in output to be worth the required increase in inequality.

personal use), has unavoidably entered the picture. After all, unattractive wage rates decrease input supplies only because their suppliers obtain some utility by keeping additional amounts for themselves. The trade-off between increased equality and output may therefore, in principle, be no trade-off at all. For reduced output means increased leisure, and as a result increased leisure sometimes entails no loss in the welfare of any individual even though it reduces some people's or even everyone's flow of material goods.[15]

How do we know that under progressive taxation complete equality is likely to entail a loss of *utility* even if it substitutes leisure for material output? The answer lies in proposition 2, which shows that with the indifference maps postulated, if tax arrangements are *absolutely* egalitarian in terms of purchasing power, society will end up with zero employment of resources and zero material goods output. We can invoke the indifference maps to show that this is surely no optimal state of affairs, but such an exercise hardly seems necessary.[16]

5   Conclusion: Toward Practical Policy

Our theory has already told us several things pertinent for policy. First, it has shown that however helpful progressive taxation may be in achieving *small* increases in equality, it can be inferred (via a continuity assumption)

15.The analysis of the possibility frontier is easily reformulated to take this issue into account. While there is no way we can add together output and leisure, we can deal with them both with the help of an ordinal utility possibility locus. For this we must take our axes to represent, rather than y_1 and y_2, the two ordinal utilities, u^1 and u^2. As usual, we have no way of comparing these two magnitudes, which can each legitimately be modified by any monotone transformation.

16. Thus, it follows that at least part of the utility frontier under progressive taxes must lie inside the frontier corresponding to wage discrimination. The use of a utility frontier rather than an output frontier does inhibit our analysis to some degree. Taking redistribution, as a matter of realism, to mean redistribution of output (purchasing) power, not equalization of utility (who ever heard of a progressive tax upon psychic utility, and what would it mean?), the solution values corresponding to our four prototype solutions—the output maximum, the welfare maximum, the egalitarian and the Rawlsian solutions—remain the same as before. However, in utility space they all lose their simple representations. Since in that space the utility indices for the two individuals are not comparable, the 45° line loses its meaning as a standard of equality, and so our devices for the representation of the egalitarian and the Rawlsian solutions no longer work. Similarly, a negatively sloping 45° line no longer represents either a fixed total output or a fixed total utility for the two parties. This is a problem that seems to have been overlooked in previous graphic analyses of the subject.

from our analysis of the extreme case of perfect equality[17] that it can impose a terrible burden upon the productive mechanism of any economy where it is used to eliminate all but minor differences in incomes. The implications for countries that have already gone far along this path may be worth noting.

Second, we have seen that, at least in theory, there may be a way out of the problem. The perfectly discriminatory pricing of inputs that our analysis used to illustrate such alternative procedures does not pretend to be, of course, a practical proposal as it stands. One cannot vary wage rates, input supplier by input supplier, in accord with fine-tuned calculations based on the individual supply functions. However, some ingenuity may be able to produce viable approximations to the discriminatory wage policy, which has been shown to be capable to getting us closer to equality without necessarily causing a catastrophic loss in output.

As with any arrangement involving effective price discrimination, some knowledge of relative elasticities is required, and it must be difficult to shift goods or services from lower- to higher-priced markets. Both of these issues can perhaps be dealt with by discriminating not among individuals but among broad groups of income earners. If doctors and ditchdiggers are fairly noncompeting groups, with little movement of labor from one to the other, a national wages policy that discriminates between them may be entirely feasible. Moreover, for such broad groups the estimation of labor supply functions is surely not out of the question. One can supplement wage rates for the one and limit wages for the other without expecting a large attrition in the supply of doctors by migration into ditchdigging. There are obvious problems besetting this process and any brief discussion of such a complicated matter is inevitably condemned to naiveté. The approach will run into trouble if large international differences in doctors' wages persist, since doctors can migrate abroad. High ditchdigger wages will discourage demand for the unskilled unless the wages are supported by public subsidy. But the fact is that real interoccupational wage ratios have been changed in a number of countries through government policy— national health programs and the earnings of their doctors providing a prime example. Thus, it *can* be done. We have not argued that it should be done, but have suggested that interoccupational wage differences can be, and have been, influenced in practice, and that these represent one measure

---

17. This is a Marshallian view of matters: *Natura non facit saltum* (or, in the words of a fortune cookie I received while this was being written, "Nature does not proceed by leaps").

that is in principle capable of producing substantial decreases in inequality without nearly the disincentive effects of means we have traditionally used for the purpose.

All economists are aware that egalitarian measures are likely to exact a cost in terms of a loss in national income. What seems not to have been considered before is the possibility that heterodox means may be able to limit this cost considerably even if the desired increase in equality is substantial.

Appendix: An Example Proving the Discriminatory Frontier Need Not Go through the Origin[*]

This section will illustrate by means of a concrete example the income versus equity trade-offs that are possible under the two redistribution measures we have discussed: progressive taxation and differentiated wage rates. By its example, it will prove[18]

Proposition 4   Under discriminatory wages it is not impossible to achieve absolute equality without zero outputs, even for normal input supply curves. Indeed, at the point of equality the boundary of the feasible set in output distribution space can be negatively sloping and concave.

Assume an input supply function for each of two individuals that, as the wage rate rises, increases rapidly at first, then more slowly and smoothly approaches a maximum. Simple functions with this property are given by[19]

$$g^i(w_i) = \begin{cases} r_i^*(1 - (1 - w_i)^2) & \text{if } 0 \leqslant w_i < 1 \\ r_i^* & \text{if } w_i \geqslant 1, \end{cases} \tag{9.5}$$

with $r_1^* = 1$ and $r_2^* = 2$. The input supply functions (9.5) are normal in the

---

[*]Dietrich Fischer is author of this appendix.

18. As Shlomo Maital once reminded me, there is a Yiddish proverb that states, "For example is not a proof." However, here we obviously have an exception, since proposition 4 merely claims that its result is logically possible. Indeed, the example goes further, showing that one needs no implausible relationships to yield the result asserted.

19. It can be shown that a family of indifference curves in income-leisure space for each individual that implies the assumed input supply behavior is given by

$$u^i(y_i, v_i) = y_i + v_i - \tfrac{2}{3}r_i^*\left(\frac{v_i}{r_i^*}\right)^{3/2} = \text{constant}.$$

Transfer payments do not affect the individuals' input supply in this example.

sense that no scheme of taxation can yield equal income without reducing output to zero.[20]

Let us now determine what total output y will be produced by the two individuals under various schemes of taxation and redistribution. Consider the following simple taxation scheme: Both individuals pay a tax at the same rate t, and the revenue obtained in this way is distributed equally between the two. (Both, of course, are paid at the same wage rate $w = w_1 = w_2$ under this first set of policy measures.) If $t = 0$, no redistribution will take place. If $t = 1$, the entire output is taxed away and distributed equally. As was shown in proposition 2, such a policy results in a maximal disincentive effect and yields a zero output. Let us now analyze intermediate cases.

Consider the simple production function[21]

$$y = f(r_1, r_2) = r_1 + r_2, \tag{9.6}$$

which permits a maximum wage rate of $w = 1$. If a tax rate t is applied, then the after-tax wage rate is $w = 1 - t$ and from (9.5) it follows that the tax revenue, T, which is to be distributed equally, is given by

$$T = r_1 + r_2 - w(r_1 + r_2) = 3t(1 - t^2).$$

This yields, as the incomes obtained after taxes and transfers,

$$y_1 = r_1(1 - t) + T/2$$

$$= (1 - t^2)(1 + t/2), \tag{9.7}$$

---

20. To see this, we note that any tax and transfer system in which the transfer payments depend on income is always equivalent to another scheme under which everybody receives the same transfer payment and only the tax levied depends on income. Now, for income equality, both individuals would have to receive the same after-tax wage income. Let $w = w_1 = w_2$ be the wage rate, $t(wr)$ be the progressive income-dependent tax rate, and $h(r) = wr[1 - t(wr)]$ be the after-tax wage income. We have assumed that $dh(r)/dr > 0$ for $0 \leqslant r \leqslant \max(r_1^*, r_2^*)$; i.e., there is never any penalty for additional input supplied (see figure 9.1 and the discussion preceding proposition 1). Thus, to obtain equal incomes the two individuals would have to supply the same amount of input. Since both face the same after-tax wage income schedule $h(r)$, they would also have to exhibit the same preference for leisure at that point. But from $du^i/dr_i = -du_i/dv_i = [(r_i^* - r_i)/r_i^*]^{1/2} - 1$ and $du^i/dy_i = 1$ we find that since $r_i^* \neq r_2^*$ we always have $dy_1/dr_1 \neq dy_2/dr_2$ for $r_1 = r_2$, except when $r_1 = r_2 = 0$; i.e., the two individuals never have the same marginal rate of substitution between input supply and leisure except when output is zero. Note that the effect of the input supply on the size of the transfer payment is not considered here. Compare footnote 3.

21. This production function would apply, for example, in a case where the input is labor and the output is measured in terms of its labor content.

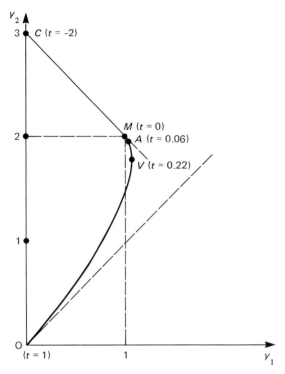

Figure 9.9

$$y_2 = r_2(1 - t) + T/2$$

$$= (1 - t^2)(2 - t/2)$$

for $0 \leqslant t \leqslant 1$.

As the tax rate t is gradually increased from 0 to 1, the incomes y_1 and y_2 move from point M in figure 9.9 through A and V to the origin.[22] The maximum output (point M) is reached when the tax rate is $t = 0$.[23] A welfare-maximizing solution (point A) was determined utilizing as the welfare function the product $y_1 \cdot y_2$. This is reached when $(1/y_1)(dy_1/dt) = -(1/y_2)(dy_2/dt)$. The various solutions are summarized and compared in table 9.1.

---

22. With a negative tax rate, the wage rate would be increased to more than 1, and a lump-sum would have to be extracted from each individual to compensate for the resulting deficit. The income-distribution frontier would then be extended from point M to C in figure 9.9, but this hardly seems realistic.

23. Since there are no externalities in this model, and there is no advantage in mutual cooperation, it is natural to find that a pure laissez-faire strategy with equal wage rates and no taxation yields the output-maximizing solution.

Table 9.1
Efficient income combinations under two types of income redistribution policies

	Output maxi-mization (M)	Welfare-maximization solution (A)	Rawlsian solution (V)	Income equalization (E)	Maximization of individual 1's income (D)	Maximization of individual 2's income (C)
Taxation with redistribution						
Tax rate	0	0.06	0.22	1	0.22	−2
Transfer payment	0	0.09	0.31	0	0.31	−3
y_1	1	1.03	1.06	0	1.06	0
y_2	2	1.96	1.81	0	1.81	3
$y = y_1 + y_2$	3	2.99	2.87	0	2.87	3
Differential wage rates						
w_1	1	1.33	1.45	1.45	1.77	0.42
w_2	1	0.83	0.77	0.77	0.42	1.19
y_1	1	1.33	1.45	1.45	1.77	0.28
y_2	2	1.62	1.45	1.45	0.56	2.38
$y = y_1 + y_2$	3	2.95	2.90	2.90	2.33	2.66

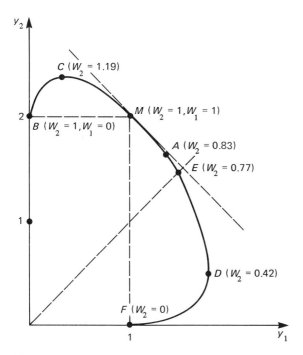

Figure 9.10

Let us now explore what the efficient income set looks like for this example if differentiated wage rates, rather than taxation and redistribution, are used as policy instruments. If individual i is paid at a wage rate $w_i < 1$, she produces more than she earns and leaves a surplus of

$$S_i = r_i - w_i r_i = (1 - w_i)r_i^*(1 - (1 - w_i)^2).$$

If $w_j > 1$, she has a deficit

$$S_j = (1 - w_j)r_j = -(w_j - 1)r_j^* < 0.$$

This deficit must then be compensated for by the surplus of the other individual. For $0 \leqslant w_2 \leqslant 1$ we obtain

$$y_1 = w_1 r_1 = w_1 \cdot 1$$
$$= 1 + 2(1 - w_2) \cdot (1 - (1 - w_2)^2), \tag{9.8}$$
$$y_2 = w_2 r_2 = 2w_2(1 - (1 - w_2)^2).$$

A similar pair of formulas applies when $0 \leqslant w_1 \leqslant 1$. The resulting output distribution frontier is shown in figure 9.10. Table 9.1 gives a summary of the various solutions obtained.

A comparison of the income combinations that are feasible under taxation with redistribution and under wage rate differentiation confirms that under rather natural assumptions about individuals' behavior, the second set of policy measures can permit far more equitable income distributions without reducing total output substantially. Indeed, in our example, complete equality merely reduces total output to 2.9 from its maximal value of 3.0.

10   On the Reality of Economic Illusion

Economists have long recognized that the welfare an individual derives from the flow of goods and services he consumes can only be evaluated properly via his utility function and not from any direct enumeration of the quantities of those goods and services, ignoring the person's psychic predispositions. The individual likes what he likes, and for welfare analysis that is taken as a datum not to be disputed with the consumer.

Yet we do not seem prepared to embrace all of what this viewpoint implies. Usually, we are willing to deal with the consumer's preferences, whatever they may happen to be, but only so long as they entail no "irrationalities" or "illusions"—however these terms are defined. This chapter will suggest that illusions may be widespread and that in these too, consumers are entitled to their own preferences. Just as there is nothing wrong with the choice of a consumer who prefers mango ice cream to strawberry, there is nothing pathological about a consumer who prefers a method of payment that actually costs him more but pleases him by making the price of his purchase *seem* lower.

I shall suggest that such considerations are pertinent for superfairness analysis, with its reliance on the preferences of the persons affected by the circumstances whose fairness is to be evaluated. I shall also suggest that failure to take illusion into account has misled at least some economists into endorsing imposition upon the public of policies that are widely disliked, presumably upon the grounds that despite their unpopularity these measures really serve the public's true welfare. An example is the widely held view that the income tax is preferable to an excise, among other reasons, because the latter is generally more regressive. I shall suggest that the contrary is likely to be true: that even considering only its distributive effects the excise may well come close to being a Pareto improvement over the income tax in terms of the pain entailed in its payment. I shall also provide an application to the theory of nonlinear pricing, which has recently attracted attention in the literature of industrial organization.

1   Illusion and Consumer Satisfaction

Illusions beset our consumption patterns and our economic activities in a variety of ways. A simple example will bring out the point. Some years ago, on a voyage by ship from England to Denmark I was distressed to discover when signing up for the trip that passengers were expected to purchase their meals and to pay just for what they ordered. Unlike a transatlantic ship voyage, the food was not "free." Needless to say, I was well aware that I was paying for my meals in either case. Yet, even though I was convinced that my view of the matter was irrational, this did not affect my attitudes and I suffered a very real loss of utility because the meals on the Scandinavian ship visibly cost me money.

Knowledge often is incapable of dispelling illusions. A psychologist friend once told me, somewhat uneasily, that despite a period of many months spent demonstrating and explaining a set of optical illusions, when he left the platform and joined the audience, they still fooled him every time. Economic illusions are similar: Those of us who are subject to them may be left with the uncomfortable feeling that we should not succumb to them; yet somehow we cannot help it.[1]

We can all cite many examples. Some of my colleagues make certain that excessive income tax deductions are taken from their salary checks so they will have little or nothing left to pay at the end of the year. Obviously, they would gain financially if they were to hold back until the last minute every tax dollar they legally can, earning interest on the money in the meantime. But, to them, avoiding the pain of writing out a large check on April 14 is apparently worth the interest forgone. It is then, surely, not their decision that is irrational, but whatever disquiet they feel in sticking to it.[2]

---

1. Another example will underscore the point. A friend of mine told me that when she recently moved to New York City she decided to keep her car and pay the enormous insurance and garage costs entailed, in order to go on the weekend trips she enjoys so much. Though she is a capable economist who understands the price relationships clearly she does this because of her awareness that she will never be able to bring herself to pay the "high" price of car rental for weekend jaunts, although over the year this would save her a great deal. She knows perfectly well that an illusion is involved, but that does not make it vanish. In light of these considerations surely her decision is entirely rational.

2. There is one related problem whose rationale I have not been able to untangle even after a number of years of pondering. My wife has long maintained that the proper strategy at a commercial smorgasbord is to fill one's plate (predominantly) with the more expensive items, regardless of preference. I argued at first that this was irrational but then reconsidered and decided that the approach does "make sense," if when we consume the same items

Illusion may also play a role in determining the amount of time spent in conferences and over the telephone. It is hard to avoid the impression that people are generally much briefer in long distance calls than they are in face-to-face conferences involving comparable distances. This may in part be a response to the rate structure that is rational in the conventional sense: The longer one talks on the telephone, the more the call costs. But most of the cost of a trip is a fixed charge so that a conferee may, perhaps subconsciously, suffer conscience pangs unless his meeting lasts sufficiently long to give his money's worth to whoever is paying the fare.

Commercial pricing policies sometimes take economic illusions into account. Prices set at $4.99 and $29.99 are an obvious response to the phenomenon. Consumers surely are not fooled—they are only made to feel better about their outlay. Some public utilities permit prepayment on anticipated monthly charges and make periodic adjustment payments to balance off the tally. It is said that their experience has led these firms to a policy of systematic *overestimation* of future payment levels on the ground that good will is engendered when the customer receives a rebate rather than a bill.

Economic illusions are also to be found in high places. In its subbasement vaults where foreign gold is stored, the Federal Reserve Bank of New York caters to them. In response to explicit demands by the central banks each nation's gold is kept in a separate and identifiable pile, despite the shortage of space and the cost of moving heavy gold bricks from one pile to another as balances change. This is done, instead of mere separation on the books of the New York Fed, presumably because of the reassurance and satisfaction provided to a visiting representative of a foreign state when he is shown the gold that is beyond any question *his*.

2 The Recent Psychological Literature on Economic Behavior

Recently several psychologists and economists have begun to explore more systematically phenomena related to those I have just described. They have carried out both formal and informal experiments describing how choices and preferences are affected by illusion created by sunk costs and other past events that economists generally consider to be irrelevant ancient history, and by the *form* assumed by the available alternatives (the

---

outside the restaurant we do so in such quantities that their relative marginal utilities are roughly proportional to their prices. If so, considerations of complementarity aside, increased consumption of the most costly items is also likely to contribute the greatest direct pleasure (as well as the indirect pleasure of beating the game).

way in which they are presented to or observed by the decision maker, so that with one form of presentation they make decisions inconsistent with those they make with another).

For example, Thaler calls our attention to a case like that of a person who bought a bottle of wine for $3 twenty years ago and finds that its market price is now $500. Though that individual would not dream of paying such a price for a bottle of wine, he refuses to sell the one he owns to a dealer. Most of us have undoubtedly made similar decisions. Whether or not we choose to call them "irrational" they are real. And they clearly entail both the illusion that sunk costs are relevant for current decisions and the companion illusion that a sunk cost is not as costly as the expenditure of exactly the same amount.

The following two passages illustrate the sort of experiments that this literature provides (Thaler [1983, pp. 12–13]):

The [following] questionnaire, given to participants in an executive development program, shows how transaction utility can influence willingness to pay (and therefore demand).

Consider the following scenario:

You are lying on the beach on a hot day. All you have to drink is ice water. For the last hour you have been thinking about how much you would enjoy a nice cold bottle of your favorite brand of beer. A companion gets up to go make a phone call and offers to bring back a beer from the only nearby place where beer is sold (a fancy resort hotel) [a small, run down grocery store]. He says that the beer might be expensive and so asks how much you are willing to pay for the beer. He says that he will buy the beer if it costs as much or less than the price you state. But if it costs more than the price you state he will not buy it. You trust your friend, and there is no possibility of bargaining with (the bartender) [store owner]. What price do you tell him?

The results from this survey were dramatic. The median price given in the fancy resort hotel version was $2.65 while the median for the small run-down grocery store version was $1.50. This difference occurs despite the following three features of this example:

1. In both versions the ultimate consumption act is the same—drinking one beer on the beach. The beer is the same in each case.

2. There is no possibility of strategic behavior in stating the reservation price.

3. No "atmosphere" is consumed by the respondent.

The explanation offered for these choices is based on the concept of transaction utility. (Acquisition utility is constant between the two cases.) While paying $2.50 for a beer is an expected annoyance at the resort hotel, it would be considered an outrageous "rip-off" in a grocery store. Paying $2.50 a bottle is $15.00 a six-pack, considerably above the reference price.

Our second example is the following (Tversky and Kahneman [1982, p. 15]):[3]

Problem 8 [*N* = 183]. Imagine that you have decided to see a play where admission is $10 per ticket. As you enter the theater, you discover that you have lost a $10 bill.

Would you still pay $10 for a ticket for the play?
Yes [88 percent]   No [12 percent]

Problem 9 [*N* = 2000]. Imagine that you have decided to see a play and paid the admission price of $10 per ticket. As you enter the theater, you discover that you have lost the ticket. The seat was not marked, and the ticket cannot be recovered.

Would you pay $10 for another ticket?
Yes [46 percent]   No [54 percent]

The marked difference between the responses to problems 8 and 9 is an effect of psychological accounting. We propose that the purchase of a new ticket in problem 9 is entered in the account that was set up by the purchase of the original ticket. In terms of this account, the expenses required to see the show is $20, a cost which many of our respondents apparently found excessive. In problem 8, however, the loss of $10 is not linked specifically to the ticket purchase, and its effect on the decision is accordingly slight.

3   Prices and the Utility Function

Illusions, by their very nature, seem likely to be unpredictable in character, and there may be no limit to the ability of the human mind to come up with surprising varieties. Still, it is easy enough to identify some of the important sources of illusion, meaning by this variables that, in the economist's sense, do not correspond to "real" phenomena, but that nevertheless enter many individuals' utility functions.[4] Prices and monetary payments are among the prime candidates. Here, the phenomenon of money illusion is suggestive. Economists are undoubtedly right when they point out that

---

3. Here *N* equals the number of respondents.
4. Yet sometimes a view that is apparently illusory turns out on closer inspection to have some basis in fact or in logic. Thus consider the following proposition (Baumol's tautology): A majority of the vehicles traveling a two-lane road will be found in the more crowded lane. Does this not help to explain the widespread impression of drivers that, more often than not, they end up in the "wrong" lane?

there is a gap in logic in the position of consumers who consider prices to be undesirably high if they have recently risen substantially, even if their money incomes have simultaneously risen proportionately. However, it may well be appropriate to curb our instinct to argue that people somehow "ought to know better." Rather, the proper lesson may be simply that a rise in prices is likely to be very painful. The rise in costs to buyers that is entailed may indeed be illusory, but the resulting loss in utility is very real and should be taken into account in our calculation.

It is important for economists to understand this because there are so many problems that we propose to resolve by a rise in prices. For example, we often recommend a Pigouvian tax upon emissions as the best means to reduce pollution. Such a tax is designed, in part, to raise the prices of outputs whose production generates pollution, in order to discourage their consumption. Similarly, if a crop fails, we generally argue against controls upon its price, and defend the subsequent increases in its price as an effective means to ration the product and to ensure that it is consumed slowly enough to prevent the shortage from becoming truly critical before the next crop arrives. I do not mean to dispute the validity of these very legitimate arguments. But I do believe that they are incomplete. For, as they stand, they do not take account of the fact that the recommended medicines are painful, even if their pain does rest on illusion. It follows in cases where there is what would otherwise be a next best policy measure, which is in all other respects "almost as good," that the inherent disutility of price increases may make the "second best" solution preferable to an unrestricted price rise. Second, it follows that even where the pricing approach is nevertheless to be preferred, it may be optimal to swallow a dose of this medicine milder than would otherwise be ideal. Slightly lower effluent charges and slightly higher rates of emission than those that appear optimal on the usual calculation may be called for. The third and most important implication is that the widespread opposition that such proposals often encounter among politicians and members of the public is not to be ascribed merely to ignorance and inflexibility. A more sympathetic view of the public's reaction to such measures may well facilitate communication and perhaps even make it easier to explain their benefits to people outside our profession.

There are at least two ways in which money and prices may significantly affect an individual's utility: (i) As we have just seen, the absolute amount of money paid out by the person at any one date may enter his utility function. The larger the payment that is required at a particular juncture, the lower the utility the individual will enjoy, given the values of all real variables. Later in the chapter we shall see an illustration of the sort of formal analysis and the policy implications to which this phenomenon may lead. (ii) The disutility produced by a given payment may be affected by the *form* taken by the payment—whether it is laid out in a lump-sum, takes the form of a fixed charge per use, or assumes some other shape. The previous section offered some examples of this phenomenon. I shall now discuss a few more examples impressionistically and in the next few sections I shall try to suggest how their formal analysis can be approached.

4   Alternative Price Structures and Their Utility Implications

I have already observed that many people derive pleasure from the prepayment of expenses, and enjoy the illusion that their subsequent consumption is "free." Many people prefer to arrange for vacations with "all expenses paid." Apparently, many persons would prefer to "buy" their telephones rather than paying a monthly rental for the indefinite future, even if the payment stream is equivalent in expected present value to the cost of buying the instrument outright. It is not difficult to find other examples.

However, one must be careful in interpreting these conclusions. There may be reasons other than the inherent attractiveness of a low (or zero) price per use that may induce people to prefer prepayment. For one thing, prepayment is sometimes a way of reducing uncertainty (though it can increase uncertainty in other cases). When one does not know what expenses may arise (as on a vacation trip) or how long payments will continue (as in telepone subscription), prepayment may be the buyer's easiest way of shifting risk to the supplier. Second, prepayment is a way of reducing the marginal cost of additional consumption. Thus the very feature of "free" supply of resources that is anathema to economists—its inducement of wasteful consumption—may be a prime source of attraction to buyers. People with large appetites are apt to like prepaid (buffet) meals, and sickly persons are likely to prefer health care programs with fixed payments.[5]

---

5. Such incentive effects are tricky matters, however. Exactly the same phenomenon can lead someone with a weight problem to avoid prepayment of meals. The same may be true of people with little self-control and weak digestions. At a recent visit to a chuckwagon restaurant with no limit on number of helpings I saw a number of customers who looked more than a little uncomfortable as they were leaving. Another example is provided by our earlier illustration of the way in which a face-to-face conference of people from scattered geographic locations is likely to encourage garrulousness, while a conference telephone call is likely to encourage brevity because the visible cost of the one is largely independent of the

Moreover, the preference for a single, large (pre)payment is not uniform and may well vary from person to person and from case to case. I have already alluded to public preference for an excise over an income tax— which comes closer to a single and large fixed payment. I have no evidence whether there are many people who simultaneously exhibit both of these apparently conflicting preferences, nor is it my goal to attempt any explanation or reconcilation.[6] Rather, I want only to emphasize the complexity of the phenomena with which we are dealing and the consequent inevitability of oversimplification in the discussion in the next few sections.

Despite the reservations and qualifications I have expressed on the subject I shall proceed on the illustrative assumption that there are a number of goods and services for which many people prefer, all other things being equal, to make their expenditure in the form of a fixed charge rather than paying a (slightly) smaller amount in total, the bulk of which takes the form of user charges.

5   Nonlinear Pricing and Price Illusion

The role of illusion in choice among pricing arrangements naturally again brings up the concept of nonlinear pricing (see, e.g., Faulhaber and Zajac [1979], which was discussed briefly in chapter 7). Nonlinear prices may be thought of as the range of pricing options intermediate between a system of fixed (parametric) prices and perfect price discrimination (which one can never achieve in practice). A prime example is a variable two-part (n-part) tariff that can be charged for commodities that cannot easily be repackaged and resold by one customer group to another. For exposition, it is convenient to think of the two prices as a license price and per unit consumption price. The first of these is the cost of a license that entitles its holder to buy any desired quantity of the good, at the associated (fixed) unit price. However, unlike the usual two-part tariff, under this arrangement the consumer can be offered his choice of a variety of such price packages. Some packages combine a high license fee with a small unit price while others do the reverse. In the extreme case, this last package is, of course, nothing else than the ordinary fixed price per unit. Similarly, one can

---

amount of time consumed while the cost of the other varies directly with the time used in the conversation. Consequently, employers who wish to minimize waste of time by their staff may on this account be led to favor conference calls over conferences with their relatively large prepaid costs.

6. For some illuminating work on explanation and analysis see Thaler [1983] and Tversky and Kahneman [1982].

construct more complicated price arrangements with n parameters (an n-part tariff). In nonlinear pricing each customer is generally permitted to select whichever of the available pricing arrangements best serves that person's interests.

Willig [1978] has proved that there always exists an appropriately designed nonlinear arrangement that is Pareto superior to any fixed price arrangement, benefiting the supplier as well as every consumer. As is often true of such a clever idea, after it has been discovered, the reason it works is not very difficult to see. From the point of view of consumers the variable multipart tariff is usually Pareto superior (and certainly never inferior) to a system of parametric prices because, as we saw in chapter 7, one of the packages that can be included in the range of options of the multipart tariff is the polar case in which the license fee is zero, i.e., the parametric price option. Since any consumer is free to select any pricing option included in the nonlinear pricing package, a utility level at least as great as that under the fixed price option is guaranteed to each purchaser. Indeed, Willig has shown that *all* consumers can be enabled to gain by the broadening of the range of choices offered by the variable two-part tariff, as long as consumer tastes are not identical. For if it is possible to select a price arrangement that benefits some consumers and that harms no one else, then continuity must permit a slight modification of these prices that brings some benefits to those who would otherwise have neither gained nor lost.

It is not quite so obvious why there must be a net gain to suppliers—the only other party involved, in the absence of externalities. They can always gain because no consumer need pay more under the nonlinear price arrangements than he would with a fixed price; and since some consumers will pay less, we can expect some increase in quantity demanded. The trick for the seller, then, is to select a set of prices for each of the price options in the nonlinear package such that marginal revenue is at least equal to marginal cost at the quantities that would be purchased at the fixed prices that constitute that option. The expansion in demand can then produce an increase in profit.

Nonlinear pricing analysis suggests how the structure of a price arrangement can be tailored to the consumers' *pricing* preferences. One may surmise that it will call for decreased reliance on the user charge compensated by an increase in the value of the entry fee component of the two-part tariff, compared to what would otherwise be optimal. There will then be a trade-off, with members of the community giving up some surplus in exchange for a more palatable pricing arrangement. In general, we may expect a loss in surplus to result from "excessive" consumption induced by

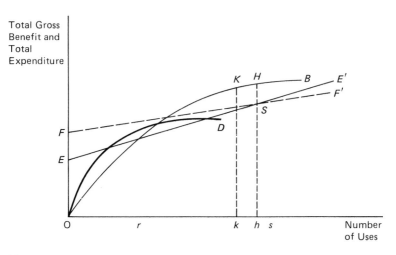

Figure 10.1

low user charges as these would be calculated in the standard welfare analysis. But offsetting effects may be expected.

Figure 10.1 describes the partial equilibrium of the individual consumer showing his purchases of the good with whose price we are concerned. The piecewise linear payments locus, OEE', indicates how the consumer's total expenditure varies with number of units of the good or service consumed. The vertical segment, OE, is the entry fee required before the buyer can purchase any of the item. The slope of EE' is, of course, the fixed user charge per unit of consumption.

In Figure 10.1 we also see that when there is a rise in fixed charge compensated by a fall in user charge the expenditure locus changes from OEE' to OFF' with the latter having the larger fixed charge ($OF > OE$) and the smaller slope. If the benefit curve does not shift, then we see that the optimal usage level of the person with benefit curve OB (the point at which the benefits curve has the same slope as the payments locus) will increase from k to h. This must certainly be true of the substitution effect—as an obvious consequence of the Slutsky theorem, for the relative price of additional use will have declined. The individual will, therefore, probably consume more than before. However, the rise in the entry fee may instead lead that person to give up consumption of the item altogether. This is likely for an individual whose net benefit curve initially never lies far above the total expenditure locus and who initially consumes a relatively small amount of the good so that the reduced charge per use does not offset the

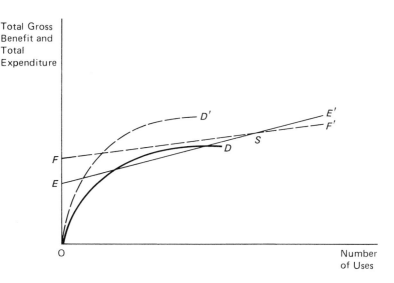

Figure 10.2

rise in entry fee. This is illustrated in figure 10.2 by gross benefit curve *OD*. Expenditure locus *OFF'* lies above benefit curve *OD* at every nonzero level of use, so it now pays this person to give up consumption of the good altogether. We are, thus, likely to end up with fewer consumers of the item each using more of it than before, and we cannot say where total use will come out on balance.

Price illusion changes matters somewhat, though by no means removing the ambiguity of the preceding conclusion. If illusion adds to consumer welfare when the pricing arrangement changes from *OEE'* to *OFF'*, the benefit curve will shift upward (the shift from *OD* to *OD'* in figure 10.2). If the upward shift is sufficient, as in the figure, it will pay the individual who would otherwise have given up consuming the item to remain in the market. It is even conceivable that people who under price regime *OEE'* do not consider purchasing any of the good will be induced to do so by pricing arrangement *OFF'*. This will, for example, be true of an impecunious person with a large appetite, to whom consumption at an ordinary restaurant is prohibitive but for whom eating at a fixed price restaurant ("eat as much as you want") may be attractive.[7]

---

7. With price illusion we can also no longer be confident that the continued user's consumption of the item will increase. With the shift in the benefit curve its slope will also change, and so we cannot be sure where his new equilibrium point will lie.

6   Illusion and Self-Selection in Nonlinear Pricing

Besides its other virtues, nonlinear pricing may be an ideal way of dealing with the allocative issues raised by illusion, for a reason that is rather evident. The pertinent feature of a nonlinear pricing arrangement is the consumer's freedom to choose among the pricing options it offers. He is given the opportunity to select a prepaid vacation package, or a pay-as-you-go program. She can rent cars at a fixed charge per mile, or a high rental charge with no payment for distance, or something in between.

This choice can, of course, be based simply on the usual pricing consider-ations; for example, the car-rental customer who has far to drive can be expected to select the rental plan with a high fixed fee and little or no charge based on distance. But the customers subject to price illusion can (and very likely will) also tailor their choices accordingly. Those who enjoy the illusion of "free meals" will select the prepaid vacation while those who are disproportionately distressed by a large payment may avoid it assiduously.

The most attractive feature of this way of dealing with the problem is its avoidance of the need for information, which may often be all but unattain-able, but which may be needed for more direct adaptation to price illusion. Under nonlinear pricing the policy maker need not know whether people prefer prepayment or the avoidance of large outlays or have some other form of preference among pricing patterns. Consumers are left to determine this for themselves and to act accordingly.

Indeed, if, as seems likely, the form as well as the strength of price illusion varies substantially from person to person, there is no other way to deal with the issue. Any price arrangements that are well suited to one person's set of pricing preferences will be ill suited to another's. But with the range of choice offered under nonlinear pricing there is room for satisfaction of all pricing tastes.

Looked at another way, pricing illusion means that consumers may benefit from differentiation of products in terms of pricing arrangements, as well as in terms of the physical or other attributes of the goods that are usually cited as examples of product differentiation. And, as usual, the market does sometimes provide such choices where they stimulate enough consumer demand to make the options profitable. But as in the standard analysis of monopolistic competition and product differentation there seems little reason for confidence that the optimal range of options will be offered. The theory of monopolistic competition suggests the possibility that this market form will extend the range too far, the number of alternatives offered perhaps exceeding what can be justified by the benefits vis-à-vis the administractive and other costs imposed by a great proliferation of options. But the presence of a variety of price illusions surely calls for the provision of a larger range of options than it would otherwise be possible to justify.

7 Application: Price Discrimination and the Burden on Consumers with Inelastic Demands

It has already been noted in chapter 1 that a case can be made for the view that a price increase in some sense affects most severely the buyers whose demands are inelastic—the consumers whom the market is likely to offer no good substitute products, who have "nowhere else to go."

Price discrimination is likely to aggravate such problems. For we know that a discriminating monopolist who "charges what the traffic will bear" generally charges customers with inelastic demands a price higher than that imposed on other buyers relative to the marginal costs incurred in serving them. We also know the same is likely to be true under Ramsey pricing, since then prices tend to vary inversely with demand elasticity. Yet, a curious example in which optimality in the presence of price illusion seems to work for discrimination against persons whose demands are relatively *elastic* is provided by the use of high prices as a means to curtail consumption, say, in order to preserve a scarce resource or to ration consumption after a crop failure. Recognizing the psychic pain caused consumers by a rise in prices, the appropriately modified *efficiency* considerations suggest that it will be illuminating to see what pattern of discriminatory prices can achieve any given level of restricted consumption with a minimal (weighted average) rise in prices to different consumers. We obtain

Proposition 1   If discriminatory prices are used to restrict consumption of a commodity to some target quantity and it is desired to do so in a way that minimizes consumer expenditure on the item, then the prices must be such that (a) no consumer will purchase a quantity at which marginal revenue is positive; (b) if all cross elasticities are zero, no consumer will purchase a quantity at which demand is elastic—i.e., any person whose demand is elastic throughout will, in effect, be faced by an "infinite price," and his consumption driven to zero; and (c) with zero cross-elasticities, among consumers who do purchase nonzero quantities of the good the more elastic the demand of an individual at his equilibrium point, the higher the price he will be charged.

Proof Let y_i be the quantity of the resource purchased by group i and let p_i be the price charged to the group. Then the problem is to

minimize $\sum p_i y_i$

subject to $\sum y_i = k$ (the target level of resource consumption), whose Lagrangian is

$$L = \sum p_i y_i + \lambda(\sum y_i - k), \quad \text{with} \quad \lambda \geqslant 0, \quad y_i \geqslant 0,$$

and whose Kuhn-Tucker conditions include

$$\text{mr}_j + \lambda \equiv \partial \sum p_i y_i / \partial y_j + \lambda \geqslant 0, \quad y_j(\text{mr}_j + \lambda) = 0.$$

Here mr_j represents the marginal revenue derive from group j.

Part (a) of proposition 1 now follows from the second of our Kuhn-Tucker conditions, for if $y_j > 0$, we must have

$$\text{mr}_j = -\lambda \leqslant 0.$$

Part (b) also follows at once from the standard relation for the case with zero cross elasticities:

$$\text{mr}_j = p_j(1 - 1/E_j) \leqslant 0 \quad \text{if} \quad E_j \leqslant 1,$$

where $E_j \geqslant 0$ is the price elasticity of demand of group j. Finally, we come to part (c) of the proposition, which follows from the result that for y_i, $y_j > 0$, with zero cross elasticities $\text{mr}_x = p_x(1 - 1/E_x) = -\lambda$, $x = i, j$, so that

$$p_i/p_j = \left(\frac{1}{E_j} - 1\right) \Big/ \left(\frac{1}{E_i} - 1\right).$$

Thus, if $1 \geqslant E_j > E_i > 0$, we have $p_i/p_j < 1$, which is our result.[8]

This conclusion suggests that in this case there are efficiency as well as equity grounds that favor lower prices to customers with inelastic demands. Even if the price adjustment is produced by a tax that is returned to consumers via rebates, so that there is little or no effect on consumers' real incomes in the conventional sense, the fact remains that payment of taxes is

---

8. We obtain a result that is more striking if we attempt to minimize not $\sum y_i p_i$, but $\sum y_i^* p_i$, where y_i^* is the fixed "initial" consumption of the resource by group i. Then the Lagrangian becomes $\sum y_i^* p_i + \lambda(\sum y_i - k)$, which yields, for $y_i > 0$, and 0 cross-elasticities, $y_i^* \, dp_i/dy_i + \lambda \equiv p_i(y_i^*/p_i)(dp_i/dy_i) + \lambda = 0$, or $p_i/p_j = E_i^*/E_j^*$, where E_i^* is the bastard elasticity $E_i^* = -(p_i/y_i^*) \, dy_i/dp_i$. In other words, in this case, the optimal prices will vary strictly proportionately with the bastard elasticity of demand.

painful. Consequently, a reduction in the tax payment needed to achieve a consumption reduction is surely a net addition to welfare. The fact that the loss in taxpayer's income is illusory is, once more, beside the point. Since it is desirable to achieve our conservation goal with as little pain and suffering as possible, there is an efficiency argument that favors the favoring of consumers with inelastic demands.

Of course, the discriminatory solution we are now discussing will not, in general, constitute a true optimum, since it takes into account none of the variables other than the prices that enter the utility functions of the affected individuals. That is, it surely is implausible that minimization of payments for the scarce resource is all there is to the pertinent social objective function. It follows that while optimality in the presence of price illusion may plausibly be expected to call for *somewhat* lower prices to consumers whose demands are inelastic than would otherwise be the case, we should not expect it to lead all the way to minimization of the total rise in payments. Rather, one should expect the optimal solution to involve a trade-off between the ordinary efficiency requirements and the disutility costs of the expenditure increase.

From the point of view of equity one may also question the desirability of the expenditure-minimizing solution if the price of only one commodity is involved. Those who are favored by it—the consumers whose demands are most inelastic—are an arbitrarily chosen group of persons who may not be particularly poor or particularly deserving on any other grounds.

Only if a considerable number of items is involved and if different persons' demands are likely to exhibit relative inelasticity of demand for the different goods, so that everyone is likely to share the benefits, is such a proposal apt to pass a test of fairness. Otherwise, this kind of discriminatory policy, though it may indeed offer benefits to those who are affected by price illusion of the sort postulated, may well be far from ideal in terms of either efficiency or equity.

8   Application: Payments Illusion—Income versus Excise Taxes

As was already noted, in the case of tax payments people may characteristically be subject to an illusion that is opposite in direction from the sort of price illusion posited in earlier sections of this chapter. There we proceeded on the hypothesis that people often prefer their payments to take the form of fixed charges rather than a user charge that extracts an additional payment with every increase in use. In taxation the evidence, such as it is, suggests that many people prefer a multitude of small payments based on quantities of goods purchased (and which they are perhaps able to conceal from themselves) rather than large periodic payments whose magnitude is independent of quantities purchased.

Illusion (or perhaps delusion) is surely at the heart of the excise tax issue. In the course of recent attempts to introduce a broad based tax in a number of states some observers seem to have been taken aback by the evidence of opposition to a progressive income tax among lower income earners, many of whom seem to prefer a sales levy. After all, the main objective of those who advocated an income tax was to avoid the shifting of a disproportionate share of the burden to those who are less affluent. But apparently the fact of the matter seems to be that many people would rather pay their taxes in small, relatively unnoticeable amounts—that to them the annual exaction of a relatively large sum or the direct reduction in the size of their paycheck through a withholding arrangement is far more painful. This is just another manifestation of the early prepayment syndrome that characterizes even some economists. Are we, then, really entitled to say that advocacy of a sales tax by a fairly impecunious individual can only stem from ignorance or irrationality? True, he may not know just how large a price he is paying for the privilege of making piecemeal payments, but it is possible that he does not *want* to know, and even this may be a rational attitude if he believes he is happier not knowing.[9]

Paradoxically, there is some evidence suggesting that the group that is most opposed to an excise tax is composed of financially more comfortable and better educated individuals whose pangs of conscience when they do not bear their proportionate share of the tax burden may motivate them to join the good fight for the "fairer" income tax. They want such a tax program for the lower income earners' "own good" even though it may be anathema to the objects of concern of the advocate of the "fairer" tax. But which of them is then being irrational or, at least, unfair?

9   Illusion and Fairness Analysis

Illusion up to this point may seem, at most, an embellishment of fairness theory. Yet it should affect even the way one defines the concept of fairness. For example, consider a case in which a homogeneous commodity is divided unequally between two persons, but individual A who receives the smaller amount is, for whatever reason, under the illusion that he has

---

9. Conversation with my wife: She: Guess how much this new dress cost. He: I would rather not know.

obtained the bulk of the item and is very pleased with the outcome. Are we to judge the outcome to be fair or unfair to A? After all, in his own judgment A received what may be described as more than half the available utility. Given the choice, he would refuse to trade with the other individual. On this view, what matters is not what the individual receives but the pleasure he derives thereby. Whether that pleasure is or is not the result of illusion is beside the point.

This interpretation has policy implications that can be significant, as we have seen. The income-excise tax controversy just discussed involves an issue similar to that in the preceding paragraph. An excise tax may extract payments from the poor greater than those under a progressive income tax. Yet, if the poorer sectors of the community uniformly consider themselves to be treated better under an excise tax, both absolutely and relative to the remainder of the community, who is to say that the excise must be less fair to the poor than the income tax?[10]

Aside from its consequences for applications of fairness analysis, illusion also has its implications for the underpinnings of the theory. Specifically, it may drive a wedge between the superfairness and the superequality criteria. Superfairness can readily adapt itself to illusion, for it relies entirely on the evaluations of the individuals concerned. This is clearest in the cake cutting game. If one of us cuts and the other chooses, each of us will end up preferring what we get to what is obtained by the other party (or will at least be indifferent between the two). This will be so whether or not our preferences are affected by illusion. The same is true of superfairness analysis in general, because it takes the participants' preferences for what they are, however illusory their basis may be. The implication is that if the utility functions used in the analysis do represent the true preferences of the individuals, the effects of illusion are automatically handled thereby.

In the case of superequality matters are not quite so straightforward. This criterion, as we know, takes the equal division point as its point of departure. But, given what Lord Robbins taught us about interpersonal comparisons, we know that there is no way we can define equal division of *utilities*. The equal division point, consequently, must correspond to assignment of identical vectors of commodities to each of the participants. We

---

10. We must, however, proceed with caution here. The discussion seems to involve both incremental fairness (that of the changeover from an income to an excise tax) and the fairness of the excise tax itself. But the relationship between the two is tenuous, at best. As we know from the set of paradoxes first suggested in the work of Feldman and Kirman, an incrementally superfair move from an initial distribution that is superfair may well yield a new distribution that is unfair (on this, see chapter 3).

can, of course, *assume* that A and B, having received identical commodity bundles, will not envy one another, and in the absence of illusion that is obviously so. However, the presence of illusion surely makes the premise shakier, and reduces our confidence in the judgment that the equal division point must be fair. However, if we can no longer use the equal division point as our reference, the entire superequality concept loses its rationale. More than that, since in a world of illusion the equal division point need not lie within a region of superfairness, it need no longer be true that the set of superequal points is a proper subset of the points of superfairness. In this way, illusion can cost us one of the fundamental relationships between superfairness and superequality.

10   Standards of Fairness and Framing by Surrounding Circumstances

Once we leave the formal theory of fairness, illusion-related considerations, rather than serving as a peripheral consideration, may come closer to constituting the heart of the matter. As we have seen, the nature of an economic illusion, that is, the mental image of a real phenomenon possessed by a member of the economy, is, apparently, heavily influenced by the *framing* of the phenomenon, i.e., by the circumstances that surround it. A $100 bottle of wine may not be considered too expensive to drink if it was purchased for $7 a decade earlier by the same person who would judge it to be far too costly if he had to purchase it today. The maximum price the thirsty individual is willing to pay for a beer depends on whether the beer seller is a small grocery or an elegant hotel.

   Zajac [1985] emphasizes that framing is equally important in common standards of fairness. An act that is generally considered "fair" in one set of surrounding circumstances is likely to be rejected as grossly unjust when peripheral conditions are different. To illustrate his point he cites the following parallel experiments, carried out by Hoffman and Spitzer [1985] (see also Selten [1978] for related results). In each of the first set of experiments a random device was used openly to select a "winner" from the two participants. The winner was, in effect, offered a choice of either x dollars that he could assign to himself unilaterally, with y dollars ($y < x$) going to the other player, or, instead, if he and the other players could reach an agreement, they could share an amount $x + y + z < 2x$, divided between them in any way they desired. In 61 percent of the cases (14 out of 22) the agreements reached in this way involved an equal or a nearly equal division of the total payoff (in an earlier experiment there was an equal division in *every* case!). Thus, while in accord with the predictions of most economic models, in 91 percent of the experiments an agreement was reached that yielded the joint maximum payoff to the two players, the agreements, far from constituting a Pareto improvement over the noncooperative equilibrium, involved a voluntary sacrifice by the winner of the (positive) amount $x - (x + y + z)/2$; that is, the winners forwent the x dollar payoff that they were permitted to assign themselves unilaterally, accepting instead the smaller equal share, presumably for the sake of fairness.

Next, the experiments were varied in two respects: The position of winner, instead of being assigned randomly, was awarded to the victor in a game of Nim. The instructions also now told the winner that he had "earned the right" to select the payoff arrangement from among exactly the same set of options as before. In this second set of 22 experiments the joint maximum was arrived at in 21 cases. But now only in 7 cases was there an approximately equal split, in 15 cases the winner received at least as much as the maximum he could achieve in the absence of cooperation, and in 12 cases he received more than this.

There was also a third (intermediate) variation of the experiment in which the winner was selected by the game of Nim, but the instructions were carefully purged of any suggestion that this gave that person any *moral* right to control over the payoffs. This time in 13 of the 22 cases there was an approximately equal division and in only 6 cases the winner received as much as he could have assigned himself unilaterally.

One suspects that these results, surprising as they were, apparently, even to the experimenters, in fact represent a widespread phenomenon. It will not do to dismiss them as a mere manifestation of irrationality. The experimental subjects, upper level undergraduate and graduate students in economics, management, and law at a major university, were surely at least as sophisticated as the population generally. Rather, it seems to me, their behavior demonstrates that Zajac is justified in concluding that framing does affect profoundly the nature of the public's standards of fairness that it accepts as applicable to a particular set of circumstances.

This is precisely the sort of phenomenon to which I allude when discussing "economic illusion." And all of it implies, consequently, that economic illusion is relevant to application of fairness theory not only because of the way it modifies the individual's evaluation of the vector of items he receives in a given allocation but, more fundamentally, because it affects his criteria of fairness themselves and thereby changes the entire fairness calculation from that which would hold in a world in which standards of equity did not bend as the framing of issues varied.

In this sense, then, "illusion" lies at the heart of the logic of fairness and certainly is far more than a mere footnote to its analysis.

Further Applications and Issues of Method

1 Asymmetry and Other Issues of Method in Applied Fairness Theory

Like the dog in Dr. Johnson's remark, what is surprising about the applications of fairness theory that this volume has offered is not the depth that they have been able to achieve but the fact that they have been achieved at all. There are obviously many economic issues other than those dealt with here that give rise to questions of fairness. This chapter will list a few of these by way of illustration. It will suggest briefly how fairness theory may be able to contribute to their analysis. Finally, and most important, it will discuss some serious impediments to such uses of fairness theory, as the theory has so far been formulated.

2 On Some Other Possible Applications of Fairness Theory

Fairness is widely cited as a consideration crucial for a variety of policy issues—among them taxation; sharing of common costs of services such as snow removal on a private street; and settlements among contending parties, as in wage negotiations or divorce arrangements. All of these lend themselves to some degree to translation into the terms of our analysis. We have already seen this for the sharing of common costs in our discussion of public utility pricing, which, at least in form, is essentially the same issue. Taxation, too, can be interpreted similarly, as the sharing of the overall costs of government activities. In all of these cases a set of resources is to be provided to a government, to the snow removal enterprise, etc., and once those resources have been transferred to such a use the Edgeworth hyperbox representing the resources available for distribution among the members of society will have shrunk correspondingly. The superfair region of the incremental Edgeworth box connecting the pre- and posttransfer circumstances then may be taken to represent the tax solutions or the cost apportionments that are fair to all those who will bear the burden.

Where resources are to be apportioned among several disputants, as in the division of inherited property or the property of a partnership that is to be dissolved or that of a husband and wife who are being divorced, the applicability of the superfairness criterion is even more direct. The divide and choose procedure in such cases simply becomes the operational embodiment of the superfairness test.

In this chapter we shall discuss several of the fairness issues that have just been mentioned. In particular, we shall consider the divorce issue as an example of the complications that can arise in a settlement among contending parties, and taxation as an example of the difficulties that can beset cost sharing solutions. In all these cases we shall see that a basic difficulty for the theory of fairness at this stage of its development is the symmetry with which it treats the parties involved, when the nature of the issue or exogenous circumstances call for asymmetry in their treatment, *as a matter of fairness.*

3   On Divorce Settlements

The literature has mentioned the cut and choose algorithm as an instrument that may possibly prove helpful in divorce settlements (see, e.g., Crawford [1977]). The discussion has focused on such matters as the advantage that can accrue to the well informed cutter, and has proposed some procedural modifications (already mentioned in chapter 2) to reduce the assymmetry in the positions of the cutter and chooser. For example, it has been shown by Crawford that if these roles are assigned randomly to the contending parties and the chooser is permitted to select the equal division collection of assets or (either) one of the collections provided by the chooser, the range of potential asymmetry will be reduced.

It is probably true that the cut and choose device can be a powerful and attractive procedure in some cases where the contending parties can find no other basis for settlement. Its advantages are clear. This form of execution of the superfairness test is widely accepted as fair. It is easy to carry out and its properties are well understood. It offers a significant degree of protection even to the party who would otherwise be in the weaker bargaining position, and it eliminates much of the stochastic element introduced via trial by (attorneys') combat. The problem of asymmetry of the advantage enjoyed by cutter and chooser may well be minor in many of the cases one encounters in practice.

Yet despite all of these attractive features of the approach, some consideration confirms that it will sometimes not get to the heart of the problem. In reality, matters are usually complicated in ways that bring them beyond the range of the cut and choose approach. The difficulties that beset property division in cases of divorce also have their counterpart elsewhere.

Divorce settlements are often complicated beyond the reach of an abstract procedure such as that called for by the superfairness or superequality criteria by the very fact that the two parties generally cannot be treated as interchangeable abstractions, as the theory assumes. Symmetry of the deserts of the two parties is at the very heart of superfairness analysis, and probably of any other fairness analyses that are currently available. Thus, it is not unknown for writers to adopt as something tantamount to an axiom the fairness requirement that a distribution between two parties, i and j, not be affected if the indicies assigned to the two parties are interchanged.[1]

The treatment of the parties in an exchange of commodities as anonymous and essentially interchangeable persons may sometimes be quite reasonable when the trade is a market (barter) transaction between two individuals. However, in divorce it is likely to miss the essence of the matter. The role of the individuals in the family as it was previously constituted, their behavior, their current earning abilities, and their likely future earning opportunities are not only relevant—they are generally the nub of the fair division issue. If both parties were working full time, did they contribute equally to family income? Did the wife give up a promising career at her husband's request? Are her prospective earnings opportunities after the divorce as promising as his? Did one party mistreat the other? Such matters can and do arise in any divorce hearing and most observers would agree that a settlement is unlikely to be fair unless it takes them into account. The problem is in part like that which arises when one deals with fairness in production, in contradistinction to pure exchange (chapter 2, sections 8–10). For the issue involves the relative weighting assigned to relative productive contribution as against the weights given to relative

---

1. It may seem on first consideration that a criterion such as that proposed by Rawls eschews such neutrality by favoring the individuals in the most disadvantagous position over other members of society. This, however, would be a misunderstanding of Rawls, who would presumably treat any impoverished individual i, just as well or as badly as equally impoverished individual j, all other things being equal. People are just as anonymous under the Rawls test as they are under superfairness, which also can take income or material possessions into account, albeit in its own manner.

"needs." We have seen what difficulties this alone can cause both for the formulation of an appropriately modified fairness criterion and for the analysis and results that such a revised criterion permits. But these difficulties may be minor compared with those likely to be introduced by other pertinent considerations. We can at least define and measure with tolerable accuracy the income contribution of each party to a divorce, using proxies such as the current market price of a housekeeper as a means to value the income contribution of housework. But what yardstick does one use to value a career forgone and how does one embed the information in a suitable fairness criterion? What about intangibles such as mistreatment of one person by the other?

Matters grow more complex still when the couple involved in the divorce is not childless. First of all, the children themselves may constitute part of collection of "items" to be bargained over. But that may be treated as an issue in a formal sense no different from the division of automobiles, houses, and pets between childless spouses, though in practice one will surely want to exercise far more care in the assignment of custody over children than in the division of inanimate objects.

The more taxing analytic problem arises once the children have been assigned to one of the parents. Suppose, for concreteness, that there are three children and that custody has been awarded to the mother. How does one now go about dividing the available assets between the father as the one party and the other four members of the family as the other? What, for example, constitutes the equal division distribution? There are many objects that are useful to adults that minors cannot use and in which they are generally not even interested. Presumably, in an equal division such items, too, should be distributed equally among the children to be used by them (or their mother acting on their behalf) in voluntary (superfair) exchanges. Thus, if all of the family's holdings are divisible and four-fifths of each item is assigned to the mother's party, one may perhaps take the result to constitute an equal division, despite the differences in the needs and preferences of children and adults.

But is that really reasonable? On one side of the matter there may be economies of scale. It is probably not four times as expensive in terms of food and shelter to keep four persons at what might be considered to constitute a given living standard than to do so for a single isolated individual. If that were the overriding consideration, it might be agreed that equality of division might assign less than four-fifths of the value of the property to the mother in our illustrative parable.

However, the matter has another side. Specially expensive outlays, notably on education, are customarily made on children. Besides, children produce no incomes—only outlays. On these scores true equality (or perhaps equity is the better term) would seem to require that far more than a proportionate share of the total assets of the family be assigned to the mother and her children.

All of the points that have just been made are common observations in the divorce courts and clever attorneys on either side have adduced many others that are at least equally difficult to encompass in the formal analysis.

The preceding discussion is, of course, not intended to constitute even the beginning of a serious analysis of the fairness issues raised by divorce. The subject is clearly too complex to lend itself to useful treatment in so brief a space. Moreover, the psychological and sociological considerations that must be taken into account in such an analysis carry it well beyond the economist's realm.

Indeed, that is the main point of the discussion, which is meant to indicate the limitations that beset application of fairness analysis to issues involving apportionment among contending parties, particularly where it is not clearly appropriate to treat the contending parties symmetrically.

4 On Fairness in Taxation

Discussions of fairness in taxes clearly precede Adam Smith's well-known treatment of the subject and have been a mainstay of texts in public finance ever since. Many of the considerations cited are quite standard—ability to pay, horizontal equity, and the notion that tax payments should somehow be related to benefits. This is not the place to review the list or to discuss its components in any detail. Rather, what I want to point out here, and it should be obvious once mentioned, is that here, too, asymmetries are certain to play a critical role of much the same sort they assume in the case of divorce settlements. Ability to pay clearly depends on the size of the taxpaying family and the ages of its members. The benefits the family derives from the public sector obviously also vary widely with many subtle characteristics of that family. It is such differences that, at least ostensibly, underlie many of the complexities of the tax laws such as exemptions for dependents, medical deductions, educational credits, and the like. There are, no doubt, solid grounds for the objections that have been raised against many such exemptions in the form they assume in reality. But one cannot simply deny the legitimacy of the asymmetry complications that fairness in taxation entails and that serve as justification for special tax provisions of the sort we have been considering. Once again, the conclusion is that there is more to fairness in taxation than symmetric principles of economic justice can readily encompass.[2]

5 Asymmetry and Fairness in General

Almost always, fairness is taken to involve some asymmetry in the treatment of different individuals. No one considers it unfair that a convicted and dangerous criminal receive treatment very different from that accorded other individuals. More generally, it seems clear that most views of fairness consider it appropriate for exceptional merit (however defined) to be rewarded and for exceptional vice at least to be shortchanged in distribution.

But that is only a peripheral consideration for our purposes. In cases where it arises the asymmetries may well be fortuitous so far as the main fairness issue is concerned. Fairness may call for unequal treatment, but not because of the nature of the case at issue. Rather, the people concerned happen to be unequal in merit and hence by some ill formulated standard of equity they happen not to deserve identical rewards.

There are other cases, as in divorce, in which the asymmetries also do not arise directly from the issue, but the asymmetries are likely to be so substantial and pervasive that they constitute the bulk of the relevant discussion. Here, to adopt Marx's phrase, the (symmetry) rule becomes the exception and the exception becomes the rule. In such cases a symmetric fairness analysis may well leave out the essence of the subject.

Finally, there are issues in which asymmetry arises out of the nature of the case. We have encountered an example in our discussion of public utility pricing and its comparative treatment of household and business customers. The issue arises here precisely because a household is very different from a firm in financial size, objectives, and a host of other

---

2. I use the term "readily" to indicate that in principle, with a sufficient number of attributes to distinguish different categories of individuals, it might be possible to treat persons anonymously within an analytic model and yet approximate to a tolerable degree of accuracy all the significant asymmetries. Thus, by treating alike every family of four with three children under the age of 18 with an annual income of x dollars (etc.) one could avoid any special treatment of individual i who happened to fall in that category. This still does not solve the associated problem of choice of an appropriate definitional (axiomatic) treatment of fairness in terms of such a list of attributes. I remind the reader of the difficulty encountered by the literature in trying to deal with two such objective attributes—the amount of labor an individual has contributed to production and the quantity of (incremental) output that labor yields.

attributes. Such differences did, indeed, cause complications for our discussion of fairness in pricing. An even clearer example is provided by wage bargaining. An employer is very different from an employee, even where the latter is represented by his trade union's bargaining agent. This makes it difficult to take even the first step of fairness analysis—the evaluation of the benefits of a proposed wage settlement to the business firm as viewed from the vantage point of the employee. That is, it is not easy to formulate the specifications of the pertinent Edgeworth box or to define what is meant by the symmetric image in that box of an indifference hypersurface of either of the parties.

Thus, asymmetries must affect fairness evaluations in a variety of ways that differ in their significance and in the degree to which they emerge intrinsically from the structure of the problem at issue.

6 A Word on Interpersonal Comparisons of Utility

Ever since Lionel Robbins provided his fundamental methodological contributions and challenging criticisms of welfare theory, economists have explored a variety of procedures, entailing various degrees of convolution, to avoid recourse to interpersonal comparisons of utility. The Hicks, Kaldor, and Scitovsky criteria were offered as supplements to the Pareto criterion, seeking to permit the theory of efficiency in resource allocation to arrive at definitive results without any need to evaluate either the relative strengths of feelings or the relative merits and deserts of different individuals.

The superfairness and superequality criteria used in this book accomplish as much, or as little. Each of these standards is constructed in such a way that the need for such interpersonal comparisons never arises in the process of use of either criterion. We need only compare the utility any pertinent individual A derives from a, the bundle of items assigned to him, with the utility A himself would derive from the bundle b, assigned to some other pertinent individual B. In this process we never compare the utility B can obtain from either bundle with the utility that it offers to A. I hope the preceding chapters have shown that this refinement, while protecting the purity of the superfairness and superequality criteria, does not rob them completely of applicability.

Yet it cannot help shrinking the domain of their applicability. As eminent analysts such as Rawls, Sen, and Lord Robbins himself were driven to conclude, many fairness issues inherently assign an indispensable role to interpersonal comparisons of utility. Perhaps the most noteworthy examples are redistribution issues such as that which arises in the choice of degree of progressivity in taxation. A moment's thought shows why in such a case, where A's gain must constitute a loss to some other person, B,[3] we cannot hope to evaluate any redistribution proposal without some basis on which to weigh the relative gains and losses of the affected persons.

That is precisely why this book has had virtually nothing to offer on issues of pure income distribution, important though they are. In at least this area, then, the prospects for application of fairness analysis remain modest at best. It seems clear that only by adoption of a forthright procedure for interpersonal comparisons, however arbitrary and subject to criticism it may be, can one hope for true progress on this front.

7   Concluding Comment

This chapter was initially intended to conclude the book. By emphasizing the fairness applications not dealt with here, and pointing to asymmetry as the major impediment to their analysis, it seemed an appropriate point to offer the customary challenge to future researchers in the field.

However, a last minute suggestion, which will be described in the next chapter, led me to turn to the recent literature on the theory and practice of arbitration. It became clear to me in the course of preparation of the chapter that arbitration is the one means that offers any immediate promise of dealing effectively with application of the principles of fairness theory to cases of fundamental asymmetry in the positions and character of the contending parties, and with the need for interpersonal comparisons.

In one sense, arbitration deals with asymmetry using Alexander the Great's approach to the Gordian knot. It solves difficult fairness problems not through analysis, but by the election of an individual to the position of authority on equitability, and an agreement simply to accept whatever he may recommend. As described so far this plainly constitutes no untangling of the complex issue. Yet, as we shall see in the next chapter, there is a good deal more to be said on the matter, and both the theory and the empirical work help us to understand not only the arbitration process, but approaches that promise to facilitate the application of fairness theory in asymmetric cases.

---

3. Again, the exception is the case that is the focus of the Hochman and Rogers literature (e.g., [1969]) in which b derives an external benefit from a utility gain to A.

12

The Arbitrator: Fairness Incarnate (or: Toward Resolution of the Asymmetry Problem)

There are a number of professions, lawyers, physicians, clergymen, among others, which deal frequently with fairness issues during the course of their work. But one activity, that of the professional arbitrator, actually specializes in the fair and equitable resolution of a variety of disputes, such as those between labor and management, between firms, and even between the parties to a divorce. They cut through the asymmetries contributed by the identities of the contending parties (e.g., labor versus management), the differences in their circumstances (e.g., who is the more impecunious), and the nature of the pertinent environment (e.g., the prospects for inflation). It is the arbitrator's task to select the fairest of the available settlement options, and consequently his main professional qualification is the ability to determine what is fair or, at least, to convince others that he can and will do so. In short, the arbitrator is the very embodiment of fairness.

It is, therefore, appropriate to examine both the theory and practice of arbitration,[1] hoping to learn thereby some of the secrets of fairness that the symmetry models alone cannot reveal. Fortunately, in the past few years there have been several major contributions to this literature that, while not as yet nearly definitive (as their authors carefully emphasize), do offer remarkable insights on the general subject. The presentation here consists largely of a summary of the pertinent portions of those writings, with little added contribution aside from selection and some bits of supplementary interpretation.

This chapter will deal first with the empirical material, to be followed by the theoretical arguments, as some of the most relevant theoretical work is

---

1. Here I shall be dealing almost exclusively with what is referred to as "interest arbitration" in labor disputes, i.e., disputes over wages and other conditions of employment, in contradistinction to grievance arbitration. Interest arbitration occurs primarily in state and local governments, particularly in disputes involving the police and fire fighters.

understandable only in terms of the institutional arrangements character-istic of the arbitration process. The descriptive section will report, among other things, that

(i) The livelihood of a professional arbitrator depends on his ability to avoid repeated rejection by either of the disputing parties in cases where his services are being considered. Consequentiy, he has a substantial stake in his reputation as a maker of fair decisions.

(ii) Where arbitrated conflicts recur repeatedly, e.g., in labor disputes, pro-fessional arbitrators tend to acquire a track record that is the basis for a persistent degree of agreement between contending parties on the arbitra-tors they prefer. That is, in actual practice (where, as we shall see, ranking is often part of the selection process), the rankings of the two parties will often turn out to be similar, presumably indicating that they feel they know who is likely to make a fair decision. Both sides seem to seek to secure that person's selection rather than pressing the appointment of someone who will be prejudiced in their favor, thereby running the risk that the selected arbitrator will be biased toward the other side.

(iii) There is a substantial degree of consistency in a given arbitrator's awards, although it is far from perfect. This observation is made possible both by institutional arrangements in labor-management arbitration that permit the quantitative comparison of awards in different cases or of the judgments of different arbitrators (fact finders) in a given case and by an ingenious interview *cum* simulation study.

(iv) Strategic positioning by contending parties seems to have a limited effect on arbitrators' awards. That is, the arbitrators seem to have an independent view of what constitutes a fair solution in the attendant circumstances, and are not substantially swayed from it by the conserva-tism or extremism of the offers put forward by the contending parties.

In other words, arbitrators appear to ignore posturing and strategic manipulation and to act rather consistently in accord with their own conception of true fairness. Moreover, those who submit to arbitration appear to feel they can identify the persons who possess the knowledge or ability to make relatively fair decisions.

Much of the theoretical writing that has been published in this field is not directly pertinent to our analysis because it deals with the strategic choices available to the disputants and the consequences of selection of a particular strategy. However, there is some work, particularly that of Craw-ford [1979B], that constitutes what may be considered an extension of superfairness or, perhaps more accurately, of superequality analysis.

This analysis interprets the work of the arbitrator as the selection of a neutral and, hence, fair decision, which can be taken to be the counterpart of the equal division point of the Edgeworth box in the applications of fairness theory in which the symmetry requirements are not violated. From this neutral point, N, it may be possible to carry out further redistributions that are Pareto superior to it and, perhaps, even incrementally superfair. Crawford not only shows us what determines the location of these solutions superior to N, but also devises an arbitration procedure whose only Cournot-Nash equilibria are such solutions. Thus, self-interested behavior may lead the disputing parties to arrive at such a point or to make it necessary for the arbitrator to reach a decision that leads to the selection of such a Cournot-Nash equilibrium. This solution is also shown to be analytically similar to the procedure Crawford has offered elsewhere [1980] for improvement of the solution that emerges from a process of cutting and choosing. This solution will also necessarily be Pareto optimal where the requisite information is available to the parties though, unfortunately, all or virtually all of the gain over the arbitrator's neutral solution will tend to accrue to one or the other of the contending parties.

Thus we see that the arbitration process makes it possible to extend at least some of fairness analysis to cases that are fundamentally asymmetric. Moreover, the analysis not only helps us to understand the logic of the arbitration process but also gives us some insight into the nature of fairness in cases where the parties involved are so fundamentally different as to preclude direct comparison as a test of the appropriateness of their payoffs.

1   Empirical Evidence: Are Fair Arbitrators Distinguishable?

There are several features of arbitration in practice (for an excellent description, see Lester [1984]) that facilitate the study of the institution and its workings. First, the number of cases in which it occurs is substantial. This is so particularly because employees in the public sector are often prohibited from striking, with the legal requirement that disputes that the contending parties cannot resolve between themselves be settled by binding arbitration. Second, in many cases, particularly where the public sector is involved, the settlement, as well as some of the process leading up to it, is a matter of public record. Third, many of the decision processes are such as to permit quantitative analysis including, in some circumstances, direct comparison with typical outcomes when other arbitration procedures are used.

This section focuses upon the selection of the arbitrators, and we shall begin to see how observation of the selection procedures can help in the analysis of behavior patterns that emerge in arbitration. Most of the material on patterns in choice of arbitrator is based on a pioneering study by Bloom and Cavanagh [1984].

Methods for selecting arbitrators vary from appointment purely by rotation from a list previously agreed to by potential disputants to elaborate systems involving systematic use of vetos and rankings by those parties.[2] The New Jersey arbitration system for police and fire fighters is of the latter variety. A roster of some 70 candidate arbitrators is maintained and revised every three years. If the parties to a dispute cannot reach agreement, the commission that governs public employment relations selects a list of seven names from this panel. Each party is provided with information about the candidates and is asked to veto three of the seven and to rank the others. The commission then selects as arbitrator the person who was not vetoed by either party and whose combined rank is highest. Records are kept of all such proceedings and are available for study.

Bloom and Cavanagh used 1980 data for a panel that had been in operation for three years, so that the unions and managements would have had maximum opportunity to assess the individual arbitrators. Information on 197 panels was collected, and 75 of them provided data ideally suited for analysis. The authors then formulated a number of questions for investigation.

The first question was whether the rankings of arbitrators by management and unions would display any consistency. They noted that if the two parties disagreed completely in their three vetoes, only one of the seven candidates would be available for ranking, while if they agreed completely, four of the candidates would survive unvetoed. The average number that remained available for ranking was in fact about 2.5, and "Over 80 percent of the panels yielded two or three jointly acceptable arbitrators" [1984, p.15].

Next, Bloom and Cavanagh correlated the rankings of the two parties and found a small but positive correlation ($\bar{\rho} = 0.13$), largely because "... the unions and the employers ranked the same individual first in 21 of the 75 panels they reviewed" (pp. 16–17). In addition, in every rank position other than first place the observed frequency of coincidence exceeded the theoretical value that one would expect had the two parties' choices been independent. Thus, while union and management views on the relative

---

2. Procedures of the latter variety are common in circumstances where arbitration is built into the system and recurs frequently. On this, see Ashenfelter [1985, pp. 12–14].

desirability of individual arbitrators were hardly identical, they were certainly far from diametrically opposed.

Next, the authors investigated which characteristics of arbitrators in the New Jersey system made a candidate attractive to both unions and employers, as indicated by their rankings. For this purpose they collected data on individual arbitrators' impartiality as measured by the relative difference between the number of cases in which they had favored the unions and those in which they had favored the employers in final offer arbitration[3] during the two previous years. They also acquired data on the candidates' training (law, economics, or other) and previous arbitration experience as indicated by several measures. A Neumann-Morgenstern utility model was then formulated, and maximum likelihood estimates of its parameters were calculated from the data on the observed rankings and the arbitrator characteristics. First, the authors found that previous experience had a positive coefficient in both the union and employer equations. Second, while there was an understandable tendency for unions to prefer arbitrators who had previously leaned toward the union side and for management rankings to go the other way, the significance levels of the two coefficients were very low. Third, both sides showed a preference for arbitrators with legal training over labor relations practitioners. Management tended to prefer economists to both these professions, while the unions tended to rank the economists last.

Finally, the authors tested the hypothesis that the observed rankings did not represent the parties' true preferences, but were, rather, a strategic attempt to deal with the expected rankings of the opposing party. As the authors describe it, "Our test for strategic behavior primarily involves the estimation of alternative random utility models which use different subsets of information available in the arbitrator rankings data. Under the null hypothesis that the data reveal the parties' true preferences, estimates of the parameters of these models should not be significantly different" (p. 24). In fact the authors found that with a single exception for one of the parameters, the equality hypothesis was never rejected: "Indeed, the closeness of the parameter estimates . . . . is a remarkable finding which provides strong evidence that the ranking data mainly reveal the parties' true preferences . . . . Overall, then, the results . . . provide no support for the hypothesis of strategic behavior of either party" (pp. 25–26).

Taken as a whole, the results of this study do not present an absolutely

---

3. In final offer arbitration the arbitrator is required to select, without modification, the offer of one of the parties. More will be said presently about this procedure and its logic.

conclusive picture of the inner mechanism of arbitrator selection. Yet for our purposes, much is suggested by the strong evidence that the recorded rankings represent true preferences rather than acts of strategy. Apparently, neither side displayed much preference for a candidate whose record might indicate bias in its own favor, and the rankings of the two parties, while far from identical, showed considerable overlap and certainly were not consistently at odds. These observations are surely not in conflict with the hypothesis that each party considers its interests to be protected most effectively by support of an arbitrator who is perceived likely to be considered fair by both sides. For all-out support by one side of candidates who appear to be biased in its direction may well prove too dangerous. If both sides play that game, it opens the possibility that the arbitrator selected will not be fair, and will be inclined to the opposing side. In this limited sense, one possible explanation of the observed overlap of rankings by the opposing parties may indeed be strategic—each party rejecting the risky option of making an all-out try for an advantageous choice. It will take the more conservative route of trying to ensure the selection of the fairest and most unbiased arbitrator possible. This also suggests that there exist criteria of fairness not yet formally described or analyzed, which are nevertheless known, perhaps intuitively, by both parties and, to a degree, accepted by them both.

2   Some Other Institutional Arrangements for Arbitration

Several investigators have been able to study the consistency of arbitrators' choices, and from their results we can hope to determine whether there exists anything like a consensus on what constitute truly fair decisions. Some knowledge of the procedures used by arbitrators is necessary to understand the analysis. These procedural options will also play a key role in the theoretical discussions later in this chapter.

The two most common forms of arbitration in the United States are *conventional arbitration* and *final offer arbitration*. The former is the obvious procedure under which the appointed arbitrator acquaints himself with the pertinent objective facts and the positions taken by the contending parties. The law sometimes suggests particular considerations (e.g., the rate of inflation, the financial health of the employer, wages in comparable occupations) that the arbitrator should take into account, but it apparently never dictates the relative weights that should be assigned to them or the way in which they should enter the final decision. The arbitrator then renders whatever decision he or she considers appropriate, and it is binding on the parties. Of course, if the arbitrator wishes to be reemployed, as is normally expected, then the decision must not be bizarre or highly unbalanced, but it is otherwise quite unconstrained.

A widespread view about this process is that because arbitrators wish to retain an appearance of impartiality they will tend to split the difference between the positions of the two parties. That, in turn, tends to induce the parties to inflate their demands in order to come out ahead in the splitting process. The net result, according to this common view, is that the availability of conventional arbitration undermines the direct negotiation process because the exaggerated offers virtually preclude serious bargaining. This is referred to in the literature as the "chilling effect" of conventional arbitration upon the prospects for amicable settlement between the parties.

To overcome this problem an alternative procedure has been devised and it is now widely used. This procedure, final offer arbitration, requires each of the contending parties to submit a firm offer to the arbitrator. The arbitrator is then required to accept one of the offers *without modifying it one iota*. The idea is that the parties will thereby be induced to submit offers that are reasonable and fair, because if one of them makes an offer that is not so, it becomes likely that the arbitrator will feel compelled to accept the offer of the other party. We shall see later that for a number of reasons the final offer device may very well fail in its purpose, and may even be the source of a chilling effect of its own. We shall also examine some modifications of final offer arbitration that, at least in theory, circumvent the problem.

More important for our immediate purposes is the fact that each of the two procedures is used rather frequently. In New Jersey, for example, nearly 70 percent of the arbitrated cases were settled by final offer procedures, while the remainder used conventional arbitration. This provides sufficient statistical data to permit direct comparison of the tailor-made awards fashioned by the arbitrators themselves (under conventional procedures) with both the formal offers of the parties, and the arbitrators' choices between them in the final offer cases. Cases of the latter variety also permit the observer to determine categorically whether an arbitrator decided in favor of labor or management, both in a particular dispute and over a specified period. Much of the recent empirical work rests on the contrast between the two types of arbitration.

Two variants of the final offer process are also pertinent. First, where a dispute involves several issues (say, wages and safety arrangements) the procedure may require packaging of the final offers or the issues may be dealt with one by one. Under the first, management's offer must describe *both* its proposed wage scale and the set of safety provisions it hopes to undertake, and a similar joint package must be provided by the union. The arbitrator is then required to accept either management's package as a whole or labor's package in its entirety. Under unbundled final offer arbitration the arbitrator can, for example, choose the union's wage offer and management's safety proposal, thereby again being enabled to go some way toward splitting the difference.

Another relevant variant of final offer arbitration is employed in Iowa (see Ashenfelter [1985 p. 24]). There the parties are offered substantial leeway to design their own arbitration procedure, but when they cannot agree even on this, a two-step process is imposed upon them. The first step is the employment of a neutral "fact finder" who recommends a settlement. Armed with this suggestion the parties may then reopen negotiations and arrive at a voluntary settlement. If that fails, however, they are required to undergo final offer arbitration of a sort that differs from the usual variety in that the arbitrator can select one of *three* proposals: the union's final offer, that of management, or that of the fact finder. This procedure, then, permits analysis of the frequency of agreement of the two neutral specialists in the making of fair decisions: the fact finder and the arbitrator.

3   On Consistency of Arbitration Decisions

The data on the outcomes in final offer and conventional arbitration settlements have been studied with care and ingenuity (see, e.g., Ashenfelter and Bloom [1984] and Ashenfelter [1985]). In addition, a very illuminating simulation study was carried out by Bazerman [1984]) and the data that emerge have been subjected to several illuminating analyses by Farber and Bazerman [1984]).

A superficial glance at the data reveals a curious appearance of partiality. The New Jersey statistics indicate that the arbitrators selected the union offer in at least 65 percent of the final offer arbitration cases in *each* of the three years for which the data are available. In Iowa, on the other hand, in most years the employers' share of the awards ranged from 66.7 to 100 percent of the total. These observations might well give rise to the suspicion that arbitrators are not as unbiased as they are supposed to be. However, a comparison of conventional and final offer awards by the arbitrators told a very different story. If it can be assumed that in final offer arbitration cases they simply select what they consider to be the fairer of the two offers, i.e., the one closest to the fair ideal, F, where a single quantitative variable, such as percentage wage increase, is at issue, one can calculate from the observed settlements the maximum likelihood value of F and of its standard deviation. That is, one can estimate the mean fair settlement value, $\overline{F}$, and the value of the standard deviation most likely to have generated the pattern of final offer settlements actually observed. This can then be compared with the mean and standard deviation of the settlements in standard arbitration cases that can, not unreasonably, be interpreted to represent the arbitrators' own view on the fairest decision value, F. This calculation was carried out for each of the three years of New Jersey data available (Ashenfelter [1985, pp. 19–20 and table 2]). In each year the two estimates of $\overline{F}$ were close, grew closer year by year, and by 1980 had reached $\overline{F} = 8.26$ percent (the selected rate of wage increase) for conventional arbitration and an estimated 8.27 percent for final offer arbitration.[4] This surely fits in with the hypothesis that arbitrators feel, consciously or subconsciously, that they know what decisions constitute true fairness and are prepared, with considerable consistency, to act accordingly.

There is a bit more to the story. Ashenfelter and Bloom went on to compare these figures with the unions' and managements' final offers. The pattern they found repeatedly in each year was that in New Jersey the unions consistently made offers that were far less extreme and, hence, less risky than managements'. For example, in 1980 the mean union offer was a wage rise of 8.54 percent, while the mean conventional compensation award was 8.26 percent and the mean management offer was only 5.7 percent.[5] This suggests that in New Jersey[6] the unions are systematically more conservative than managements in their final offers, as judged by the standard of conventional arbitration awards. The fact that unions won final offer cases more frequently in New Jersey is, consequently, consistent with my interpretation that the arbitrator thinks he knows what fairness is, and tends to act accordingly.[7]

Another test of consistency, as already noted, was carried out by Farber

---

4. The corresponding standard deviation figures were also fairly close, but not nearly to the same degree. The poorest correspondence occurred in 1980, which yielded a standard deviation of 2.10 percent for conventional arbitration and a 1.48 percent estimate for final offer arbitration.

5. In 1979 the mean union offer was actually lower than the mean conventional award.

6. Curiously, in Iowa in most years patterns were completely reversed, with managements making the more conservative offers and winning more often.

7. This view is also consistent with the fact that management was usually the more frequent victor in Iowa, and that in 1983, the one year in which the Iowa unions made the apparently more conservative offer on the Ashenfelter-Bloom calculation, the union offers were adopted in 57 percent of the cases.

and Bazerman. They submitted a set of twenty-five hypothetical scenarios to a number of experienced professional arbitrators. In each case they included the hypothesized representative "facts" on items such as the rate of inflation, the financial state of management (its ability to pay), the terms of current settlements in other analogous cases (which seem in practice to be among the most critical considerations in what arbitrators consider to be fair), etc., as well as the accompanying (equally invented) union and management offers. These circumstances were, of course, varied systematically among the cases. The arbitrators were then asked to render a decision in each case, first under conventional arbitration and, then, under final offer arbitration. Sixty-four arbitrators provided usable responses.

The most pertinent conclusions from the authors' statistical analysis of the results were that

(i) the decisions of arbitrators as a group under conventional arbitration were highly consistent with those they made under final offer arbitration, with the award in the final offer case generally going to the party whose offer was closer to the arbitrator's conventional arbitration decision; and

(ii) arbitrators' decisions were far more heavily dependent on the objective facts about the case than on the offers of the parties, the influence of the latter declining systematically as the two offers grew further apart.

So far, then, the results do not conflict with the hypothesis that an arbitrator acts with consistency on the view that he knows what decision is truly fair, and that the views of the parties themselves do not affect that absolute truth. However, the evidence also suggests that arbitrators do not all hear one voice on that vision of true fairness. In his analysis, Bazerman [1984] found that there was "little consistency" among different arbitrators' decisions and, hence, in the weights each implicitly assigned to different pertinent facts. A similar conclusion emerges from the Iowa data for the cases in which the arbitrator chose among the (earlier) fact finder's recommendation and a final offer by management and by the union. In about one-third of the cases the arbitrator did *not* select the fact finder's recommendation. Moreover, this figure changed negligibly in the (nearly 50 percent) of the total cases in which one of the contending parties' final offer coincided with the fact finder's recommendation(!).

This suggests two conclusions important for our purposes:

First, though each arbitrator may have a view of fairness that to him seems definitive, the fairness evaluations of different professional evaluators may differ significantly. Second, it suggests that the contending parties are likely to be uncertain about at least an unknown arbitrator's views on fairness and hence about the decision that that person would consider most evenhanded. This observation will play an important role in the theoretical discussion that follows.

4   On Arbitration Theory: The Farber Model

The institution of arbitration has elicited a variety of theoretical investigations, some of which, though important in themselves, have only peripheral relevance to the applied fairness analysis that is our central concern. Other work, to which I will turn in section 6, fits in directly with the superfairness literature.

The formal discussion of arbitration has naturally directed itself to behavioral issues such as the strategic options it opens to the contending parties. Noteworthy is the recent work by Farber (see, e.g., [1981] in which he provides some basic models of the behavior of arbitrators and shows their implications for the reaction of disputants. Farber starts off from the widely suggested view that arbitrators characteristically seek to reach an equitable compromise between the proposals of the contending parties. However, he assumes also that the arbitrator has an independent notion of what constitutes a fair settlement of the issue. Farber then postulates that an arbitrator can be taken to act as though he were maximizing an objective function that assigns weights to his own fair solution and to the proposals of both the parties.

However, in these circumstances, if the contending parties have some idea of the arbitrator's behavior pattern, which experience may plausibly be expected to reveal to them, they will be induced to adapt their own positions so as to increase their expected payoffs.

What is optimal from the viewpoint of the interests of one of the parties clearly depends on the likely reaction of the opposition—i.e., on the likely resulting modification of the offer of the other party. We are thus back into the complexities of small numbers bargaining analysis and all their game theoretic implications. Farber deals with this issue by examining only the properties of the Cournot-Nash equilibrium.[8]

Farber is able to show that in such a model a Cournot-Nash equilibrium

---

8. It will be recalled that such an equilibrium is one in which each party selects those values of his decision variables that would maximize his own payoff if the other party were to leave its own decisions fixed. That is, if $A(y_a, y_b)$ and $B(y_a, y_b)$ are the two parties' respective payoff functions and y_a, y_b their respective decision variables, then the equilibrium is characterized by the two conditions $A_a = 0$, $B_b = 0$, where A_a is the partial derivative of $A(\cdot)$ with respect to y_a, etc.

tends to entail positions by the two parties in which they deliberately place themselves on opposite sides of the arbitrator's independently selected fair solution. In fact, in circumstances that are not implausible they will make final offers approximately equidistant from what they believe to be the arbitrator's fair solution. The implication is that in such a case, while superficial observation may indicate that the arbitrator is simply splitting the difference between the contenders' offers, it will in fact be these offers that place themselves at an equal distance from his preferred solution. Paradoxically, it will then be the arbitrator's independent views that control both the parties' offers and the ultimate decision, to the exclusion of other considerations, and despite the arbitrator's postulated desire to give some weight to the views of the two opponents.

While the Farber model may absolve the conventional arbitration process from the standard "chilling effect" criticism, the author nevertheless concludes that the process does impede full and effective bargaining in another way. That is, while it means that the parties really do not gain by inflating their claims, as they would if the arbitrator were simply to split the difference between their offers, strategic considerations may nevertheless deter them from making offers sufficiently conciliatory to permit a voluntary agreement. For each may fear that an offer less demanding than that corresponding to the Nash equilibrium, even though acceptable in itself, may nevertheless elicit an arbitrator decision in which the party that makes the conciliatory offer is left with the short end of the stick.

More important for our purposes, as we shall see presently, is the role of uncertainty in the Farber analysis. Each party feels itself required to act in accord with the requirements of the Nash equilibrium because it is not quite sure how the arbitrator or the other party will react to an offer that is less extreme. We shall see later how the analysis can change if there is no uncertainty about the arbitrator's objective function. (On the case of uncertainty about the arbitrator's preferences, see also Crawford [1981, 1982].)

5   On Arbitration, Fairness, and Game Theory

An early recognition of the link between fairness and arbitration occurs in the classic volume by Luce and Raiffa ([1957, pp. 121–154]). They start off by reminding us of the wide range of possible outcomes that may remain in the Neumann-Morgenstern solution set for a cooperative game, i.e., a game in which the participants combine to assure attainment of their maximal combined payoff and then bargain (or, perhaps, battle) over the division of the spoils.

They then suggest that such a conflict may be resolvable only by "... an arbiter, an impartial outsider [who] sincerely envisages his mission to be 'fairness' to both players ..." (p. 121). They then go on to "... define an *arbitration scheme* to be a function, i.e., rule, which associates to each conflict, i.e., two-person non-strictly competitive game, a unique payoff to the players" (p. 121).

They use as their main illustration of such a scheme the Nash solution of the bargaining game, which we must avoid confusing with the Cournot-Nash equilibrium concept, whose definition has just been reviewed. The Nash solution concept is a rather abstract concept whose applicability is not entirely obvious. Indeed only its derivation offers us an intuitive grasp of what may be involved, and it has been suggested that the seductiveness of its axiomatic foundations may be misleading rather than helpful.

Assume that the preferences of each of the contending parties is describable by a Neumann-Morgenstern utility function, u_i, that is unique up to a linear transformation. The Nash solution then requires the arbitrator to impose that division of the combined payoffs that maximizes the product, $u_1 u_2$, of the two parties' utility functions. Neither the fairness nor the viability of this solution is immediately obvious. However, there is a standard proof that this solution satisfies the following four axioms, which some writers have suggested as reasonable requirements of any fair solution. Moreover, and rather surprisingly, it is not difficult to prove that *no* arbitrated decision other than the Nash solution satisfies those four axioms. Making no attempt at rigor, the four axioms can be restated to require

1. *utility invariance:* the arbitrated decision must not change if, *ceteris paribus*, either party's utility function is reexpressed either in new units or a different origin, i.e., it is subjected to any transformation that is linear and that, consequently, does not change the information it conveys about the party's preferences;

2. *Pareto optimality:* the decision must be such that neither party can gain from any feasible change without the other party being harmed;

3. *symmetry:* if the positions of the two parties happen to be completely interchangeable, then the arbitrator should award identical utility payoffs to them; and

4. *independence of irrelevant alternatives:* Imagine two conflicts, A and B, each of which gives rise to bargaining between two parties, with A offering every settlement option available under conflict B, and that A offers several additional options besides. If the two parties' initial positions are the same in the two cases, and if A^*, the arbitrated settlement of conflict A, is also

among the options available in conflict B, then A^* must also be the arbitrated settlement for B. That is, if none of the *additional* options available in conflict A is the fairest solution, A^*, of A, then A^* must also be the fairest solution of B, because its fairness must be unaffected by the irrelevant additional solutions available under A.

As I have said, these axioms are appealing. However, there are commentators who feel that their appeal exceeds their merits. For example, it has been argued that the innocent appearance of the axiom on the independence of irrelevant alternatives enables it to sneak in some powerful but questionable constraints requiring, for example, that neither party's ranking of an option be affected by the range of alternatives available, or, if that ranking is affected in this way, that any "fair" arbitrator decisions not take such preference behavior into account. There is no point in going into further detail here on the perils of the axiomatic approach to the derivation of a criterion of fairness. This subject has already been pursued in chapter 7 in the discussion of cost allocation schemes as a basis for fair treatment of the different groups of customers of a regulated firm. There we saw in some detail how persuasive axioms can turn out, on closer inspection, unintentionally to conceal requirements that few of us will be prepared to accept. Moreover, it was suggested that when a set of axioms displays a remarkable power to derive surprisingly definitive results, that alone constitutes grounds for suspicion that there is much more to the axioms than meets the eye—and that where this is so, let the analyst beware.[9] The procedures that constitute the basis of this book's analyses are certainly very different in spirit from the axiomatic approaches, and my provisional conclusion that the Nash solution approach is unlikely to recommed itself to practitioners does not seem to me to represent an exceedingly narrow-minded view of the matter.

The most relevant feature of the Luce and Raiffa discussion, then, is their pioneering recognition of the relationship between the concepts of arbitration and fairness, and their demonstration of the opportunities for formal analysis that this observation opens.

6   Final Offer Arbitration with Known Arbitrator Preferences

Vincent Crawford's important contributions to fairness theory have been cited several times in earlier chapters. Now we turn to a fundamental piece

---

9. It is no coincidence that Luce and Raiffa derive as an alternative arbitration criterion, for another type of game, the same Shapley value relationship that has usually emerged from the axiomatic approach to cost allocation discussed earlier in this volume.

he has written on the theory of arbitration [1979B]. It should come as no surprise that this will be the piece of arbitration analysis most immediately pertinent to the subject matter of this book.

The basic difficulty besetting extension of superfairness analysis and the concepts related to it to cases in which there is a fundamental asymmetry between the parties is that we do not even have a straightforward base such as the equal allocation point that can serve as an obviously fair solution from which other fair distributions can be derived. When a divorce involves a husband on one side and wife and three children on the other most of us would suspect that equal division of their joint assets might be far from equitable. When management bargains with labor over wages and safety provisions it is not even clear what equal division may mean.

More than that, in such circumstances there is no obvious test for the fundamental criterion of superfairness theory— absence of envy, which in the symmetric case can be judged by one party's unwillingness to exchange its allocation with that of the other party. The very different character of a management and a union makes it clear that such a test is not readily extended to the sort of bargaining to which they are normally the parties.

Crawford's analysis, supplemented by some of the empirical work described earlier in this chapter, offers us a way of overcoming these difficulties, at least to some degree. Here I refer to two of our repeated observations: first, that the contending parties appear to have at least some measure of agreement on the identity of a "fair arbitrator," i.e., one who knows what is fair and will act accordingly, and, second, that individual arbitrators seem to render consistent decisions, indicating that they act on the basis of a criterion of fairness that is implicitly defined, though it may not be consciously known and recognized even by the arbitrator himself.

One may then follow Crawford in assuming that the arbitrator acts in accord with a well defined equity function, $e(z)$, where z is a possible settlement of a dispute that is subject to arbitration. Thus, z^*, the value of z that maximizes $e(z)$, may be taken as the fairest decision, at least in the view of the arbitrator—a view that, as has been said, commands some respect from the contending parties, a conclusion supported both by the institutional arrangements for the selection of arbitrators and by the empirical evidence.

We may observe immediately that z^* can be used in a modified Edgeworth box analysis of fairness, as a substitute for the equal division point, to serve as a basic fair solution that constitutes the benchmark for further analysis. We shall see presently how that observation can be built upon.

First, however, we must review Crawford's use of the arbitrator's equity function to analyze the implications of final offer arbitration under the extreme assumption that the parties are completely certain about the arbitrator's views on fairness, as encompassed in $e(z)$.

It will be recalled that final offer arbitration is an arrangement devised to avoid the alleged chilling effect of conventional arbitration if the parties come to believe that the arbitrator will merely split the difference between the offers proffered by the contending parties. Ashenfelter has observed most cogently [1985 p. 5] that if this is really what arbitrators do, or are believed to do, final offer arbitration may not really get around the problem. For if in their allegedly excessive zeal to avoid the wrath of either party, arbitrators were simply to toss coins to decide between the two parties' final offers, and if this became known, the incentive for inflation of offers by the parties would become just as strong as under conventional arbitration with arbitrators splitting the difference between the offers directly.

Crawford has shown that final offer arbitration can chill effective negotiation in yet another way in cases where both parties know the arbitrator's view on fairness. He proves, using four very plausible assumptions, that in these circumstances the only Cournot-Nash equilibrium is that in which both parties adopt as their final offer the settlement, z^*, that maximizes the arbitrator's equity function! That is, in this plausible model, both parties may well end up feeling themselves forced to adopt the arbitrator's preferred solution, whatever their feelings about it may be. Moreover, as we shall see, such a response pattern can also prevent the attainment of alternative settlements even if they are both Pareto optimal and Pareto improvements over z^*.

Crawford's four premises, which he uses to show that a final offer of z^* by each party is a Cournot-Nash equilibrium, and is the only such equilibrium under final offer arbitration with full information on the arbitrators preferences, are the following:

(1) z^*, the value of z that maximizes $e(z)$, is unique (i.e., to the arbitrator there is just one most equitable settlement).

(2) $e(z)$ is continuous, so that for any $z \neq z^*$ there exists a z' in every neighborhood of z such that $e(z') > e(z)$ (i.e., the arbitrator considers z' more equitable than z).

(3) For each party i, there exists in each neighborhood of z^* a settlement, z, that i prefers (selfishly) to z^* even though it may be detrimental to the other party.

(4) For any value of $e \neq e(z^*)$ any solution that is optimal (utility maximizing) for one of the parties will not be utility maximizing for the other.

Of these, only (4) is in any respect more than a routine sort of assumption, and (4) only tells us that there is sufficient disagreement between the parties to prevent them from reaching some negotiated settlement other than z^*.

Crawford's theorem is now easy to derive heuristically. It is clear that if party J makes the offer $z^j \neq z^*$, then by assumptions (2) and (3) there will exist a counteroffer, z^i, by the other party, I, which yields a higher value of e than z^j does and so, by continuity, there will exist an offer z' that is a slight modification of z^i and that is better for I than z^j is and for which, simultaneously, $e(z') > e(z^j)$. Consequently, if J's final offer were $z^j \neq z^*$ and I's final offer were z', the arbitrator would select the latter under a final offer arbitration process. Thus, z^j could not be J's final offer in a Cournot-Nash equilibrium. Nor could z' be an equilibrium final offer for I unless it maximized I's utility given the value $e(z')$ of e. But then, by assumption (4), unless $z' = z^*$, J could make a counteroffer that simultaneously increased the value of e and J's own utility payoff. This shows that no offer other than z^* is compatible with Cournot-Nash equilibrium under the circumstances postulated. The proof that z^* *is* a Cournot-Nash equilibrium now follows from the uniqueness of z^*, and the fact that the arbitrator will select the offer of the party that proposes z^* if the other does not.

It is to be noted that Crawford's problem arises even if neither party knows the arbitrator's true preferences. So long as each party believes it has a shrewd idea of the arbitrator's preferred settlement, z^*, that party will find itself subject to the Crawfordian incentives for the selection of its estimated value of z^* even where the estimates of z^* adopted by the parties do not coincide. So much, then, for final offer arbitration as a sure cure for the chilling effect of arbitration on the effectiveness of the negotiation process.

7 Superequity

It is obvious that while z^* may serve as an effective substitute for the equal division point in the symmetric case dealt with by standard superfairness theory, z^*, like the equal division point, need not be Pareto optimal, and Pareto improvements from z^* may well be possible. The situation is depicted in the Edgeworth diagram figure 12.1, which is a slight modification of Crawford's [1979B, p. 148].

It is assumed here that the conflict involves two issues that are not directly substitutable (here, wages and union representation on the

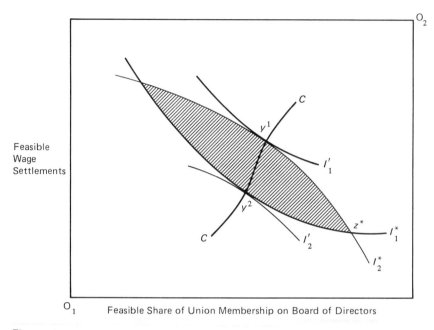

Figure 12.1

company's board of directors are offered as suggestive illustrations). The length and height of the box are taken to represent the range of offers not leading to total breakdown of negotiations. Here z^* is the benchmark settlement, whose fairness is presumably agreed upon by all the affected parties. I_1^* and I_2^* are the respective indifference curves of parties 1 and 2 through point z^*.

It is clear that any point in the shaded area is a settlement Pareto superior to the arbitrator's equitable point, z^*. We may therefore refer to the shaded area as the region of superequitable settlements. Let I_1' be 1's indifferences curve that is tangent to I_2^* at point y^1 and define I_2' and y^2 symmetrically (with CC the contract curve). Then y^1 and y^2 will be the superequitable points that maximally favor the interests of parties 1 and 2, respectively. Obviously, y^1 and y^2 are also Pareto optimal.

All this has a direct relation to some propositions in superfairness analysis. It will be recalled from chapter 2 that in the symmetric case if one substitutes the equal division point, H, for z^*, then the region of super-equality (the set of points Pareto superior to H in the shaded region of figure 12.2) will, under the usual assumptions about the utility functions of the two parties, be contained entirely in the region of superfair solutions

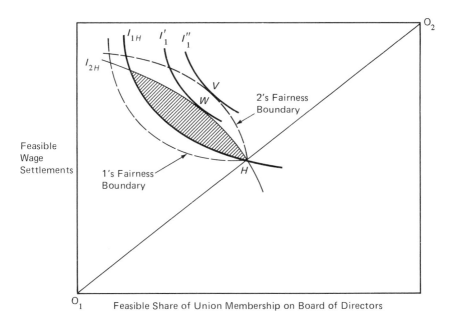

Figure 12.2

that lie between the superfairness boundaries of the two parties. Now, as
we have seen, if the choice of distributions represented by points in this
diagram is to be decided by a divide and choose procedure, and if the
divider knows the other party's preferences, then that individual will have a
substantial advantage over the chooser. Thus, suppose the role of divider is
assigned to party 1. Then 1 will select a distribution that offers 2 an option
slightly preferable to 2 over the choices represented by point V, at which
2's fairness boundary coincides with the highest of 1's indifference curves
that intersect the region of superfairness.

Crawford [1980] showed that some protection can be offered to the
parties by assigning the role of divider randomly and modifying the remainder of the process by giving the chooser the option of either one of
the divider's offers or the equal division point. It is easy to see that now the
divider's best strategy becomes more favorable to the chooser. For
example, if the random process again selects 1 as divider, he must now
offer 2 something slightly better than W, the choices represented by the
point of coincidence of 1's highest indifference curve intersecting the
shaded superequality region and the northeast boundary of that region, 2's
indifference curve through the equal division point, H.

In the arbitration case, just as z^* corresponds to H in the symmetric analysis, y^1 in figure 12.1 corresponds to W in figure 12.2 and offers similar protection to the interests of party 2. We shall see next how Crawford proposes to modify the rules of arbitration so as to provide this sort of protection to the two contending parties.

8   More on Arbitration and Asymmetry: Multiple Offer Arbitration

As a cure for his version of the "chilling effect" of ordinary final offer arbitration described in an earlier section, Crawford proposes a modification of a scheme that had appeared previously in the literature, and that, as will soon be seen, provides the contending parties the sort of protection that has just been discussed. Under this arrangement each party is asked to submit not *one* final offer but several, though these need not differ from one another. In what follows I shall deal for simplicity with the case in which two is the number of such final offers required. Thus, party I may submit offers y^i and z^i and J may provide offers y^j and z^j. The arbitrator is then required to select either I's *pair* of offers or J's, but the arbitrator is not permitted to make the final settlement. Instead, that settlement is arrived at in one more step. Suppose, for concreteness, that the arbitrator selects I's pair of offers. In that case it is J who gets to choose between the two alternative settlements, y^i and z^i, that I has proposed. J's choice is then final. *If any pair of the offers of the two parties agree, the arbitrator is required to choose between the parties randomly*, say, by the toss of a coin, and if, say, I wins the toss, J still gets to make the final choice between the two offers made by I.

Crawford then proves, under assumptions slightly extended from those listed earlier, that a Cournot-Nash equilibrium exists in which $z^i = z^j = z^*$ and y^i is selected so as to maximize I's utility given what choice he believes J will make between y^i and $z^i = z^*$, and y^j is selected by J analagously. Moreover, this offer must leave each party at least as well off as he is under the arbitrator's equitable settlement, z^*, and if each party is informed about the other's preferences, that final offer will also be Pareto optimal.

In terms of our diagram (figure 12.1) in the Cournot-Nash equilibrium where each party knows the preferences of the other, party 1 will submit the offers $z_1 = z^*$ and y^1 while party 2 will provide the offers $z_2 = z^*$ and y^2.

Why is this so? For the same reasons as before, no Cournot-Nash equilibrium will be possible in which a party fails to include z^* as one of its offers. Roughly, this is so because any party I that fails to do so leaves its opponent J the opportunity to formulate a package of proposals more attractive both to the arbitrator and to itself (i.e., to party J). Then the arbitrator will select J's offer over I's, an outcome I can improve over by selecting z^* as one of its offers.

Now, if both parties select z^* as one of their offers, by the rule on coincidence of offers the choice between I's and J's offer packages must be made, not by the arbitrator, but by a random device. In that case I has nothing to lose in selecting as his second final offer, y^i, the outcome most favorable to himself in case he should turn out the winner in the random selection process. The same is clearly true of J. This is the Cournot-Nash equilibrium that has just been described.

It is obvious that the process leaves both parties with nothing to lose and much plausibly to be gained vis-à-vis more conventional arbitration processes when the contending parties are informed about the arbitrator's preferences. For we have seen that then under either standard arbitration or final offer arbitration z^* constitutes the unique Cournot-Nash equilibrium. But under the Crawford scheme party I is sure that it will, at worst, have option z^* to select if it is the loser in the random process, so that the settlement must be chosen from between the other party's pair of offers. Alternatively, if I is the winner of the random draw, it will have selected its offers so that it normally has something (and possibly a good deal) to gain over the settlement z^* that the arbitrator considers the fairest possibility. Obviously, the other party, J, enjoys the same protection, and the Crawford proposal thereby guarantees a superequitable solution when both parties know the arbitrator's preferences. Of course, an arbitrator who understands the logic of the process may find it appropriate to facilitate its workings by making no secret of his views on the most equitable solution before the contenders formulate their bundle of final offers.

The only unfortunate property of the Crawford solution, one that the author himself emphasizes, is its tendency to let one or the other of the parties appropriate virtually all the gains offered by a move from z^* to a point on the contract curve. In terms of figure 12.1 we see that the ultimate settlement can be expected to fall either next to y^1, where almost all of the gains accrue to party 1, or near point y^2, where party 2 is virtually the sole beneficiary. The search for an automatic process that automatically leads toward what may be considered a more neutral solution point on contract curve segment y^1y^2 continues to be a challenge to arbitration theory.

9   Concluding Comment

This chapter makes little pretense to originality. What minor insights it does offer involve slightly extended interpretations of the very illuminating work others have recently carried out in the analysis of arbitration. Perhaps the only one of these extensions that is of any substance is the observation that arbitration theory to some degree permits applied work in the spirit of superfairness analysis to go beyond the rather confining case of fundamental symmetry.

Lest the preceding paragraph appear excessively apologetic let me emphasize again the importance of the analyses described in this chapter. To be able to offer an exposition of so illuminating a body of ideas and observations is accomplishment enough.

The chapter also concludes this little book. I close with the impression that we seem to have been fortunate in being able to find a number of applications of fairness theory that do not involve structural symmetries so severe that they preclude virtually all illuminating analysis. Indeed, what is surprising is the broad range of issues with which the fairness theory is able to begin to grapple. We have touched on some of the favorite policy recommendations of the microeconomists, among them peak load pricing, the use of marginal and incremental cost as guides to the regulation of public utility rates, the employment of Pigouvian taxes for the control of externalities, and the establishment of a white market in ration coupons in times of shortages. The range is indeed considerable.

I end the book as I began, with two general observations. The one broad pattern that seems to emerge from the formal analyses is the frequency with which fairness theory tends to support the equity judgments of noneconomist observers. In cases where they have exhibited suspicion of the fairness of policy measures recommended by microeconomists such as myself, on grounds of economic efficicency, the fairness analysis often seems to confirm that there is something that does really merit suspicion.

Second, I believe the discussion here shows that fairness analysis is far more than an intriguing formal exercise. It has already borne some fruit, however fragile and tender; in the hands of others, I am confident that it can yield a crop that is far more abundant.

Bibliography

Acworth, W. M., *The Railways and the Traders*, J. Murray, London, 1891.

Alexander, E. P., *Railway Practice*, G. P. Putnam's Sons, New York and London, 1887.

Allingham, M., "Fairness and Utility," *Economie Appliquée*, 29(2), 1977, 257–266.

Archibald, G. C., and Donaldson, D., "Notes on Economic Equality," *Journal of Public Economics*, 12(2), 1979, 205–214.

Areeda, Philip, and Turner, Donald, "Predatory Pricing and Related Practices under Section 2 of the Sherman Act, *Harvard Law Review*, 88, 1975, 637–733.

Ashenfelter, Orley, "Evidence on U.S. Experiences with Dispute Resolution Systems," Princeton University, February 1985 (unpublished).

Ashenfelter, Orley, and Bloom, David, "Models of Arbitrator Behavior: Theory and Evidence," *American Economic Review*, 74, March 1984, 111–124.

Atkinson, A. B., "How Progressive Should The Income Tax Be?" in M. Parkin (ed.), *Essays in Modern Economics*, Longman, London, 1973.

Austinsmith, D., "Fair Rights," *Economics Letters*, 4(1), 1979, 29–32.

Barkai, Haim, "Incentives, Efficiency, and Social Control: The Case of the Kibbutz," in William Baumol (ed.), *Public and Private Enterprise in a Mixed Economy*, MacMillan, London, 1980, pp. 233–249.

Baumol, W. J., *Welfare Economics and the Theory of the State*, G. Bell and Sons, London, 1952 (2nd ed., 1965).

Baumol, W. J., Testimony, FCC Docket 18128, July 1970.

Baumol, W. J., and Oates, W. E., *The Theory of Environmental Policy*, Prentice-Hall, Englewood Cliffs, N.J., 1975 (new edition forthcoming).

Baumol, W. J., Fischer, Dietrich, and ten Raa, Thijs, "The Price-Iso Return Locus and Rational Rate Regulation," *Bell Journal of Economics and Management Science*, 10, Fall 1979, 648–658.

Baumol, W. J., Panzar, J. C., and Willing, R. D., *Contestable Markets and the Theory of Industry Structure*, Harcourt, Brace, Jovanovich, New York, 1982.

Bazerman, Max H., "Norms of Distributive Justice in Interest Arbitration," *Industrial and Labor Relations Review*, 1984 (forthcoming).

Billera, Louis J., and Heath, David C., "The Allocation of Shared Costs: A Set of Axioms Yielding a Unique Procedure," *Mathematics of Operations Research*, 7, 1982, 32–39.

Bloom, David E., and Cavanagh, Christopher L., "An Analysis of the Selection of Arbitrators," Harvard University, June 1984 (unpublished).

Brock, W., and Scheinkman, J., "On Just Savings Rules," University of Chicago, 1977 (unpublished).

Coase, Ronald H., "The Problem of Social Cost," *Journal of Law and Economics*, 3, October 1960, 1–44.

Cooter, R., and Helpman, E., "Optimal Income Taxation for Transfer Payments under Different Social Welfare Criteria," *Quarterly Journal of Economics*, 88, November 1974, 656–670.

Crawford, V. P., "A Game of Fair Division," *Review of Economic Studies*, 44, June 1977, 235–247.

Crawford, V. P., "A Procedure for Generating Pareto-Efficient Egalitarian-Equivalent Allocations," *Econometrica*, 47, January 1979 [1979A], 49–60.

Crawford, V. P., "On Compulsory Arbitration Schemes," *Journal of Political Economy*, 87, February 1979 [1979B], 131–160.

Crawford, V. P., "A Self-Administered Solution of the Bargaining Problem," *Review of Economic Studies*, 47, January 1980, 385–392.

Crawford, V. P., "Arbitration and Conflict Resolution in Labor-Management Bargaining," *American Economic Review*, 71, May 1981, 205–210.

Crawford, V. P., "Compulsory Arbitration, Arbitral Risk and Negotiated Settlements: A Case Study in Bargaining under Imperfect Information," *Review of Economic Studies*, 49, 1982, 69–82.

Crawford, V. P., and Heller, W., "Fair Division with Indivisible Commodities," *Journal of Economic Theory*, 21(1), 1979, 10–27.

Diamond, P. A., and Mirrlees, J. A., "Optimal Taxation and Public Production: II," *American Economic Review*, 61, June 1971, 261–278.

Dorfman, Nancy S. (assisted by Arthur Snow), "Who Will Pay for Pollution Control?—The Distribution by Income of the Burden of the National Environmental Protection Program, 1972–1980," *National Tax Journal*, 28, March 1975, 101–115.

Dorfman, Robert, "Incidence of the Benefits and Costs of Environmental Programs," *American Economic Review*, 67, February 1977.

Engels, Frederick, *Anti-Dühring*, International Publishers, New York, 1939 [3rd ed., 1894].

Fair, R. C., "The Optimal Distribution of Income," *Quarterly Journal of Economics*, 85, November 1971, 551–579.

Farber, Henry S., "Splitting the Difference in Interest Arbitration," *Industrial and Labor Relations Review*, 35, October 1981, 70–77.

Farber, Henry S., and Bazerman, Max H., "The General Basis of Arbitrator Behavior," Working Paper 1488, Massachusetts Institute of Technology, November, 1984 (unpublished).

Faulhaber, G. R., and Levinson, S. B., "Subsidy-Free Prices and Anonymous Equity," *American Economic Review*, 71, December 1981, 1083–1091.

Faulhaber, G. R., and Zajac, E. E., "Some Thoughts on Cross Subsidization in Regulated Industries," Bell Laboratories Discussion Paper 48, 1976.

Faulhaber, G. R., and Zajac, E. E., "Cross-Subsidization in Public Enterprise Pricing," in J. T. Wenders (ed.), *Pricing in Regulated Industries: Theory and Application*, II, Mountain States Telephone and Telegraph Co., Denver, 1979.

Feldman, Allan, and Kirman, Alan, "Fairness and Envy," *American Economic Review*, 64, December 1974, 995–1005.

Feldstein, M., "On the Optimal Progressivity of the Income Tax," *Journal of Public Economics*, 2, November 1973, 357–376.

Foley, Duncan, "Resource Allocation and the Public Sector," *Yale Economic Essays* 7, Spring 1967, 45–98.

Freeman, A. Myrick, III, "The Distribution of Environmental Quality," in A. Kneese and B. Bower (eds.), *Environmental Quality Analysis: Theory and Method in the Social Sciences*, The Johns Hopkins Press, Baltimore, 1972.

Fussel, Paul, *The Great War and Modern Memory*, Oxford University Press, London, 1975.

Gaertner, W., "Envy-Free Rights Assignments and Self-Oriented Preferences," *Mathematical Social Sciences*, 2, 1982, 199–208.

Hadley, A. T., *Railroad Transportation*, G. P., Putnam's Sons, New York and London, 1886.

Hochman, H. M., and Rogers, J. D., "Pareto Optimal Distribution," *American Economic Review*, 59, September 1969, 542–557.

Hoffman, E., and Spitzer, M., "Entitlements, Rights, and Fairness: An Experimental Examination of Subject's Concepts of Distributive Justice," *Journal of Legal Studies*, 1985 (forthcoming).

Holcombe, Randall G., "Applied Fairness Theory: Comment," *American Economic Review*, 73, December 1983, 1153–1156.

Kolm, Serge-Christophe, *Justice et Equité*, Éditions du Centre National de la Recherche Scientifique, Paris, 1972.

Kolm, Serge-Christophe, "Super-Equité," *Kyklos*, 26(4), 1973.

Kuhn, Harold, "On Games of Fair Division," in M. Shubik (ed.), *Essays in Mathematical Economics in Honor of Oskar Morgenstern*, Princeton University Press, Princeton, 1967, pp. 29–37.

Lester, Richard A., *Labor Arbitration in State and Local Government*, Industrial Relations Section, Princeton University, Princeton, 1984.

Lewis, W. Arthur, *Overhead Costs: Some Essays in Economic Analysis*, Rinehart, New York, 1949.

Littlechild, Stephen P., "Peak-Load Pricing of Telephone Calls," *The Bell Journal of Economics and Management Science*, 1, Autumn 1970, 191–210.

Loehman, Edna, and Whinston, Andrew, "A New Theory of Pricing and Decision Making for Public Investment," *Bell Journal of Economics*, Autumn 1971, 606–625.

Loehman, Edna, and Whinston, Andrew, "An Axiomatic Approach to Cost Allocations for Public Investment," *Public Finance Quarterly*, April 1974, 236–251.

Longfield, Mountifort, *Lectures on Political Economy*, R. Milliben and Son, Dublin, 1834 (reprinted by the London School of Economics, 1938).

Luce, R. Duncan, and Raiffa, Howard, *Games and Decisions*, John Wiley & Sons, New York, 1957.

Marx, Karl, *Critique of the Gotha Program*. International Publishers, New York, 1970 [1875].

Marx, Karl, and Engels, Frederick, *The German Ideology (Collected Works)*, International Publishers, New York, 1972 [1845–1846].

Mirrlees, J. A., "An Exploration in the Theory of Optimum Income Taxation," *Review of Economic Studies*, 38, April 1971, 175–208.

Nozick, R. *Anarchy, State and Utopia*, Basic Books, New York, 1974.

Ordover, J. A., and Phelps, E. S., "The Concept of Optimal Taxation in the Overlapping-Generations Model of Capital and Wealth," *Journal of Public Economics*, 12, August 1979, 1–26.

Pazner, E. A., and Schmeidler, David, "A Difficulty in the Concept of Fairness," *Review of Economic Studies*, 41, July 1974, 441–443.

Pazner, E. A., and Schmeidler, David, "Egalitarian-Equivalent Allocations: A New Concept of Economic Equity," *Quarterly Journal of Economics*, 92(4), 1978, 1–45.

Peskin, Henry, Leonard Gianessi, and Wolff, Edward N., "The Distributional Effects of Uniform Air Pollution Policy in the United States," *Quarterly Journal of Economics*, 93, May 1979, 281–301.

Phelps, E. S., "Taxation of Wage Income for Economic Justice," *Quarterly Journal of Economics*, 87, August 1973, 331–354.

Philpotts, Geoffrey, "Applied Fairness Theory: Comment," *American Economic Review*, 73 December 1983, 1157–1160.

Posner, Richard, "The Ethical and Political Basis of the Efficiency Norm in Common Law Adjudication," *Hofstra Law Review*, 8, Spring 1980.

Rawls, John, *A Theory of Justice*, Harvard University Press, Cambridge, MA, 1971.

Robbins, Lionel, *The Theory of Economic Policy in English Classical Political Economy*, Macmillan, London, 1952.

Robbins, Lionel, *Political Economy, Past and Present*, Columbia University Press, New York, 1976.

Schmeidler, David, "The Nucleolus of a Characteristic Function Form Game," *SIAM Journal of Applied Mathematics*, 17, November 1969, 1163–1170.

Schmeidler, David, and Vind, Karl, "Fair Net Trades," *Econometrica*, 40, July 1972, 637–642.

Schmeidler, David, and Yaari, Menahem E., "Fair Allocations" (unpublished: 1971?).

Schotter, Andrew, and Schwödiauer, Gerhard, "Economics and the Theory of Games: A Survey," *Journal of Economic Literature*, 18, June 1980, 479–527.

Selten, Reinhard, "The Equity Principle in Economic Behavior," in H. W. Gottinger and Werner Leinfellner (eds.), *Decision Theory and Social Ethics, Issues in Social Choice*, D. Reidel Publishing Co., Dordrecht, 1978, pp. 289–301.

Sen, Amartya, *On Economic Inequality*, Clarendon Press, Oxford, 1972.

Sheshinski, Eytan, "The Optimal Linear Income-Tax," *Review of Economic Studies*, 30, July 1972, 297–302.

Sheshinski, Eytan, "Income Taxation and Capital Accumulation," *Quarterly Journal of Economics* (forthcoming).

Sobel, J., "Fair Allocations of a Renewable Resource," *Journal of Economic Theory*, 21(2), 1979, 235–248.

Steiner, Peter O., "Peak Loads and Efficient Pricing," *Quarterly Journal of Economics*, 71, November 1957, 585–610.

Steinhaus, H., "The Problem of Fair Division," *Econometrica*, 16, 1948, 101–104.

Svensson, L., "Some Views on a Fair Wage Structure," *Ekonomiska Samfunddets Tidskrift*, 33(3), 1980, 385–392.

ten Raa, Thijs, "Supportability and Anonymous Equity," *Journal of Economic Theory*, 31, October 1983, 176–181.

Thaler, Richard, "Toward a Positive Theory of Consumer Choice," *Journal of Economic Behavior and Organization*, 1, March 1980, 39–60.

Thaler, Richard, "Using Mental Accounting in a Theory of Consumer Behavior," Cornell University, 1983 (unpublished).

Thomson, W., "Equity in Exchange Economies," *Journal of Economic Theory*, 29(2), 1983 217–244.

Thomson, W., and Varian, H. R., "Theories of Justice Based on Symmetry," in L. Hurwicz, D. Schmeidler, and H. Sonnenschein (eds.), *Social Goals and Social Organization: Essays in Memory of Elisha Pazner*, Cambridge University Press, New York, 1985.

Titmuss, R. M., *The Gift Relationship: From Human Blood to Social Policy*, Pantheon Books, New York, 1971.

Tobin, James, "A Survey of the Theory of Rationing," *Econometrica*, 20(4), October 1952, 521–553.

Tversky, Amos, and Kahneman, Daniel, "The Framing of Decisions and the Psychology of Choice," in R. Hogarth (ed.), *New Directions for Methodology of Social and Behavioral Science: Question Framing and Response Consistency*, No. 11, Jossey-Bass, San Francisco, 1982.

Ulph, D., "On Labor Supply and the Measurement of Inequality," *Journal of Economic Theory*, 19(2), 1978, 492–512.

Varian, H. R., "Equity, Envy and Efficiency," *Journal of Economic Theory*, 9, September 1974, 63–91.

Varian, H. R. "Distributive Justice, Welfare Economics, and the Theory of Fairness," *Philosophy and Public Affairs*, 4, 1975, 223–247.

Varian, H. R., "Two Problems in the Theory of Fairness," *Journal of Public Economics*, 5, 1976 [1976A], 249–260.

Varian, H. R., "On the History of Concepts of Fairness," *Journal of Economic Theory*, 13, December 1976 [1976B], 486–487.

Varian, H. R., "Redistributive Taxation as Social Insurance," *Journal of Public Economics*, 14, 1980, 49–68.

Varian, H. R., "Dworkin on Equality of Resources," University of Michigan, October 1984 (unpublished).

Wagstaff, P., "A Benthamite Wages Policy," *Review of Economic Studies*, 42, October 1975, 571–580.

Wasow, B., "Optimal Income Distribution with Variable Factor Supplies: A Graphical Exposition," Center for Applied Economics, New York University, 1975 (unpublished).

Willig, R. D., "Pareto Superior Nonlinear Outlay Schedules," *Bell Journal of Economics*, 9, Spring 1978, 56–69.

Willig, R. D., "Consumer Equity and Local Measured Service," in J. A. Baude et al. (eds.), *Perspectives on Local Measured Service*, Telecommunications Industry Workshop, Kansas City, 1979, pp. 71–80.

Zajac, E. E. "Perceived Economic Justice: the Example of Public Utility Regulation," in H. Peyton Young (ed.), *Cost Allocation: Methods, Principles and Applications*, North Holland, Amsterdam, 1985 (forthcoming).

Index